A Guide to
European Community Law

AUSTRALIA
The Law Book Company Ltd.
Sydney : Melbourne : Brisbane

CANADA AND U.S.A.
The Carswell Company Ltd.
Agincourt, Ontario

INDIA
N. M. Tripathi Private Ltd.
Bombay
and
Eastern Law House (Private) Ltd.
Calcutta
M.P.P. House
Bangalore

ISRAEL
Steimatzky's Agency Ltd.
Jerusalem : Tel Aviv : Haifa

MALAYSIA : SINGAPORE : BRUNEI
Malayan Law Journal (Pte.) Ltd.
Singapore

NEW ZEALAND
Sweet & Maxwell (N.Z.) Ltd.
Auckland

PAKISTAN
Pakistan Law House
Karachi

A Guide to European Community Law

by

P. S. R. F. Mathijsen

Director-General with the Commission
of the European Communities
Professor of Law, University of Nijmegen

Preface

by

J. D. B. Mitchell
Salvesen Professor of European Institutions
University of Edinburgh

Third Edition

London
Sweet & Maxwell
1980

First Edition 1972
Second Edition 1975
Second Impression 1976
Third Edition 1980
Published in Great Britain by
Sweet & Maxwell Ltd. of
11 *New Fetter Lane, London*
Computerset by
MFK Graphic Systems (Typesetting) Ltd
Saffron Walden, Essex
Printed in Great Britain by Page Bros. (Norwich) Ltd.

British Library Cataloguing in Publication Data

Mathijsen, Petrus Servatius Renoldus Franciscus
A guide to European community law. – 3rd ed.
1. Law – European Economic Community countries
2. European communities
I. Title
341.24′2 Law
ISBN 0-421-25900-0
ISBN 0-421-25910-8 Pbk

To my daughters Claire
Bénédicte
Stéphanie
Valérie
Olivia
Daphné

ACKNOWLEDGEMENT

In preparing this third edition I was greatly helped by the comments, criticisms and suggestions of my Nijmegen assistant Mr. Janssen. I am also thankful to him and to Mr. Wellens for reading and correcting the proofs; my daughter Daphné was of great assistance in preparing the manuscript.

I am much indebted to Professor Mitchell who, once more, was ready to discuss the manuscript and write the preface.

For typing and retyping I am most thankful to Mrs. Christiane Fannes.

Finally I am pleased to mention the precious help given by my wife Beverly and daughters Valérie, Olivia and Daphné in establishing the Index.

The author is an official of the Commission of the European Communities; the views expressed in this book are his and may not be attributed to any of the Community organs.

FOREWORD TO THE THIRD EDITION

THE first edition of this book covered the development of Community law up to the middle of 1972 and was published shortly before Denmark, Ireland and the United Kingdom joined the European Communities.

The second edition, which consisted mainly in an updating of the first, appeared in June 1975, just after the negotiations regarding Britain's continued membership of the European Communities were concluded.

This third edition comes out just before the accession of Greece. It is rather different from the previous ones: the structure of the book has been profoundly modified. The considerations regarding Community law now constitute the last chapter, as a kind of conclusion, rather than an introduction as was the case before. Also the chapters on the Institutions and the Community acts have been brought forward in order to allow the reader to grasp the formal aspects before tackling the substantive law. As regards the latter, the emphasis still is on the characteristics of the common market, agricultural policy, competition and external relations, but the chapter on regional policy also receives particular attention.

To simplify the text and facilitate the reading everything not strictly essential to the matter under discussion, together with the references to treaty provisions and the case law of the Court of Justice, have been transferred to the footnotes, which consequently have increased in size and importance.

The object of the book has not changed, *i.e.* to give the reader an overall view of the state of development of Community law. This development has to be placed, necessarily, within the larger context of the progress made by the European Communities as such. In this respect it will be noted that in the past five years they have not merely survived the economic and energy crisis but have continued to develop both internally and externally. The most impressive of the various events which marked the last five years should be briefly mentioned.

The relations between the Community and a number of developing countries took a new turn : in 1975, the first Lomé Convention was signed with 46 African, Caribbean and Pacific States; four years later, the second Lomé Convention was signed with 58 States, thereby considerably enlarging the Community's influence in the third world. The European Unit of account was adopted and is now widely used; the European University Institute in Florence was officially instituted; in the British referendum of 1975, 67.2 per cent. voted in favour of the United Kingdom remaining as member of the Community, while Greece, Portugal and Spain applied to join; freedom to provide services and in certain cases the right of establishment for doctors, lawyers, dentists and veterinary surgeons took effect; the Court of Auditors replaced the Audit Board and a trade agreement was concluded with China.

Then there are the Declaration on Human Rights, the establishment of the European Monetary System, the signature of the Greek Accession Treaty, the first elections to the European Parliament by direct universal suffrage and the conclusion of the multilateral trade negotiations.

All these events bear witness to the remarkable vitality of the European Communities and the economic and political integration which take place within their context.

As for the law of the European Community it will be seen that it not only continues to develop in scope, but also in precision, thanks mainly to the Court of Justice. It might be useful in this respect to mention, *e.g.* the judgment in the *Defrenne* case where the Court held that the principle of equal pay for men and women is directly applicable, the *Kramer* case where it was stated that in the field of external relations the Community enjoys the capacity to enter into international commitments over the whole field of the objectives defined in Part One of the Treaty and the Court's opinion in the *International Agreement on Natural Rubber* case where the Community's exclusive competence to conclude certain agreements was reaffirmed. Finally, in the competition field the Commission and the Court continued to clarify certain basic concepts such as "abuse of a dominant position" in cases like *United Brands* and *Hoffman-La Roche.*

Notwithstanding the slowness of the progress and the inevitable failures, the European Community remains for all of us a fascinating experience which is bound to succeed for the simple reason that there is no political or economic alternative for the peoples of Europe.

PREFACE

PROFESSOR Mathijsen's book first appeared at the time of enlargement from Six to Nine. The third edition comes out at a time when the Treaty for the next enlargement to Ten has been signed (and on the institutional side takes account of that) and at a time when negotiations for further enlargement to Twelve are in hand. In between times the second edition had appeared when one might have assumed that a "running-in" period was nearing its end. Yet that edition had to deal with a so-called re-negotiation. Writing in March 1980 one has then to look back, to look forward, and also to look at the current scene. One must confess that it is easier to lecture on the Communities than it is to write about them: easier because (without any loss of face) the dogmatism that one may use in one Autumn term may be changed, as a result of continuous observation, into speculation by the next. The printed word is harsher. Writing now some of the certainties which one might have expressed in 1975 or 1976 might perhaps be expressed with more circumspection. In short, even the ambition that Professor Mathijsen first had of presenting a photograph of the Communities at any one point of time becomes more difficult.

Looking back over the years between the second edition and this one, three events stand out. Two are obvious. Internally there was the fact of Direct Elections to the European Parliament. Win, lose, or draw that event matters, even though its consequences are not yet clear, and will only become apparent in the context of the shifts of balance in other institutional relationships. Externally there has been the signing of the second and enlarged Lomé Convention and the creation of the STABEX system, which demonstrates at least an evolution of the Communities in the eyes of others. There has been movement, even if not as much as might have been hoped, and movement which provokes fresh thought. Hence the third "event"—which may be miscalled—it is the arrival of a mood of formal introspection. In their different ways both the Spierenburg Report and the Report of the Three Wise Men, though springing from quite different sources, mark that mood. Both can be called technical in the sense that they lack the fundamental quality of the Spaak Report and its progenitor declarations. It is this combination of circumstances which makes a new edition even of an established *Guide* important. Even against a background of major hopeful happenings, there are immediate uncertainties of varying orders of significance to which must be added the problems springing from the perspective of further enlargement. Any judgment on those uncertainties, and any answers which one may give in that questioning require as clear a knowledge as is possible of where we are and how we have got to wherever that may be.

It is helpful, in making such assessments, that Professor Mathijsen has brought forward the passages on the structure of the Communities before entering on the consequences of that structure. It is also helpful that, although the book is called a guide to Community law, the content deals also with the substance of policies. What has happened at lower levels also matters (though a Director General of Regional Policy may not like the evolution of the Regional Development Fund being thus classified). In that respect Professor Mathijsen has correctly used the information available to him as a member of the Commission staff. Even details may matter, such as, in the Budgetary debate, the information that he gives on terms like commitment and appropriation payments. The *Guide* then serves its own purposes and also gives the background for the debate which should go on. Indeed one commends the virtue of those who set out to write a *Guide* and, even in the third edition, keep the book that way.

Because it remains a guide, but because it proclaims itself as one to Community law, a final point should be made, which will no doubt irritate the professional political scientists. No-one can discuss, or even understand, the problems of Community/Member State relationships, or even some of the evolution (or hesitancies in the evolution) of policies without the background of the "legal basis" in question. In March 1980 one writes that sentence with many underlying thoughts in mind. In that respect too things are no longer simple, and a realistic guide becomes all the more useful.

In life, and in writing, I will no doubt (as in the past) happily continue to argue with Pierre Mathijsen about things in and out of this book. Meanwhile it is a pleasure to write a preface to a *Guide* coming from the pen of one who knows so well the machinery from the inside.

March, 1980 J. D. B. Mitchell

CONTENTS

TABLE OF CASES

Court of Justice of the European Communities

Commission Decisions

TABLE OF EUROPEAN TREATIES

TABLE OF COMMUNITY SECONDARY LEGISLATION

TABLE OF UNITED KINGDOM LEGISLATION

ABBREVIATIONS

A.C.P.	African, Caribbean and Pacific countries, signatories to the Lomé Conventions I and II.
Act of Accession	Act concerning the conditions of accession and the adjustments to the treaties establishing the ECSC, EEC and EAEC, annexed to the Treaty of accession.
Adaptation Decision	Council Decision of the European Communities of January 1, 1973, adjusting the instruments concerning the accession of Denmark, Ireland and the United Kingdom to the European Communities, O.J. 1973, L 2. These adjustments were necessary because Norway, although a signatory to the Treaty of accession, did not become a member of the European Communities.
Budgetary Treaty	Treaties of April 22, 1970, and July 22, 1975, amending Certain Budgetary Provisions of the Treaties establishing the European Communities and of the Treaty establishing a Single Council and a Single Commission of the European Communities.
Bull.	Bulletin of the European Communities edited by the Secretariat of the Commission; there are 12 issues per year.
C.M.L.R.	Common Market Law Reports.
C.M.L.Rev.	Common Market Law Review.
[E.C.R.]	Official reports of cases before the Court of Justice in English.
ECSC	European Coal and Steel Community.
EEC	European Economic Community.
E.L.Rev.	European Law Review.

Euratom — European Community of Atomic Energy.

General Report — General Report on the activities of the Communities, published yearly by the Commission. The year mentioned after the word Report refers to the period covered by the Report.

J.O. — *Journal Officiel:* French edition of the *Official Journal of the European Communities.*

Remarks

1. This Journal was published under the name *Journal Officiel de la Communauté Européenne du Charbon et de l'Acier* from 1952 to April 19, 1958; on April 20, 1958, the first issue of the *Journal Officiel des Communautés Européennes* appeared, without modifying the structure of the Journal itself; this lasted until December 31, 1967.

References to publications in the *Journal Officiel* for the period 1952 to July 1, 1967, are made by mentioning the page and the year: such as J.O. 849/65. Between July 1 and December 31, 1967, each issue is paged separately.

2. After January 1, 1968 (see J.O. 1968, L30), the Journal was divided into two separate editions designated by the letters "L" (legislation) and "C" (communications).

Legislative texts are published in the edition marked "L" and are again subdivided in two categories:

I. Acts for which publication is a condition for their application (see EEC, Art. 191);

II. Acts for which publication is not required.

All other texts appear in the edition marked "C".

References to publications in the *Journal Officiel* after January 1, 1968, are made by mentioning the letter "L" or "C", the No. of the issue and the year, for instance J.O. 1970, 31.

J.O. 3. Starting on January 1, 1973, the Journal was also published in the Danish and English languages. See O.J.

4. In accordance with Article 155 of the Act of Accession, provision was made in Council Regulation 857/72 of April 24, 1972, for special editions of the *Official Journal* for the publication *inter alia* of the English text of acts of the institutions of the Communities adopted and published before accession. Consequently an authentic English translation now exists of the most important Community acts.

This special edition was published in November and December 1972 and a subsequent edition was published in 1974.

5. The numbering of the pages is the same in the French, English and other language editions.

Merger Treaty Treaty of April 8, 1965, establishing a Single Council and a Single Commission of the European Communities.

O.J. *Official Journal of the European Communities;* see *supra* J.O.

Rec. *Recueil de la Jurisprudence de la Cour,* Official reports of cases before the Court of Justice in French.

CHAPTER 1

THE LAW OF THE EUROPEAN COMMUNITIES

WHEN the first European Community was established in 1952, the drafters of the Coal and Steel Treaty coined the word "supranational" to indicate the particular character of their creation and of the law it embodied. Although it was set up by an international agreement similar to many others concluded between sovereign states, the signatories were conscious of having drafted something that was different from international law, the law of nations. They were not, like so many countries before them, merely creating mutual obligations between them[1]; they were doing much more: they were limiting their own sovereign rights, transferring them to institutions over which they had no direct control and endowing them with powers they did not always possess themselves. Furthermore they were not only binding the states they represented to assume new rights and obligations, they were also directly including their citizens, who became subjects of the Community.

By contrast with ordinary international treaties, the European treaties have thus created their own legal system to which the term "international" could not apply; the term "supranational" would therefore indicate the difference: the law of the Community is not international law.

On the other hand, the terms and the spirit of the European treaties make it impossible for the Member States, as a corollary, to accord precedence to their national law over a legal system accepted by them on a basis of reciprocity. The executive force of Community law cannot vary from one state to another in deference to domestic laws without jeopardising the attainment of the objec-

[1] Case 26/62 *Van Gend en Loos* v. *Nederlandse Administratie der Belastingen* [1963] E.C.R. at 12.

tives of the treaties.[2] The law of the European Communities cannot therefore be regarded as national law; it is different and independent from it, it stands apart, it is not national law; since it is common to nine nations, it is "supranational."

The term has now fallen into disrepute and is no longer current. This does not change the specific nature of the law created by the treaties; more important, the concept is now universally accepted and expressed by the words "Community law."

Community law is to be found mainly in the European treaties and the secondary legislation. Originally there were the treaties setting up the European Coal and Steel Community, the European Atomic Energy Community and the European Economic Community. The first two can be designated as sectoral treaties while the third one, the EEC Treaty, covers the economy in general (hereinafter "the Treaty" means the EEC Treaty signed in Rome in 1957). Reference must also be made to the successive texts which conflicted and amended the basic texts: the Convention on certain institutions common to the three Communities, the Treaty establishing a single Council and a single Commission, the Decision creating the Communities' own resources, the Treaty amending certain budgetary provisions, the Treaty of accession of Denmark, Ireland and the United Kingdom, the Treaty amending certain financial provisions, the Act concerning direct elections for the European Parliament and, finally, the Treaty concerning Greek accession. However those only constitute the charter, the point of departure.

Community law has gradually evolved and developed over the past 27 years, from the 100 Articles of the Coal and Steel Treaty, into an impressive body of law comprising thousands of regulations, directives, decisions, resolutions, agreements, programmes and other measures, and above all the case law of the Court of Justice.

It is impressive, not because of its sheer volume but because of its original character and its growth potential. It is worthwhile considering this particular nature of the body of Community law: except for the basic treaties mentioned earlier, none of the Communities' acts find their origin in the traditional institutions, bodies and organs, lawyers and citizens are familiar with and over which they exercise, through democratic elections, some sort of control.

[2] Case 6/64 *Costa* v. *Enel* [1964] E.C.R. at 594.

Community regulations, directives, decisions, etc., are issued outside most citizens' own country, according to procedures they often cannot grasp and too remote to be controlled; they are nevertheless directly involved. Not only do those measures impose obligations upon them, without the possibility of their national authorities controlling either their implementation or their enforcement, but they confer upon them rights which they in turn can ask their national courts to uphold against fellow-citizens, undertakings and even their own government. And indeed, these rights arise not only where they are expressly granted by the Treaty, but also by reason of obligations which the Treaty, in a clearly defined way, imposes upon individuals as well as upon the Member States and upon the institutions of the Community.[3]

They can also challenge the legality of Community measures directly in the Community Court, when they are directly and individually concerned. The apparent aloofness of the European authorities combined with this direct involvement is sometimes bewildering, although the recent direct election of the members of the European Parliament has made most people in the Member States familiar with at least some of the aspects of Community law. But, if democratic control through directly elected representatives is to become a reality some knowledge of the basic rules and procedures of the Community is required.

Since all the citizens are concerned, it seems that not only the law student but also the practitioner, the politician and the general public must understand what it is all about. Unless one realises what the objectives are and what means and procedures have been provided to attain them, no participation is possible, no criticism is justified, no suggestion can be pertinent. The objectives are clearly set out in the Treaty: to promote throughout the Community harmonious development of economic activities, a continuous and balanced expansion, an increase in stability, an accelerated raising of the standard of living and closer relations between the Member States.[4] The means provided by the Treaty are rather limited; there is first the establishment, functioning and development of a common market and second the progressive approximation of the economic policies of the Member States. But while the Treaty provides precise rules and timetables for the former, the second is

[3] See n. 1, *supra*.
[4] EEC, Art. 2.

described in very general terms. However, notwithstanding this vagueness, Community activities have penetrated more and more social, economic and connected domains, some of which are not explicitly provided for under the Treaty, *e.g.* energy, regional policy, environment, consumer protection and the European Monetary System.

Community law is therefore also impressive because of its continuous growth since next to the coal and steel and nuclear sectors, the EEC Treaty aims at integrating the entire economies of the Member States. The dynamics of the Communities is not the only proof of their vitality; notwithstanding a decade of economic recession and political crises of all kinds, they not only held together but expanded both geographically and politically, which seems to indicate that they fulfill a basic need and respond to a profound aspiration.

But this expansion carries with it the risk of dilution, while on the other hand, the dangers of a return to protectionism and nationalism are certainly not imaginary; but it so happens that the inbuilt system of check and balance has until now preserved the Community from those pitfalls. It is, therefore, essential to understand this system where the balance is based on a carefully designed relationship between Council, Commission and Parliament and where the check is mainly in the hands of the Court of Justice. As will be seen, the Council is the central piece of the institutional set-up endowed with large legislative and budgetary powers, but the former can, generally speaking, only be exercised at the initiative of the Commission and the latter are shared more and more with the European Parliament. This structure risks being upset by the recent *de facto* creation of the European Council whose activities are not subject to any rules, controls or procedures. However useful the incentives and guidelines issued by this new organ, the procedures provided for in the Treaty are essential, since they constitute the only safeguard against the arbitrary use of power. It is, therefore, imperative that all those who are affected by Community activities know and understand the rules of the game: this is particularly true for the institutions of the Community, their composition, their powers and their relationship with the other organs. In the first place, it is the legislative power of the Community which directly interests all those who are subject to the Community's jurisdiction; the decision-making process should therefore be understood, but also the possibilities which are provided by the Treaty to challenge the legality of Community measures in the Court of Justice.

This institution plays an essential role not only by providing judicial protection and, when justified, reparation for damages caused by Community action, but mainly by defining, interpreting and developing Community law. It is thanks to the Court of Justice that the rule of law remained the basis for defining the obligations of the Member States, both in their relation to one another and with the Community institutions, with regard to the rights individual citizens derive from those obligations. It is this particular effect of the Community rules which constitutes the most interesting aspect of Community law: if the law has developed so intensely through the case law of the Court of Justice, it was very often thanks to the initiative of the legal or natural persons: their keen awareness of the advantages which could derive for them from the implementation of Community law, has conferred upon them a major role in its development. This direct involvement of the citizen is the consequence of the doctrine of direct effect of Community rules, as developed by the Court of Justice; it has become the keystone of the juridical system. It also has created a close link between the national and the Community judge; although, generally speaking, the former only applies while the latter interprets, it is clear that both have greatly contributed to the development of the new legal order. The fact that individuals and undertakings can ask the national courts to uphold the rights which derive for them from Community law and can request those courts to refer to the Court of Justice questions regarding the validity and the interpretation of Community provisions has proved to be an extremely effective way both to guarantee a satisfactory implementation of Community measures throughout the member countries and to stimulate development of the law. However, this momentum can only be maintained if, besides acquiring an understanding of the institutional structure and decision-making process; those who come within the Community jurisdiction keep abreast with the evolution of the law in the various fields of action.

It is important to understand how the law has evolved in several domains and especially in regard to the basic freedoms, agriculture, competition, regional policy and external relations, without therefore neglecting the other areas, namely those where activities of the Community were not specifically provided for in the European treaties.

Parliamentary democracy is characterised by the attribution to an elected body of legislative and budgetary powers. A few years ago, the Assembly of the European Communities had none of those attributes; but here also things have improved: the Budgetary Treaty gave Parliament some real powers in the adoption of the Community budget and on June 10, 1979, the citizens of the Community elected their representatives to this Assembly for the first time. But these changes have not created a situation which allows one to speak of a democratic system of decision-making within the Communities, but at least the citizens of the Member States are now in a better position to influence the course of events.

This whole complex of rules, procedures, institutions, powers and controls constitute the main elements of European Community law. However, the existence of this new legal order also raises questions in regard to its relation with internal, *i.e.* national law and with the law of nations. It was necessary to clarify what solutions for instance the national judge must apply in case of conflict between Community and national rules, under which conditions legal and natural persons can invoke the Community rules, what are the international obligations of the Community and the Member States, which have assumed obligations under both international law and the European treaties. Is there a possibility of conflict and if so, who decides on the solutions to be applied? These questions and others must be examined and solutions must be found. It is important to note that not only the Court of Justice has defined the rules and priorities but that, generally speaking, national courts and tribunals have concurred; it is this unity of perception concerning the meaning and consequences of Community law that makes its uniform application throughout the Community possible.

Chapter 2

HISTORY

1. Introduction

Every institution is the product of a series of historical events and at the same time reflects the convictions, hopes and concerns of those who were instrumental in establishing it. The European Communities are no exception to this. For a full understanding and correct interpretation of the European treaties some knowledge as to the historical background therefore seems required.

Although the expression "United States of Europe" was already used by Victor Hugo in 1849,[1] there is no need to go that far back! The end of the Second World War seems a fair starting point, notwithstanding the existence before then of a very active but not too influential Pan-European Movement inspired by Count Coudenhove-Kalergi.

2. Churchill's speech

The agreement made at Yalta in 1945 by the United Kingdom, the United States and the U.S.S.R. left Europe more divided than ever and the growing antagonism among the victorious "Allies" spelt only more tensions and catastrophes. It was on September 19, 1946, in a speech at Zurich University, that Winston Churchill proposed a "sovereign remedy," *i.e.* to "recreate the European family, or as much of it as we can, and provide it with a structure under which it can dwell in peace, in safety and in freedom. We must build a kind of United States of Europe." And he went on "to say something that will astonish you. The first step in the recreation of the European family must be a partnership between France and Germany." As will be seen, it was this (British) idea which also inspired the French Government in 1950 to propose the establish-

[1] See Henri Brugmans, *L'Idée Européenne*, 1920–1970 (Bruges, 1970).

ment of the European Coal and Steel Community. Towards the end of his Zurich speech, Churchill also proposed to start by setting up a regional structure and to form a Council of Europe.[2]

3. OEEC

If Churchill's words were well received, the European states in those days lacked the necessary stamina to proceed with such far-reaching plans, as they were preoccupied by their daily fight for economic survival. Once again the United States came to the rescue. In another famous University speech, at Harvard this time, George Marshall, United States Secretary of State, announced on June 5, 1947, that the United States would do "whatever it is able to do to assist in the return of normal economic health in the world." But he added that "before the United States' Government can . . . help start the European world on its way to recovery, there must be some agreement among the countries of Europe. . . . The role of this country should consist of friendly aid in the drafting of a European programme and of later support of such a programme. . . . The programme should be a joint one, agreed to by a number of, if not all, European nations." This offer was accepted by 16 European countries on July 15, 1947, and so the Marshall Plan was born; but more important for the future of European integration was the setting up of the Organisation for European Economic Co-operation (OEEC)[3] in 1948; this was in response to the American request for an agreement among Europeans.

Thus Europe's economic destiny became closely linked, for at least two decades, with that of the United States; this dependence was formally extended to the field of defence by the signature in Washington on Apil 4, 1949, of the North Atlantic Treaty (NATO).

4. May 9, 1950: Robert Schuman

In the meantime, Churchill's words about a partnership between France and Germany had not been forgotten and on May 9, 1950 Robert Schuman, French Foreign Minister, declared that a united Europe was essential for world peace and that a gathering

[2] The treaty establishing the Council of Europe was signed in London on May 5, 1949.

[3] In 1961, it became the Organisation for Economic Co-operation and Development (OECD), with the participation of the United States and Canada.

of the European nations required the elimination of the century-old opposition between France and Germany. As a first practical step towards this end he proposed "to place the whole Franco-German coal and steel production under one joint High Authority, in an organization open to the participation of the other countries of Europe." He described this pooling of production as the "first stage of the European Federation." Germany, the Netherlands, Belgium, Luxembourg and Italy accepted in principle and negotiations started at once. But, as Huizinga[4] writes, "what did Britain do? Challenged to put her European cards on the table at last, she attempted to hide them by refusing to say yes or no. . . . And so we got the sorry spectacle . . . of British statesmen and diplomats, dutifully echoed by even the best organs of the British Press, endlessly and plaintively repeating that they were full of sympathy for Mr. Schuman's plan, but that they really had to have more details before they could decide, and that they should not be asked to 'take a leap in the dark' or to 'sign on the dotted line' or to 'commit themselves in advance to surrender certain fundamental rights.' As if anyone had asked them to do so; as if there were any details and as if there were any plans even, beyond the proposal to try and see whether those of us who accepted the federal principle could work out a first instalment of federal organization."

5. European Coal and Steel Community

The negotiations progressed rapidly and were simplified by the fact that all the future partners had accepted the proposed principles; the work consisted mainly in giving them a legal form. A sense of urgency was probably added to the existing goodwill by the communist invasion in South Korea. The treaty establishing the European Coal and Steel Community (ECSC) was signed in Paris, on April 18, 1951.

Ratification by the national parliaments met with little opposition and on July 25, 1952, the Treaty entered into force. Although political considerations came first, the experience gained in the economic field from this first community was vital for future developments. It showed that the system with its institutions and decision-making process was viable in organising international trade, but it also showed the difficulties of limited economic integration.

[4] H. H. Huizinga, *Confessions of a European in England* (London, 1958), p. 177.

6. European Defence Community

The following two years were difficult. It has been said that the easing of the international political situation—Stalin died on March 5, 1953 and July 27, 1953 marked the end of the Korean war—diminished the necessity for "closing the ranks." In any case, two additional proposals for close co-operation among the "Six"—in the form of a European Defence Community and a European Political Community—failed miserably.

7. EEC and Euratom

Undaunted by those setbacks, the Benelux countries proposed in 1955, to their partners in the Coal and Steel Community, to take another step towards economic integration by setting up a common market and jointly developing transportation, classical and atomic energy. This led to the conference of Messina in the same year, at which Mr. Spaak was asked to report on the feasibility of those plans. At that time an invitation was issued also to the British Government to join the negotiations of the Six; alas, to no avail.[5]

The "Spaak Report" was ready in 1956, and was discussed in Venice, where the decision was taken to start negotiations for drafting treaties that would establish a "common market" and an Atomic Energy Community. With incredible speed (June 1956–February 1957) these two complex treaties were prepared for signature in Rome on March 25, 1957, and on January 1, 1958, the European Economic Community (EEC) and the European Community for Atomic Energy (Euratom) became a reality.

On this occasion the economic considerations were so much in the foreground that only one paragraph of the preamble to the EEC Treaty makes a vague reference to Europe's political future: "determined to establish the foundations of an ever closer union among the European peoples."

In 1961, the British Government decided to apply for negotiations to determine whether satisfactory arrangements could be made to meet the needs of the United Kingdom, of the Commonwealth and of EFTA. The Government were "baulked in their objective, so that it was not possible to determine whether satisfactory conditions of entry could be obtained."[6]

[5] See Hans Joachim Heiser, *British Policy with regard to the unification efforts on the European Continent* (Leyden, 1959), p. 96.

[6] *The United Kingdom and the European Communities,* July 1971, Cmnd. 4715, 6.

8. Merger Treaty

On April 8, 1965, the institutional set-up of the Communities was simplified by the treaty establishing "a Single Council and a Single Commission of the European Communities," commonly referred to as the "Merger Treaty." This treaty became effective on July 1, 1967; as from that date there was therefore one Council, one European Commission, one European Court and one Assembly for all three Communities. See further Chapter 3, *infra*.

9. The Customs Union

The Customs Union was fully operative in the EEC on July 1, 1968. It meant that tariff and quota restrictions between Member States had by then been completely abolished and that the replacement of the national external tariff by the common external tariff had been completed. The Community was 18 months ahead of the schedule laid down in the Treaty.[7]

10. British membership

After a debate in both Houses of Parliament, at the end of which the Government's decision was approved in the Commons by a majority of 426, the British Government applied for membership of the Communities on May 10, 1967. By December of the same year it was clear however that the "Six" could not reach the unanimity necessary under the Community treaties to return a reply to Britain's application. Thus ended the second endeavour of the United Kingdom to enter "Europe." The British Government, however, decided to maintain their application for membership and it was discussed at many meetings of the Council of the Communities in the following two years.

At the meeting of heads of state and government, on December 1 and 2, 1969, in The Hague, it was finally agreed to open negotiations between the Communities and the states which had applied for membership. Other important decisions taken at this "Summit" concerned the economic and monetary union and the Community's own resources, *i.e.* Community's direct income system.

The Treaty of Brussels relating to the accession of the United Kingdom, Ireland, Norway and Denmark was signed on January 22, 1972; this Treaty entered into force on January 1, 1973, except

[7] Twelve years, see EEC, Art. 8 and Acceleration Decisions (J.O. 1960, 1217 and J.O. 1962, 1284).

for Norway which, as a result of a referendum on the subject, did not ratify the Treaty. Consequently, several provisions of this Treaty and of the "Act concerning the conditions of accession and the adjustments to the Treaties" attached thereto were modified by the Council Decision of January 1, 1973, adjusting the documents concerning accession of the new Member States to the European Communities (hereinafter referred to as the "Adaptation Decision").[8]

11. Treaty amending certain budgetary provisions

Mention should also be made of the Treaty of Luxembourg of April 22, 1970, which entered into force on January 1, 1971, relating to the Community's budget and the replacement of the financial contributions of Member States by other resources of the Community itself, namely the revenue accruing from the common customs tariff, the agricultural levies and part of the value added tax.

12. Treaty amending certain financial provisions

This treaty was signed in Brussels on July 22, 1975, and entered into force on June 1, 1977; the preamble states that the complete replacement of financial contributions of Member States by the Communities' own resources requires a strengthening of the budgetary powers of the Assembly. Among other things this treaty provides for the establishment of a Court of Auditors and entrusts the European Parliament with the task to give discharge to the Commission in respect of the implementation of the budget.

13. Direct elections to the European Parliament

On September 20, 1976, the Council adopted a decision and annexed to it an Act concerning the election of the representatives of the Assembly by direct universal suffrage. This Act entered into force on July 1, 1978. It provides for the number of representatives to be elected in each Member State and conditions under which the election would take place. The first direct elections were held from June 6 to 10, 1979. See further Chapter 3, *infra*, p. 17.

[8] O.J. 1973, L2/1.

14. Further enlargement

On June 12, 1975, Greece applied for membership to the European Communities and the Treaty of Accession, together with an Act concerning the conditions of accession and the adjustments to the Treaties were signed at Athens on May 28, 1979[9]; it was ratified by the Greek Parliament on June 28, 1979. On March 28, 1977, Portugal and on July 28, 1977, Spain applied for membership. Formal negotiations with Portugal started on October, 16, 1978, and with Spain on February 5, 1979.

[9] O.J. 1979, L 291/1.

CHAPTER 3

THE INSTITUTIONS AND OTHER ORGANS OF THE COMMUNITY

AMONG the various bodies established by, or in pursuance of the European treaties,[1] four are referred to as "institutions": the Assembly (European Parliament), the Council, the Commission and the Court of Justice.[2] What distinguishes an institution from another community organ is the fact that it is empowered to take decisions binding upon Member States, institutions or person (natural or legal).[3] The other bodies generally speaking act in an advisory capacity only.

[1] For bodies set up by the treaties, see, *e.g.*: the Consultative Committee (ECSC, Art. 18); the Scientific and Technical Committee (Euratom, Art. 134); the Economic and Social Committee (Euratom, Art. 3 and 165 EEC, Arts. 4 and 193; the Court of Auditors (EEC, Art. 4 (3)), see Art. 11 of the Treaty amending certain financial provisions; the European Investment Bank (EEC, Arts. 3 (*j*) and 129); the Monetary Committee (EEC, Art. 105 (2)) and the Committee of Permanent Representatives (Merger Treaty, Art. 4).

For bodies set up by the institutions in pursuance of the powers conferred upon them by the Treaties, see, *e.g.*: the Committee for medium-term economic policy, Dec. 64/247 (J.O. 1964, 1031); the Management Committees in Agriculture, *e.g.* Reg. 2727/75, Art. 25 (O.J. 1975 L 281/1) and the Regional Policy Committee, Dec. 75/185 (O.J. 1975, L 73/1). Numerous committees and commissions have been set up by the Council and by the Commission. Indications as to their legal status, tasks and powers are to be found in answers to written questions No. 149/76 (O.J. 1976, C 167/21), No. 188/76 (O.J. 1976, C 203/6) and No. 1318/77 (O.J. 1978, C 137/32).

[2] See EEC, Art. 4 (1).

[3] Only the institutions are endowed "with sovereign rights, the exercise of which affects Member States and also their citizens"; Case 26/62 *Van Gend en Loos* v. *Dutch Fiscal Administration* [1963] E.C.R. at 12. For the Council and the Commission this follows directly from EEC, Art. 189; for the Court of Justice this power is provided for in EEC, Arts. 171 (Member States), 176 (institutions) and 172 (persons). The power of the Assembly to take binding decisions is defined in EEC, Art. 144, together with Merger Treaty, Art. 11 (Commission and Member States) and EEC, Art. 203 (Council and Member States).

Although "each institution shall act within the limits of the powers conferred upon it by this treaty,"[4] only the Community itself has legal personality and capacity[5]; when it acquires property or is a party to legal proceedings (outside the Court of Justice)[6] it may only be represented by the Commission. On the other hand for the conclusion of agreements between the Community and one or more states or an international organisation the Community is represented by the Council.[7]

The first European institutions—the High Authority, the Common Assembly, the Special Council of Ministers and the Court of Justice—were set up by the Treaty of Paris of 1951 establishing the European Coal and Steel Community.[8] Similar institutions—an Assembly, a Council, a Commission and a Court of Justice—were created by the two Treaties of Rome of 1957 for the European Economic Community and for the European Community for Atomic Energy. The result would, therefore, have been three Assemblies, three Councils, three Commissions (High Authority) and three Courts, had not a convention[9] signed the same day provided for a single Assembly and a single Court of Justice.

Nonetheless this left three Councils and three Commissions (High Authority) beside the one Assembly and one Court: a total of eight institutions. A further rationalisation was introduced by the Merger Treaty of 1965[10] establishing a "Council of the European Communities" and a "Commission of the European Communities," to replace the existing Councils, Commissions and High Authority of the ECSC, EEC and Euratom. It might be interesting to note that according to the preamble of this treaty the

[4] EEC, Art. 4 (1).

[5] EEC, Arts. 210 and 211. It is beyond the scope of this book to analyse the nature of this personality in the context of private and public law and international law; but see Court of Justice, Cases 43, 45 and 48/59 *Lachmüller et al.* v. *Commission* [1960] E.C.R. 463 at 472; Opinions 1/75 [1975] E.C.R. 1355; 1/76 [1977] E.C.R. 741 and 1/78 [1978] E.C.R. 2151.

[6] It follows from EEC, Arts. 173 and 175 that each institution has the authority to bring an action before the Court of Justice. Art. 1 (2) of the Staff Regulations (O.J. 1968, 30) assimilates the Economic and Social Committee to the institutions so it can act as defendant in disputes with its own staff.

[7] EEC, Art. 228 (1).

[8] ECSC, Art. 7.

[9] Convention relating to certain institutions common to the European Communities, of March 25, 1957, annexed to the EEC and Euratom Treaties.

[10] This Treaty entered into force on July 1, 1967 (J.O. 1967, 152/2).

creation of single institutions is seen as a step in the direction of the "unification of the three Communities." The four single institutions now exercise the powers and jurisdiction conferred on the institutions they replace in accordance with the provisions of the relevant treaties.[11]

Neither the Treaty of Brussels of January 22, 1972, concerning the accession of Denmark, Ireland and the United Kingdom[12] nor the Treaty of Athens of May 28, 1979, concerning the accession of Greece have modified this institutional structure; these treaties merely provide for increases in the number of members of each institution in order to accomodate nationals from the new Member States.

I. *The Assembly (European Parliament)*

All the European treaties[13] refer to this institution as the "Assembly."[14] It was the Assembly which, back in 1962, decided to call itself the "European Parliament."[15] All the institutions, except for a while the Council,[16] have adopted that denomination; the acts of the institutions which require prior consultation of the Assembly now refer to "the opinion of the European Parliament."[17] The

[11] Convention of March 25, 1957, Arts. 1–4 and Merger Treaty, Arts. 1 and 9.

[12] The documents concerning accession were also signed by Norway (J.O. 1972, L 73/1); this signatory, however, did not become a Member State and adjustments had to be made to the Treaty and the Act of Accession; see Council Decs. of January 1, 1973 (O.J. 1973, L 2/1).

[13] Including the latest, the Accession Treaty signed at Athens on May 28, 1979, and also Dec. 76/787 (O.J. 1976, L 278/1) and the Act concerning the election of the representatives of the Assembly by direct universal suffrage. See, however, the two Yaoundé Conventions (J.O. 1964, 1142 and J.O. 1970, L 282/1) and the Lomé Convention between the EEC and the ACP countries, of February 28, 1975, Art. 80 (O.J. 1976, L 25/1); also the Association agreements with Greece and Turkey (J.O. 1963, 354 and J.O. 1964, 3685).

[14] Or "Common Assembly," ECSC, Art. 7.

[15] Resolution of March 30, 1962 (J.O. 1962, 1045). On March 20, 1958, the Assembly decided to call itself "European Parliamentary Assembly" (J.O. 1958, 6).

[16] Answer to questions No. 398/77 concerning denomination of the European Parliament in the Communities' official documents: the Council replied that the denomination of any one of the institutions could only be amended by a Treaty amending the existing Treaties (O.J. 1977, C 270/18) and No. 1085/78 (O.J. 1979, C 92/22).

[17] See, *e.g.* Reg. 214/79 concerning the European Regional Development Fund (O.J. 1979, L 35/1).

Court of Justice has also used the terms "Parliamentary Assembly" and "Parliament" since 1959.[18]

Whether the Assembly was well advised in changing its name is questionable, not so much because this institution lacks the powers that are characteristic of democratic parliaments, *i.e.* the powers to legislate and to raise taxes, beside controlling the Administration, but because by calling itself a Parliament it has created the illusion that democratic control already exists within the Communities.

1. Members of Parliament[19]

According to the Treaty, the European Parliament consists "of representatives of the peoples of the states brought together in the Community." When the Court of Justice considered, in one of its judgments, that the EEC Treaty was "more than an agreement which merely creates mutual obligations between the contracting states," it found confirmation for this view in the fact that the nationals of the Member States are "called upon to co-operate in the functioning of this Community through the intermediary of the European Parliament."[20]

(1) *Direct elections*

Until June 1979—date of the first direct elections for the European Parliament—the members of the Assembly were not "direct" representatives of the citizens of the Community, since the Treaty provided[21] that the "Assembly shall consist of delegates who shall be designated from among their members by the respective Parliaments in accordance with the procedure laid down by each Member State."[22] However, this method of designation of the

[18] See Opinion of December 17, 1959 [1959] E.C.R. 273.

[19] It will be noted that the EEC Treaty refers to "representatives" in Art. 137 and to "delegates" in Art. 138. The Act concerning the direct election refers only to "representatives" (O.J. 1976, L 278/1).

[20] Case 26/62 *Van Gend en Loos* v. *Dutch Fiscal Administration* [1963] E.C.R. at 12.

[21] EEC, Art. 138. Art. 14 of the Act concerning the election provides that EEC, Art. 138 (1) and (2) shall lapse on the date of the first sitting of the first directly elected Assembly (O.J. 1976, L 278/1).

[22] In the U.K. the delegates came from both Houses. The first resolutions creating the delegation are in 848 H.C. Deb. 1293 and 337 H.L. Deb. 1114. In both Houses the motion was moved by a Minister (see *Encyclopedia of European Community Law* (Sweet and Maxwell, 1974), Vol. B, B 10–314. In the Netherlands, *e.g.* a royal decree of February 11, 1958, provided that the delegates were nominated by both Houses, according to a procedure jointly laid down by them.

members was intended as a temporary procedure (although it lasted 27 years!): ECSC, Art. 21 (3) provides for the Assembly to be elected by direct universal suffrage. Agreement concerning the implementation of this provision was finally reached at the Summit Conference held in Paris on December 9 and 10, 1974.[23] A month later, Parliament adopted a new draft convention[24] and on September 20, 1976, the representatives of the Member States meeting in Council agreed on the conditions for the elections. On July 25, 1978, the Council decided to hold the elections between June 7 and 10, 1979.[25]

The elections by direct universal suffrage must be held "in accordance with a uniform procedure in all Member States,"[26] but agreement on such a procedure could not be reached in time for the first election and the 1979 elections were held in accordance with the method of voting decided nationally.[27] One of the first tasks of the newly elected Parliament will be to draft a uniform electoral procedure.[28]

The present directly elected European Parliament is composed of 410 representatives (as against 198 in the previous one) distributed as follows: 81 for the Large Member States (Germany, France, Italy, United Kingdom), 25 and 24 for the Netherlands and Belgium respectively, 16 and 15 for Denmark and Ireland and 6 for

[23] See Bull. 12–1974, 8 (para. 12 of official communiqué).

[24] Resolution of January 14, 1975 (O.J. 1975, C 32/15). The first draft convention was adopted by Parliament on May 17, 1960 (J.O. 1960, 834).

[25] See Act concerning direct election (O.J. 1976, L 278/1). The last notification of parliamentary ratification was deposited by France on June 23, 1979. In accordance with Art. 16 of the Act concerning direct election, the latter entered into force on July 1, 1978 (O.J. 1978, L 173/30) and the date of the election was fixed on July 25, 1978 (O.J. 1978, C 203/6).

[26] EEC, Art. 138 (3).

[27] Act concerning direct election, Art. 7 (2). The electoral system chosen in the U.K. is laid down in the European Assembly Election Act of 1978 and is for England, Scotland and Wales, simple majority in single-member seats ("first-past-the-post") and in Northern Ireland, single transferable vote in 3-member seats. Most other Member States opted for proportional representation via party lists. For the national legal texts concerning electoral procedures see European Parliament doc. PE 54.524, PE 54.757 and PE 57.047; see also Twelfth General Report (1978), 360. For election results, see Bull. 6–1979, 19; the names of the representatives are to be found in O.J. 1979, C 203/6. See Thirteenth General Report (1979), 27.

[28] Act concerning direct election, Art. 7 (1).

Luxembourg.[29] On January 1, 1981, when Greece becomes the tenth Member of the Communities, the total will increase to 434; the first Greek representatives will not be elected by universal suffrage but designated by the Greek Parliament according to national rules laid down for that purpose by the Hellenic Republic.[30]

(2) *Mandate*

Members of Parliament are elected for a term of five years.[31] Anybody can stand for the European Parliament,[32] it being understood that upon election the rules concerning incompatibility[33] must be applied. In case an elected candidate does not wish to relinquish an office which is incompatible with that of representative to the European Parliament he will be replaced, pending the entry into force of the uniform electoral procedure, according to procedures laid down by each Member State.[34] Under the old provisions, members of the European Parliament had to be members of a national Parliament; under the present Act it is simply stated that there is no incompatibility between the two offices.[35]

During the sessions, the representatives enjoy the privileges and immunities accorded to members of national parliaments when in their own state and immunity from detention and legal proceedings when on the territory of any other Member State.

[29] In the U.K. the seats were distributed as follows: England 66, Scotland 8, Wales 4 and Northern Ireland 3. In Belgium: 13 for the Flemings and 11 for the Walloons and in Denmark one of the 16 seats was allocated to Greenland. All other Member States had national lists.

[30] See Act for Greek Accession, Art. 23 (2). In 1984, when the next European elections are held, the Greek representatives will be elected like all the other members of Parliament (O.J. 1979, L 291/1).

[31] See Act concerning direct election, Art. 3 (1).

[32] Included, in the U.K., peers and ministers of religion who are excluded from elections to Westminster.

[33] Act concerning direct election, Art. 6 (1) and (2): membership is incompatible, *e.g.* for active servants and officials of the European institutions and bodies. Incompatibility can also result from national rules pending the entry into force of the uniform electoral procedure. See also rules of procedure, Art. 4 (4), as amended by Resolution of March 12, 1979 (O.J. 1979, C 93/13).

[34] *Ibid.* Art. 12 (1).

[35] *Ibid.* Art. 5.

2. Internal organisation[36]

The internal organisation of the European Parliament is broadly comparable to that of any national Parliament; it is based on a double structure: the political parties and the parliamentary committees.

(1) *Political groups*

Representatives sit in seven multinational political groups[37] (plus a few independents): in a few cases, the elections gave rise to the creation of European political parties: the European People's Party and the European Progressive Democrats; the other groups are the Communists and Allies, the Socialists, the European Democrats (formerly the Conservatives), the Liberals and Democrats and the Technical Coordination Group for the Defence of the interests of the Independent Groups and Members. However, the Act concerning the elections stipulates that representatives shall vote on an individual and personal basis and that they shall not be bound by any instructions nor receive a binding mandate.[38]

The rules of procedure of the European Parliament require for the formation of a political group 21 representatives when they belong to one single Member State, 15 when they come from two Member States and 10 when the number of Member States is three or more.[39]

[36] See rules of procedure (J.O. 1967, 280 and for the last modification O.J. 1979, C 93/13).

[37] In the first elected European Parliament the strength of the political groups was as follows:

Communists and Allies	44
European Democrats	64
Socialists	113
European Progressive Democrats	22
European People's Party: Christian-Democrats	107
Liberals and Democrats	40
Technical Coordination and Defence of Independent Groups and Members	11
Independents	9

See Thirteenth General Report (1979), 27, situation on Dec. 31, 1979.

[38] Act concerning direct election, Art. 4 (1); there are no party whips in the European Parliament.

[39] Rules, Art. 36. See also Art. 36 *bis*: members who do not belong to a political group form the "independents"; they delegate two members to the enlarged Bureau; they have at their disposal administrative services and a secretariat and they are members of the parliamentary committees on the same basis as the political groups (see Art. 37).

(2) *Parliamentary committees*

With regard to the parliamentary committees, the rules of procedure provide for standing or temporary, general or special committees, which can be set up by Parliament which determines their task.[40]

Generally speaking the committees prepare the decisions to be taken by Parliament in plenary session; when Parliament is consulted by the Council on Commission proposals, these are examined by the relevant committee(s) which reports to Parliament. The latter expresses its opinion in the form of a resolution.[41]

(3) *Bureau*

The European Parliament elects a president and 12 vice-presidents which together constitute the "Bureau" (*i.e.* the executive body); this Bureau drafts the agenda of the sessions, decides on matters of competence and makes up the preliminary draft of Parliament's budgets.[42] The Rules also provide for an "enlarged Bureau" consisting of the Bureau and the presidents of the political groups; it is this enlarged bureau which *de facto* constitutes the ultimate centre of decision for all internal matters. Parliament has its own staff grouped in a "secretariat" headed by a Secretary-General.

(4) *Sessions*

The European Parliament holds annual sessions; it meets without requiring to be convened on the second Tuesday in March.[43] Parliament may also meet in extraordinary session. Meetings are

[40] Rules, Art. 37. A parliamentary Committee was set up for each of the following items: Political Affairs; Agriculture; Budgets; Economic and Monetary Affairs; Energy and Research; External Economic Relations; Legal Affairs; Social Affairs and Employment; Regional Policy and Regional Planning; Transport; Environment, Public Health and Consumer Protection; Youth, Culture, Education, Information and Sports; Development and Co-operation; Budgetary Control; Rules of Procedure and Petitions and an *ad hoc* Committee on Women's Rights (O.J. 1979, C 203). Most committees consist of about 27 members.

[41] Rules, Arts. 37–44.

[42] Rules, Arts. 5–7, 12 and 50.

[43] Except after the elections which are held every five years between a Thursday morning and the following Sunday; Parliament then meets automatically on the first Tuesday after expiry of an interval of one month from the above-mentioned Sunday (Act concerning the election, Art. 9 (1)); the first elections were held between Thursday, June 7 and Sunday, June 10, 1979, and the first elected

held alternatively in Strasbourg and Luxembourg.[44] Members of the European Commission may attend all meetings. The Council has agreed to be represented at all the plenary sessions.

The minutes of the meetings are published in the *Official Journal of the European Communities* ("C" series) and the full debates are published in an Annex to the *Official Journal*. Except for the adoption of the motion of censure, and the budgetary procedure,[45] the Assembly acts by a majority of votes cast. There is a quorum when the majority of the representatives is present.[46]

3. Tasks and powers of the European Parliament

According to the Treaty, the European Parliament exercises only "advisory and supervisory" powers; in fact the Treaty of April 22, 1970, amending certain budgetary provisions of the original treaties and of the Merger Treaty has conferred upon Parliament certain budgetary powers which directly bind the Member States. Nevertheless, the European Parliament has no real jurisdiction with regard to Community secondary legislation, neither can it, in any way, directly bind natural and legal persons within the Community.

The main tasks of the European Parliament are to:

- participate in the legislative procedure;
- put questions to the Commission and the Council;
- adopt a motion of censure in case it disapproves of the activities of the Commission;
- discuss the annual General Report submitted to it by the Commission;

European Parliament met on Tuesday, July 17, 1979. See Rules 1 (3) (O.J. 1979, C 93/13), EEC, Art. 139. Parliament is understood to be "in sesssion" from that moment on, even if not actually sitting, until the session (yearly or extraordinary) is declared closed. See Case 101/63 *Wagner* v. *Fohrmann und Krier* [1964] E.C.R. 195.

44 In 1979, *e.g.* the European Parliament held 11 plenary part-sessions; one each month except in August when the House was in recess; two were held in Luxembourg and nine in Strasbourg. See for other activities Thirteenth General Report (1979) 27 and 332.

45 For the motion, see EEC, Art. 144 and p. 27, *infra* under Tasks and Powers of the European Parliament; for the budget, see EEC, Art. 203 (6) and (8) and *infra*, p. 29.

46 Except that under Art. 33 (3) of the Rules, votes (except nominal votes) are always valid when the President has not been formally requested, before the vote, to ascertain the number of members present.

- participate in the budgetary procedure;
- initiate procedures in the Court of Justice against the Council or the Commission in case they fail to act;
- participate in other activities of the Communities.

(1) *Participation in the legislative procedure*

There are 23 instances[47] in the EEC Treaty where consultation of the European Parliament is required as part of the process leading to a formal decision, regulation or directive of the Council. Generally speaking the Treaty provides for consultation on all important matters such as Community policies (agriculture, transport, competition) and association agreements[48]; however, there is no consultation provided, for instance, on economic policy, social policy and the admittance of new members to the Community; but, the Council has agreed to, and does in fact, consult Parliament in many cases where this is not specifically required by the Treaty. When the Council enacts decisions, directives and regulations on the basis of proposals submitted to it by the Commission; consultation of Parliament is initiated by the Council on the basis of those proposals. When provided for in the Treaty, consultation constitutes an "essential procedural requirement" and failure to comply with it constitutes a ground for annulment of an act by the Court of Justice.[49]

The opinions of Parliament are given further weight by the fact that "as long as the Council has not acted, the Commission may alter its original proposal, in particular, when the Assembly has been consulted on that proposal,"[50] but the Commission is not bound to do so. Opinions, such as those of Parliament, have no

[47] See EEC Treaty, Arts. 7, 14 (7), 43 (2), 54 (1), (2), 56 (2), 57 (1), (2), 63 (1), (2), 75 (1), 87 (1), 100, 106 (3), 126, 127, 133 (2), 201, 212, 228 (1), 235, 236 and 238.

[48] EEC, Art. 228 provides that international agreements are concluded by the Council "after consulting the Assembly when required by this treaty"; the only case where it is required is Art. 238 which provides for "agreements establishing an association."

The Council agreed in 1973 to a greater participation of the Parliament in the conclusion of commercial agreements. Seventh General Report (1973), 64.

[49] EEC, Art. 173, first para. For this reason also the EEC Treaty provides that decisions, directives and regulations "shall refer to any proposals or opinions which were required to be obtained pursuant to this treaty," EEC, Art. 190.

[50] EEC, Art. 149, second para.; see, *e.g.* information management, Twelfth General Report (1978), 230.

binding force[51] and therefore, although mention must be made in the act of the fact that the Assembly was consulted, the Treaty does not require the Council to mention whether the expressed opinion was positive or negative, or to refute, in case of a negative one, the arguments brought forward by the Assembly.[52] Finally, it should be noted that if the Commission itself does not modify its proposal, the Council can adopt an act constituting an amendment to that proposal, but then only with an unanimous vote.[53]

Parliament's participation in the legislative process is therefore still rather limited,[54] notwithstanding a slight improvement which was introduced in 1977: the *conciliation procedure* in the event of the Council departing from the opinion of the Parliament. This procedure was instituted by a Joint Declaration of the European Parliament, the Council and the Commission.[55] The aim is to give Parliament an effective participation in the procedure for preparing and adopting acts of general application which give rise to important expenditure or revenue and therefore to seek an agreement between Parliament and the Council, if the latter intends to depart from the Parliament's opinion. The Joint Declaration provides that "when the positions of the two institutions are sufficiently close, the European Parliament may give a new opinion, after which the Council shall take definitive action. The conciliation procedure should normally not take more than three months."[56]

[51] EEC, Art. 189, fifth para.

[52] See Case 6/54 *Government of the Kingdom of the Netherlands* v. *High Authority* [1954 to 1956] E.C.R. 103 at 111. Nevertheless the Commission undertook, starting with the July 1973 session of Parliament to systematically inform Parliament of action taken on its opinions.

[53] EEC, Art. 149; renewed consultation of the European Parliament in such cases is only required if the modifications introduced by the Council do affect the essence of the proposal; see Case 41/69 *ACF Chemiefarma* v. *Commission* [1970] E.C.R. 661.

[54] In 1971, the Commission set up a group to examine the possible reinforcement of the legislative and budgetary powers of the European Parliament. The group's report—the Vedel Report—proposed, *i.e.* a phased extension of the legal powers of the European Parliament, the objective being co-decision and legislative initiative (Bull. Suppl. 4/72). See n. 94, *infra*.

[55] O.J. 1975, C 89/1. The Joint Declaration was adopted on March 4, 1975, during the negotiations for the Treaty amending certain financial provisions.

[56] Unfortunately, the practice has been very different. See, *e.g.* Reg. 214/79 (O.J. 1979, L 35/1) amending Reg. 724/75 (O.J.1975, L 73/1) establishing a European

Irrespective of the opinions issued following consultation by the Council, the European Parliament has always felt free to formulate other resolutions whenever it considered this necessary.[57] The Rules of procedure provide only that such resolutions must concern matters falling within the activities of the Community.

(2) *Parliamentary questions*

The Commission must reply orally or in writing to questions put to it by the Assembly or its members.[58] This obligation, originally only provided for the Commission, is an important aspect of the supervisory powers of Parliament. It is difficult to compare this Community's practice with the national parliamentary procedures, since most questions put by members of the European Parliament are in writing, due to the fact that Parliament assembles in Strasbourg and Luxembourg only during a limited number of days every year.[59] This right of Parliament to obtain answers to its questions was extended considerably over the past years and is widely used.[60]

In the first place, although the Treaty only imposes the obligation to answer on the Commission, the European Parliament itself

Regional Development Fund. Agreement on the proposed regulation within the Council was reached at the meeting of June 26 and 27, 1978. Two conciliation procedures took place on July 24 and October 17; no agreement could be reached. After several exchanges of correspondence between Parliament and Council, a Council declaration was inserted in the minutes and the Reg. was finally adopted without further modifications on February 6, 1979, *i.e.* about seven months after the Council reached agreement. See Annual Report (1978) of the Regional Fund, para. 2.

[57] Rules of procedure, Art. 25; in 1979 the European Parliament adopted 250 resolutions of which 102 are embodying opinions. Parliament even made proposals for legislation; see Resolution of May 11, 1979, containing a draft proposal for a regulation of fishfarming (O.J. 1979, C 140/117).

[58] EEC, Art. 140, third para.

[59] In 1979, the days in session numbered 52.

[60] In 1979, 2,200 questions (written and oral) were put by members of Parliament. Answering a written question is a cumbersome procedure; the reply is prepared by the staff of the Council or of the Commission, formally accepted by these institutions, translated into five other languages, informally discussed with the other institution and finally sent to the European Parliament and published in the *Official Journal*.

extended this obligation to the Council[61] in 1958 and the latter agreed. Secondly, in 1962, the European Parliament introduced the procedure of oral questions followed by a debate[62] which was accepted by the Council and by the Commission with the proviso, however, that, where the Council is concerned, the debate may not be concluded by a vote on a resolution concerning the debated question. Thirdly, in 1973, Parliament introduced the question time in which Council and Commission agreed to participate.[63] Here also a distinction is made between those two institutions since only the answers of the Commission can give rise to a debate. This distinction is of great interest since it confirms the essential difference in the relationship between the Parliament on the one hand, and the Council and the Commission on the other. The supervisory powers referred to above concern only the Commission; the latter is under the political control of the Assembly. This does not apply to the Council whose relationship with Parliament is rather one of political co-operation and partnership and tends to find expression in a dialogue between the two institutions. Once a year Parliament meets with the President of the Council, in the presence of the Commission, to discuss matters of general interest on which the Council has not yet decided—the so-called "colloquies." Similarly, a representative of the Council presents three times a year, to Parliament an oral report on the activities of the Council, and the President of the Council makes a statement to Parliament on the outcome of the meetings of the European Council. Similarly a "programme of the Presidency" is presented by the incoming President of the Council every six months, at the beginning of his six months' term, and a survey of significant developments at the end of the Presidency. Finally, the Chairman of the Conference of Foreign Ministers reports once a

[61] Rules, Arts. 44, 45 and 46. It should be noted, however, that the position of the Council in this respect is very different from that of the Commission. The latter, sitting without interruption can define a position at any time, while the Council does reach a position only at the moment an act is formally adopted during one of its limited sessions (except for rare written procedures). It was therefore agreed that parliamentary questions could only concern decisions taken by the Council.

[62] Rules, Art. 47.

[63] *Ibid.* Art. 47*bis*. At its 257th session on October 15, 1973, the Council agreed to take part (Seventh General Report (1973), 64). The hour originally provided was extended in 1975 to one and a half hours (Ninth General Report (1975), 17).

year on the progress of European political co-operation,[64] this report may be followed by a debate. These addresses, more than any other form of co-operation, give the members of Parliament an opportunity to impress upon the Council their views on the future developments of the Community.

(3) *The motion of censure*

If the European Parliament disagrees with the activities of the Commission, it may adopt a motion of censure, thereby forcing the members of the Commission to resign as a body.[65] This is by far the most impressive power vested in the Assembly, but although several motions have been tabled in the past,[66] never yet has such a motion been carried. The procedural requirements are very heavy. In the first place, the Treaty prescribes a "reflexion time" of three days between the time the motion is tabled and the actual open-vote. Secondly, the Treaty requires that a majority of the representatives cast their vote and that two-thirds of them vote for the motion.[67] Thirdly, the motion must be moved either by a political group or by one-tenth of the members. It seems, furthermore, that this power is more apparent than real, since it only affects the Commission. The consequences of this are twofold. In the first place, the Council which, as the decision-making institution, bears the ultimate responsibility for the activities of the Community,[68] remains outside the reach of the Assembly. In the second place, a motion of censure might very well remain without practical effect. After the members of the Commission have been forced to resign as a body, "they shall continue to deal with current business until they are replaced in accordance with Article 158."[69]

[64] See Ninth General Report (1975), 17 and, *e.g.* Bull. 10–1979, 129.

[65] EEC, Art. 144.

[66] The first time was in November 1972 and was based on the failure of the Commission to submit proposals concerning the reinforcement of the budgetary powers of Parliament; it was later withdrawn.

[67] EEC, Art. 144, second para.

[68] This is true notwithstanding the fact that in most cases the Council can only act on a proposal from the Commission, since the Council is not bound by the contents of the proposal; it may unanimously adopt an act constituting an amendment to that proposal: EEC, Art. 149.

[69] EEC, Art. 144, second para., Merger Treaty, Art. 11 provides that the members of the Commission are appointed by common accord of the Governments of the Member States.

From there on, the decisions are no longer in the hands of Parliament since it has no influence on the choice of the Commissioners; the governments of the Member States could very well reappoint the same members, for instance on national political grounds.

Whatever its ultimate effects, the motion of censure remains the clearest symbol of parliamentary control within the Communities. Furthermore, the real influence of an institution cannot, of course, be judged on the basis of legal provisions alone, it depends in great part on the expertise of its members and their force of persuasion.

(4) *The General Report*

Each year the Commission must publish a general report on the activities of the Communities, not later than one month before the opening of the session of the Assembly.[70] This report is submitted to the European Parliament which discusses it in open session. There exists an obvious link between the discussion of the annual report on the activities of the Communities and the motion of censure on the activities of the Commission,[71] but the Parliament would certainly not wait for the publication of the report to censure the Commission.

The discussion by the Parliament of the annual General Report gives rise to a general debate on all the facets of Community activity, since the report covers all the institutions and bodies, although the work of the Council and the European Investment Bank for instance is described in detail in their own annual reports.[72] The General Report is furthermore supplemented by an Annual Report on the Agricultural Situation in the Community,[73] a Report on the Development of the Social Situation in the Community,[74] and a Report on Competition Policy.[75] The Commission also presents an annual Report on the Regional Fund,[76] on the

[70] Merger Treaty, Art. 18. According to EEC, Art. 139, first para., the Assembly convenes for its annual session on the second Tuesday in March.

[71] In the ECSC Treaty both subjects are provided for in the same Art. 24.

[72] See the Reviews of the Council's work published by the Secretariat-General of the Council and Annual Reports of the EIB.

[73] See Declaration of the System for Fixing Community Farm Prices contained in the Accession Documents of January 22, 1972 (J.O. 1972, L 73/200).

[74] EEC, Art. 122.

[75] Undertaking given by the Commission to Parliament on June 7, 1971; see Resolution (J.O. 1971, C 66/11).

[76] Reg. 724/75 as amended, Art. 21 (O.J. 1979, C 35/1).

State of the Environment[77] and on Consumer Protection and Information Policy.[78]

All those reports constitute an invaluable source of information on the activities of the Communities, the problems they encounter and the proposed and adopted solutions. They are less important for the supervisory function of the European Parliament since it is kept well informed by the permanent contacts it maintains with the Commission mainly through the work of the Parliamentary committees in which the Commission always participates.

More important, however, is the programme-address which the President of the Commission presents to Parliament at the beginning of every year and which gives rise to a general debate.

(5) *Participation in the budgetary procedure*

Originally, the European Parliament, having received the draft budget drawn up by the Council, could only propose modifications to the Council which would then adopt the Community budget. Important modifications were introduced in this procedure which substantially increased the powers of the Parliament in this field.[79] The present budgetary procedure and the role of the European Parliament can be summarised as follows.[80]

The Commission draws up a preliminary draft budget and sends it to the Council, not later than September 1, for the financial year starting the following January 1. The Council establishes the draft budget and forwards it to the Parliament, not later than October 5.

[77] See First and Second Programmes (O.J. 1973, C 112/1 and 1977, C 139/1) and First (1977) and Second (1978) Reports.

[78] See Action Programme (O.J. 1975, C 92/1) and First Report (1977).

[79] In this respect reference must be made to
- the Council Decision of April 21, 1970 on the Replacement of Financial Contributions from Member States by the Communities' own resources (O.J. 1970, 224 and J.O. 1970, L 94/19); this decision entered into force on January 1, 1971;
- the Treaty amending certain budgetary provisions of the Treaties establishing the European Communities and the Merger Treaty of April 22, 1970 (J.O. 1971, L 2/1), entered into force on January 1, 1971.
- the Treaty amending certain financial provisions of the Treaties establishing the European Communities and the Merger Treaty of July 22, 1975 (O.J. 1977, L 359/1), entered into force on June 1, 1977.
- the concertation procedure in budgetary matters is provided for in the third Resolution recorded in the minutes of the meeting of the Council on April 22, 1970 (Treaties establishing the European Communities, European Communities 1978, 885.

[80] EEC, Art. 203.

The European Parliament can then take one of several actions:

(a) approve the draft budget within 45 days; the budget then stands as finally adopted;

(b) refrain from amending it or proposing modifications, within 45 days; the budget then is deemed to be adopted;

(c) adopt amendments and/or propose modifications;

- with regard to expenditure necessarily resulting from the Treaty or from acts adopted in accordance therewith, ("obligatory expenditure"[81]) the European Parliament, acting by an absolute majority of the votes, may only propose modifications;
- with regard to other expenditures, the European Parliament may, acting by a majority of its members, amend the draft budget, but within a maximum rate of increase communicated by the Commission.[82] The draft budget together with the amendments and proposed modifications is forwarded to the Council;

(d) reject the budget.[82a]

The Council then can act under the following conditions:

- with regard to the amendments (expenditures not necessarily resulting from the Treaty or the acts), it may modify them within 15 days by a qualified majority; in the absence of such majority, the amendments stand;
- with regard to the proposed modifications, the Council may reject them (a difference being made between proposed modifications which increase the total amount of expenditures and the others), also by a qualified majority (generally referred to as "reversed majority").

If the Council does not modify the amendments and accepts the proposed modifications, the budget is deemed to be finally adopted and the European Parliament is informed accordingly.

If, on the other hand, one or more amendments have been modified, or proposed modifications rejected or modified, the modified draft budget is returned to the Parliament.

At this stage the powers of the European Parliament are limited

[81] Also referred to as "compulsory expenditure." See *infra*, p. 229.

[82] This maximum rate of increase results from the trend of GNP within the Community, the average variations in the national budgets and the trend of cost of living. EEC, Art. 203 (2).

[82a] EEC, Art. 203 (8); see Bull. 12–1979, 93 and 120.

to the expenditures other than those necessarily resulting from the Treaty or from acts adopted by the institutions, and for which it has a right of amendment as described above. Parliament may, within 15 days, amend or reject the modifications made by the Council to its amendments, acting by a majority of its members and three-fifths of the votes cast. The European Parliament then adopts the budget and the President of the Assembly declares that the budget has been finally adopted.

From this lengthy procedure[83] it follows that the European Parliament now has the final decision within the limits of the maximum amount of increase, with regard to the non-obligatory expenditures[84] and actually adopts the budget. The European Parliament also exercises control over the implementation of the Community budget; in this task it is assisted by the Court of Auditors.[85]

The European Parliament also gives a discharge to the Commission in respect of the implementation of the budget. To this end the Commission submits annually to Parliament and to the Council the accounts of the preceding financial year together with a financial statement of the assets and liabilities of the Communities.[86] The Council and the Assembly in turn examine the accounts and statement together with the annual Report of the Court of Auditors. In giving a discharge to the Commission, the European Parliament acts on a recommendation from the Council.

(6) *Procedures in the Court of Justice*

Apart from intervening in cases before the Court,[86a] instituting third party proceedings to contest a judgment and applying for interpretation of judgment, the European Parliament may bring an

[83] It should be noted however that the provisions of EEC, Art. 203 have been differently interpreted by the Parliament and by the Council and this gave rise to considerable difficulties for the adoption of the 1979 budget; see Twelfth General Report (1978), 51.

[84] The non-obligatory expenditures represented about 25 per cent. in the 1979 Budget, which in total exceeded 14 billion EUA; see Twelfth General Report (1978), 49.

[85] The Court of Auditors was set up by the Treaty amending certain financial provisions of the European treaties and the Merger Treaty; Art. 11.

[86] Treaty amending certain financial provisions, Arts. 14 and 17 or EEC, Arts. 205a and 206 for 1977, see O.J. 1979, L 331/1).

[86a] See Res. of Dec. 14, 1979 (O.J. 1980, C 4/52) to intervene in Cases 138 and 139/79.

action before the Court of Justice against the Council of the Commission for failure of these institutions to act in infringement of the treaties.[87]

This important supervisory power has never been used by the Parliament. If failure to "act" is understood in the sense of failure to "issue a binding act," this right must be seen as intended mainly to induce the Council, the decision-making institution, to take the measures prescribed by the treaties. The problem is that the only action open to the Court of Justice is to declare the failure to act contrary to the Treaty, so that the Court action remains virtually without direct consequences. It should therefore be compared to the motion of censure which the Parliament can use against the Commission. Both constitute external signs of parliamentary control within the Community.

(7) *Participation in other Community activities*

Several agreements of association between the Community and third states provide for a joint Parliamentary Committee. This is the case for the EEC-Greece[88] and the EEC-Turkey[89] associations; 18 representatives of the European Parliament sit in each one of these committees. Similarly the Lomé ACP-EEC Convention[90] provides for a Consultative Assembly of which 98 representatives of the European Parliament are members. Finally, it should be noted that, the European Parliament holds an annual joint meeting with the Consultative Assembly of the Council of Europe.[91]

[87] EEC, Art. 175, first and second paras. It may not, however, challenge the legality of an act of the Council or the Commission under Art. 173.

The European Parliament can, like all the other institutions, be called upon to appear as defendant before the Court of Justice in disputes with its servants. The very first case brought before the Court of Justice by an official of the Communities concerned the Common Assembly of the ECSC, Case 1/55 *Kergall* v. *Assembly* [1954 to 1956] E.C.R. 151. Theoretically, it could also be called upon to compensate for damage under Arts. 178 and 215.

[88] The EEC-Greece Committee is based on Art. 71 of the agreement (J.O. 1963, 354); for the 1978 meeting, see Bull. 11–1978, 65.

[89] See Art. 27 of the agreement (J.O. 1964, 3687); for the 1978 meeting, see Bull. 10–1978, 71.

[90] Art. 80 of the Convention (O.J. 1976, L 25/1); for the 1979 annual meeting, see Bull. 10–1979/81.

[91] See Bull. 1–1978, 74.

4. Conclusion

Until June 1979, the European Parliament played a role of increasing importance within the institutional system of the Communities. This was due partly to the quality of its members and partly to the fact that dual membership gave them a real political power base in their own country. In most cases the latter has disappeared with direct elections.

In the second edition of this book it was stated that "election by universal suffrage only has sense if at the same time the formal powers of the Assembly are increased."[92] The only improvement in this respect is to be found in the budgetary and in the conciliation procedure, and the previous Parliament has clearly shown it knew how to use the newly acquired influence.[93] But no progress was made in other fields such as those proposed by the "Vedel Report,"[94] *i.e.* mainly legislative co-decision. It remains therefore to be seen whether a directly elected European Parliament whose members do not necessarily enjoy the same kind of national political support, will be able to maintain the present momentum and institute a real democratic control within the European Communities.

II. *The Council of the European Communities*[95]

To attain the objectives assigned to the Community, the Treaty provides two means: the establishment of the common market and the progressive approximation of the economic policies of the

[92] *Op. cit.* p. 173.

[93] With regard to the resources of the Regional Fund, *e.g.* the European Parliament was able to override a decision of the European Council.

[94] In 1971, the Commission set up a group to examine the reinforcement of the powers of the European Parliament. The report was published in March 1972 (Supp. 4/72 to Bull.). Taking as a starting point the necessity to reinforce the democratic element in the Communities, the report proposed: (1) a phased extension of the legal powers of the Parliament, the goal being co-decision and legislative initiatives; (2) participation in the drafting of the economic policy programme; (3) co-decision in budgetary matters—the report underlines that this is a secondary problem as compared to legislative co-decision; (4) an increased use of regulations as opposed to directives in the case of legislative co-decision; (5) increased control and (6) election through universal suffrage.

[95] This is the official name of the institution which in accordance with the Merger Treaty, Art. 2, took the place of the Special Council of Ministers of the ECSC, the EEC and the Euratom Council. It will be referred to hereinafter as "Council."

Member States.[96] The common market was established in accordance with the detailed rules and time-limits, laid down mainly in Part Two and Titles I and III of Part Three of the Treaty, and it is the Commission's task to ensure the proper functioning and development of this common market.[97] The second of the two means, on the other hand, is the proper task of the Council: to "ensure co-ordination of the general economic policies of the Member States."[98]

Contrary to the rules applying to the setting up and functioning of the common market, those referring to the economic policies are very general and do not impose precise obligations upon the Member States. It is in the course of the elaboration of the necessary policies that more concrete rules are formulated by the Council. The latter somehow continues the fundamental legislative task of the drafters of the treaties establishing the Communities. It seems logical, therefore, that in the policy field the necessary powers were given to the Council—composed of representatives of the governments of the Member States—rather than to the Commission—an independent body; the more so, since all decisions taken at Community level in the economic policy field, generally limit the corresponding national powers. Those limitations and the corresponding transfers of sovereign rights to the Community institutions are more or less extensive depending on whether the "co-ordination" of the general economic policies of the Member States results in the simple acceptance of general rules to be applied by each government individually[99] or in joint policies[1] or even in Community policies complementing[2] or replacing[3] the national policies.

Whatever the case, all the decisions to be taken by the Council in this field must aim at the greatest possible convergence of the economic policies of the Member States—this is a necessary complement to the common market—and without which the objectives set out in the Treaty cannot be achieved.

[96] EEC, Art. 2.
[97] EEC, Art. 155.
[98] EEC, Art. 145.
[99] See, *e.g.* the medium-term economic policy programmes (O.J. 1977, L 101/1).
[1] European Monetary System (see *infra*).
[2] Regional Policy, Industrial Policy (see *infra*).
[3] Commercial Policy (see *infra* under *External Relations*).

1. Organisational aspects

(1) *Members of the Council*

The Council consists of representatives of the Member States. Each government delegates to it one of its members.[4] Being representatives of their respective countries, the members of the Council act on the basis of instructions or mandates received from their governments.[5] However, they do not constitute a conference of government representatives comparable to those existing in international organisations,[6] neither are they personally designated to fulfil a Community function in the way representatives, commissioners or judges are. They constitute an institution of the Communities and as such their instructions should be directed at achieving the Community objectives, and they must always act in the Community interest. Contrary to what happens at diplomatic conferences, the members of the Council must not, therefore, only further the national interests by negotiating the best deal for their country, but discuss and decide on the best solutions for their common interests. It is not evident that this is always clearly perceived by all participants at the Council meetings.

With regard to the question of who is a "member" of a national government in the absence of indications in the Treaty or in the Rules of procedure, the Community practice shows that governments often delegate persons who strictly speaking do not—according to their own constitution—belong to the government.[7]

Community legislation is also silent on which member of the national government should attend the Council meetings, but the Treaty provides that it is to be "one" member, which indicates that

[4] Merger Treaty, Art. 2, first para. (1); this article is identical to EEC, Art. 146, first para. which it replaced.

[5] For the members of the European Parliament and the Commission, the Treaty specifically provides that they are not to receive instructions or mandates; see respectively Act concerning the election, Art. 4 (1) and Merger Treaty, Art. 10 (2).

[6] *e.g.* the Committee of Ministers of the Council of Europe, Statute, Arts. 13 *et seq.* or the Council of the Organisation for Economic Co-operation and Development, Convention, Art. 7.

[7] This is the case, *e.g.* for the Italian "Secretario del Stato" and the German "Staatssekretär." Whatever the exact position of the representative in his home country, the drafters of the Treaty clearly intended to have persons with political responsibility at government level. This practice dates back to the ECSC and it might very well be that this explains why the ECSC's "Special Council of Ministers" was simply named the "Council" in the EEC and Euratom Treaties and the

each Member State normally has one vote.[8] Often two or more members of a given government will attend the same session.[9] Besides the "general" Council, normally attended by the Ministers of Foreign Affairs, "specialised" Council meetings take place to deal with specific subjects such as agriculture, transport, social affairs. Consequently, it is not unusual to have various Council meetings in session at the same moment. When no member of a government can be present at a Council meeting, the Member State in question may delegate a civil servant[10]; the latter, however, has no vote. But in case of absence, a member may ask another member to vote on his behalf; no member may act on behalf of more than one other member.[11]

Acts of the Council on an urgent matter may be adopted by a written vote (referred to as "written procedure"), *i.e.* the decision is taken while the Council does not actually meet. This procedure may only be adopted when all the members and the Commission are in agreement.[12]

Neither the Treaty, nor the Rules of procedure[13] of the Council refer to a quorum. However, since the Council can only, in the simplest of cases, act by a "majority" of its members[14] (at present nine), no decision can be taken unless five votes are cast, which means that a minimum of three members must be present.[15]

"Council of the European Communities" in the Merger Treaty.

[8] See voting procedure, *infra*.

[9] *e.g.* in 1976 a new development took place, *i.e.* the organisation of joint Council meetings attended by ministers having different responsibilities with a view of finding Community solutions to complex political problems and obtaining an overall view of Community policies in different sectors. Tenth General Report (1976), 33. See *e.g.* Bull. 4–1979, 104.

[10] Rules of procedure, Art. 4 (O.J. 1979, L 268/1); usually, this is the Permanent Representative, see *infra*. [11] EEC, Art. 150. [12] Rules, Art. 6.

[13] The Rules of procedure were adopted by the Council on April 15, 1958; see Merger Treaty, Art. 5 (previously EEC, Art. 151); (O.J. 1979, L 268/1).

[14] EEC, Art. 148 (1); for further details, see *infra*: voting procedure.

[15] When a *qualified majority* is required for an act which does not need a Commission proposal (EEC, Art. 148 (2) last indent) there is the additional requirement of weighted votes representing at least six Member States, but three members could be sufficient, each one acting also on behalf of another member. Finally, when *unanimity* is required, the quorum obviously becomes five, with four members voting on behalf of one other member each. Those figures will not change with Greek accession. It should be noted that abstention by members present or represented does not prevent the adoption of Acts which require unanimity (EEC, Art. 148 (3)).

Council meetings are convened by the President on his own initiative or at the request of one of its members or of the Commission.[16] The office of President is held for a term of six months by each member of the Council in turn.[17] The same rotation applies to all the subordinate bodies such as the Committee of Permanent Representatives[18] and to other meetings of ministers such as those on political co-operation.[19]

The meetings of the Council are not public; they are attended by the Commission[20] represented by its President and those members more particularly responsible for the items under discussion.

(2) *Voting procedure*

The basic rule is that "the Council shall act by a majority of its members"[21] except where otherwise provided in the Treaty.[22] Since most provisions do provide otherwise, the general rule is in fact the exception. The other voting procedures are:

(1) *Qualified majority when the Council is acting on a proposal from the Commission*; this is the normal case[23]; the votes of the Council members are weighted[24] and at least 41[25] votes in

[16] Merger Treaty, Art. 3.

[17] The office of President is held in the following order: Belgium, Denmark, Germany, (Greece), France, Ireland, Italy, Netherlands, United Kingdom, Merger Treaty, Art. 2, second para. and Act concerning Greek accession, Art. 11.

[18] See, *infra*. [19] *Ibid*. [20] Rules of procedures, Art. 4 (*a*) (*b*).

[21] Since there are presently (1980) nine members the majority is five; after Greek accession, this will become six.

[22] EEC, Art. 148 (1).

[23] See, *e.g.* EEC, Arts. 20, 28, 33 (2), 43 (2), 44 (5), 54 (2), 56 (2), 57, 63 (2), 69, 75 (1), 101.

[24] The votes are weighted as follows: (see EEC, Art. 148 (2) and Act concerning Greek accession, Art. 14).

1980		*After Greek accession*	
Belgium	5	Belgium	5
Denmark	3	Denmark	3
Germany	10	Germany	10
France	10	Greece	5
Ireland	3	France	10
Italy	10	Ireland	5
Luxembourg	2	Italy	10
Netherlands	5	Luxembourg	2
United Kingdom	10	Netherlands	5
		United Kingdom	10
Total	58	Total	63

[25] After Greek accession this becomes 45: Act concerning Greek accession, Art. 14.

favour are required; this means, *inter alia*, that the four "large" Member States (France, Germany, Italy and the United Kingdom) cannot impose their will on the "small" ones, but that the latter acting together and also two large Member States can block qualified majority decisions;

(2) *Qualified majority when the Council acts without a proposal from the Commission*; such cases are less numerous[26]; the votes of the Council members are weighted in the same way as in the preceding case and at least 41[27] votes are required, but with the additional condition that those should be cast by at least six[28] members; this means, *inter alia*, that at least two of the small countries besides the large ones have to agree with the measure or that a two-thirds majority of the Member States is required.

(3) *Unanimous vote;* This has become common practice, although it is only required by the Treaty in a limited number of cases[29] and each time it has been used the Council wants to amend a Commission proposal.[30]

The present practice stems from the arrangement regarding majority voting adopted by the Council at its meeting of January 28 and 29, 1966,[31] in Luxembourg, improperly referred to as the "Luxembourg agreement or accords." This arrangement ended the most serious crisis the Community has known[32] in the following terms:

[26] See, *e.g.* EEC, Arts. 73 (2), 106 (2), 108 (2) and (3), 109, 111, 113, 114, 154 and 206.

[27] See n. 23.

[28] After Greek accession this figure remains unchanged, Act concerning Greek Accession, Art. 14.

[29] In many cases, the Treaty provides for a unanimous vote during a certain period after the entry into force of the Treaty (all these time periods have now elapsed) and qualified majority afterwards, see EEC, Arts. 28, 33, 42–44, 54, 56, 57, 63, 69, 75, 87, 101 and 111–114. Unanimous vote was required from the beginning by EEC, Arts. 14 (7), 45 (3), 59, 76, 93 (2), 136, 188, 200, 223, 227.

[30] EEC, Art. 149.

[31] See Sweet and Maxwell, *European Community Treaties* (4th ed., 1980), at p. 235.

[32] The crisis occurred in June 1965, when the Commission submitted a rather ambitious proposal to the Council providing for the definitive establishment of the common agricultural policy linked with the introduction of direct revenue for the Community and increased budgetary powers for the European Parliament. For various reasons the French Government (read: de Gaulle) took offence and embarked upon the "empty-chair" policy, *i.e.* absence from all non-technical meetings. The Luxembourg arrangement concerns both the collaboration between the Council and the Commission and majority voting.

1. Where, in the case of decisions which may be taken by majority vote on a Commission proposal and very important interests of one or more partners are at stake, the members of the Council will endeavour, within a reasonable time, to reach solutions which can be adopted by all the members of the Council while respecting their mutual interests and those of the Community, in accordance with Article 2 of the EEC Treaty.
2. With regard to the preceding paragraph, the French delegation considers that, where very important interests are at stake, the discussion must be continued until unanimous agreement is reached.
3. The six delegations note that there is a divergence of views on what should be done in the event of failure to reach complete agreement.

There seems to be no disagreement about the fact that following this arrangement the Member States should try to reach unanimity on very important issues. Disagreement, however, persists with regard to the next stage, *i.e.* what happens if, after a reasonable time-limit, unanimity is not reached? For five Member States the rules of the Treaty then apply and decisions can be taken with qualified majority; for France, discussions should continue until unanimity is reached.[33] It is obvious that, in taking this position, France is refusing to apply the Treaty rules and there is no doubt that this attitude—which has on occasion been followed by other Member States—has had a disruptive effect on the functioning of the Community. In the communiqué published after the Conference of Heads of State and Government in Paris on December 9 and 10, 1974, it was, therefore, stated that "in order to improve the functioning of the Council of the Community, they consider that it is necessary to renounce the practice which consists of making

[33] There seems therefore to be an error of interpretation in the statement of the British Government according to which "on a question where a government considers that vital national interests are involved it is established that the decision should be unanimous" (Cmnd. 4715, 29). It might be so that, in the past, questions that were implicitly recognised as being important were always decided by unanimous vote, but is it "established" that it should be so? The statement under para. 70 of the same document is therefore more correct: "... where Member States vital interests are at stake, it is Community practice to proceed only by unanimity."

agreement on all questions conditional on the unanimous consensus of all the Member States, whatever their respective position may be regarding the conclusions reached in Luxembourg on January 28, 1966."[34]

(3) *The Committee of Permanent Representatives*

The Committee of Permanent Representatives[35] has moved in a few years from semi-obscurity to full limelight; it fulfils a task which even the wording of the Merger Treaty[36] does not adequately express. In the ECSC Treaty, there is no mention of such a Committee, but from 1953 on, there was a co-ordination Committee[37] composed of civil servants which met to prepare the Council meetings; in those days it already fulfilled an important role.

The creation of the Committee of Permanent Representatives stems from the fact that the Council meets for no more than a few days a month and that with the increase of Community business a more permanent presence seemed required. The Permanent Representatives—national civil servants with the rank of ambassador—follow the various Community activities practically on a day-by-day basis, although they are not empowered to take decisions. They constitute a subordinate organ of the Council and are not a gathering of deputies of the members of the Council; indeed, the latter (like the other institutions) may not delegate its powers of decision.

Nevertheless, once COREPER has reached agreement, for instance on a proposal from the Commission, the decision of the Council can for all practical purposes be considered as having been taken. This is expressed by the fact that in such a case the matter is put on the agenda of the next Council meeting as an "A point." The practice is that the Council accepts all such points and thereby

[34] Bull. 12–1974, p. 8, Pt. 6 of the Communiqué; it will be noted that the expression "Luxembourg Agreement" is not used.

[35] Commonly referred to as COREPER (Comité des Représentants Permanents).

[36] Merger Treaty, Art. 4: "a Committee consisting of permanent representatives of the Member States shall be responsible for preparing the work of the Council and for carrying out the tasks assigned to it by the Council." This provision replaced EEC, Art. 151: "the Council shall lay down its rules of procedure. These rules may provide for the setting-up of a Committee consisting of representatives of the Member States."

[37] This Committee was known as COCOR (Comité de Coordination).

transforms them into one of the binding legal acts provided for in the Treaty. However, it must be emphasised that the Council is in no way bound to accept the "A points" and any member is free to ask for a discussion on the subject, in which case it is placed on the agenda of the next meeting, but as a "B point."

When no agreement can be reached on a subject at COREPER level, but it is thought that a solution could be found at ministerial level, or such is explicitly requested by one of the ambassadors, the subject is placed on the Council agenda as a "B point," *i.e.* a point on which discussion is needed since no ready solution has been found.[38]

COREPER is assisted in its work by a whole series of working groups, which in turn prepare its work and indirectly the work of the Council. These working groups are composed of senior national officials and convene whenever necessary to examine subjects which fall within their competence. When a Commission proposal is sent to the Council, it is examined in the first place by COREPER who decides either to examine it further itself or ask one of the working groups to study it and report to the Committee.

Practically all these meetings: Council, Committee and working groups are attended by the Commission. Each one of those meetings is presided over by a national of the Member State whose representative holds the office of the President of the Council.[39] The great advantage of these working groups composed of national civil servants is that the national view is clearly expressed in Brussels, while the national administrations are informed through these direct contacts of the opinion of the Commission and the other Member States.

In the same way, it can be said that the Permanent Representative fulfils a double function: he defends the national interest within the Community and at the same time he represents the Community viewpoint at home; he thus constitutes a precious link between the national administration and the European institutions.

[38] For the "petite histoire" it should be mentioned that there also exist unofficially "false B points"; those are subjects on which agreement exists but which, for some reason or other, are placed on the agenda for discussion anyway.

[39] See Merger Treaty, Art. 2.

(4) *The European Council*

When important decisions were no longer taken by qualified majority and when the subjects to be decided upon became more and more vital for the general economic development of the Member States, the decision-making process within the Community practically came to a halt. Consequently, it became obvious that new impulses had to be given and new methods of decision-making had to be provided. Since the Council is already a gathering of high-level politicians, the solution was sought more and more in the Conferences of Heads of State or Government[40] which would take the necessary decisions at the highest political level. One such summit conference was held at The Hague in December 1969, with the participation of the Commission. Notwithstanding that, it took several years of hesitation and disagreement before the decisions taken at that conference—economic and monetary union and enlargement of the Community—were implemented. However, it "provided proof of the government's refound and dramatically reaffirmed willingness to press ahead with fresh political vigour to complete the construction of the Community.[41]

Several other "Summit Conferences" were held which allowed the Community to make progress in a certain number of fields.[42] At the 1974 Summit Meeting the Heads of Government, "recognizing the need for an overall approach to the internal problems involved in achieving European unity and the external problems

[40] The Conference was intended to assemble the Heads of Government and Foreign Ministers. However, in France, due to the quasi-presidential system, the Head of State had to attend. The first such conference was held at Paris on February 10 and 11, 1961, see communiqué in Bull. 3–1961, 13 and the second at Bonn on July 19, 1961, see communiqué providing *inter alia* for regular meetings, Bull. 7–8, 1961, 40.

[41] Third General Report (1969), 18.

[42] They were held at the following places and dates, and took decisions regarding *inter alia* the following subjects:
- Paris, October 19 to 21, 1972: European Monetary Co-operation Fund, Regional Development Fund, Political Co-operation, European Union. See Declaration, Sixth General Report (1972), 6;
- Copenhagen, December 1973: establishment of a Community Audit Board and strengthening of the role of the European Parliament in budgetary matters. See Declaration, Seventh General Report (1973), 487;
- Paris, December 9 to 10, 1974: Heads of Governments decide to meet, accompanied by the Ministers of Foreign Affairs, three times a year, the first endowment of the Regional Fund, confirmation of the system of own resources. See Communiqué, Eighth General Report (1974), 297.

facing Europe—consider it essential to ensure progress and overall consistency in the activities of the Communities and in the work on political cooperation—[and] have therefore decided to meet, accompanied by the Ministers of Foreign Affairs, three times a year and, whenever necessary, in the Council of the Communities and in the context of political cooperation."[43]

From 1975 the Heads of State or Government meet three times a year as the European Council. It is presided over by the Head of Government whose representative holds the office of President of the Council and the Secretariat is provided by the General Secretariat of the Council.

Although the European Council, meeting as the Council of the European Communities,[44] is empowered to adopt regulations, directives and decisions—on condition that the requirements provided for in the Treaty are fulfilled[45]—it has, to date, mainly confined itself to issuing general guidelines which have been acted upon by the Council proper and the Commission.[46] Nevertheless, the risk of confusion is great[47] and notwithstanding the fact that "the prospect of regular European Council meetings acted as a catalyst, expediting certain Council work at ministerial level,"[48] it happens that matters are not decided at Council level but left to fill the agenda of the European Council; fortunately, the European Council has nearly always refused to decide on technical matters and confined itself to matters of policy.

Besides meeting in the capacity of an institution of the Community, the European Council also meets in the context of political

[43] Eighth General Report (1974), 297 (2) and (3).

[44] Indeed, nothing prevents a government from delegating the Head of Government rather than any other Minister to a Council meeting. The only question is whether the French President is a "member" of the French Government.

[45] These conditions concern mainly the submission of a proposal by the Commission and the consultation of the European Parliament, when so required.

[46] Ninth General Report (1975), 19.

[47] A typical example was the decision taken by the European Council in December 1977 concerning the endowment of the Regional Fund for the period 1978–1980 (Bull. 12–1977, 51). The expenditures of this Fund constitute, however, "non-compulsory" expenditures for which the European Parliament is, within certain limits, exclusively competent (see, *supra:* participation in budgetary procedure). This created an institutional crisis which ended when the Council of the European Communities accepted a decision reversing the one taken by the European Council. See Bull. 12–1978, 128 and 3–1979, 126.

[48] Ninth General Report (1975), 19.

co-operation and as an informal gathering of top politicians where all major political problems can be freely and privately discussed. One of the characteristics of the European Council is that it is strictly limited to the Heads of Government, their Foreign Ministers and the President and a Vice-President of the Commission. No officials attend the meetings.

At the European Council meeting in London on June 29 and 30, 1977, agreement was reached on a framework for the organisation of the meetings.[49] It was also agreed that "for discussions aimed at reaching decisions or issuing statements there should be a record of conclusions, which should be issued on the authority of the Presidency.[50]

Notwithstanding the existence of some unsolved problems with regard to the relations between the European Council and the other institutions, particularly the European Parliament, this new Community organ has fulfilled a very important role in determining policies, both within the Community and towards third countries.

(5) *Representatives of the Member States in Council*

In accordance with the Treaties, certain decisions must be taken by the Member States acting by "common accord"[51] in such cases the Members of the Council meet as a "conference of representatives of the Governments of the Member States."[52] This conference, and the acts it issues, are to be distinguished from the meetings of the "representatives of the Governments of the Member States meeting within the Council," and their decisions, the latter not being provided for in the Treaties. As to the legal character of such meetings *within* the Council (not: *of* the Council), and of its decisions, the same problems arise in principle as are faced in qualifying the European Council and its "decisions."[53] In practice, meetings within the Council deal with matters for which the Community itself lacks competence, but which, directly or

[49] See Bull. 6–1977, 83.

[50] Those "conclusions" are published in the *Bulletin of the European Communities;* see, *e.g.* the conclusions of the Presidency released at the end of the European Council which met at Paris on March 12 and 13, 1979, in Bull. 3–1979, 9.

[51] See EEC, Art. 167; Merger Treaty, Art. 11.

[52] See EEC, Art. 236.

[53] See *supra*.

indirectly, affect the Community's powers,[54] or are connected with its activities.[55]

2. Tasks and powers of the Council

(1) *Decision-making*

As was pointed out before, under the EEC Treaty it is the Council which must "ensure that the objectives set out in this treaty are attained."[56] The Commission on the other hand is entrusted with the task to "ensure the proper functioning and development of the common market."[57] Obviously the Council is the central institution of the Communities endowed with the "power to take decisions"[58]; but the balance of power is such that in most cases the Council can only act on the basis of a proposal from the Commission and under the judicial control of the Court of Justice. Particularly important is the right of legislative initiative conferred upon the Commission; when the Council meets to "make regulations, issue directives, take decisions,"[59] it does so on the basis of a draft put before it by the Commission and therefore, one might presume, formulated in a way which furthers the Community interest. If the Council wishes to adopt an act constituting an amendment to that proposal it may only do so acting unanimously. But clearly, this latitude does not extend to adopting

[54] See, *e.g.* the Agreement of the Representatives of the Governments of the Member States meeting in the Council of May 28, 1969, providing for standstill and notification, attached to the General Programme for the elimination of technical barriers to trade which result from disparities between the provisions laid down by law, regulation or administrative action in Member States (J.O.) 1969, C 76/9); this agreement is considered as a gentleman's agreement. See also the Resolution of the Council and the Ministers of Education meeting within the Council, of February 9, 1976, on the action programme in the educational field (O.J. 1976, C 38/1).

[55] As stated in Act of Accession, Art. 3 (1) "The new Member States accede by this Act to the decisions and agreements adopted by the Representatives of the Governments of the Member States meeting in Council. They undertake to accede from the date of accession to all other agreements concluded by the original Member States relating to the functioning of the Communities or connected with their activities."

[56] EEC, Art. 145.

[57] EEC, Art. 155.

[58] *Ibid.* although the Commission is also endowed with its own power of decision, see *infra* under *Commission.*

[59] EEC, Art. 189, first para.

an act which bears no resemblance to the original proposal. It seems one must apply here, by analogy, the Court's view on the requirement of renewed consultation of the European Parliament by the Council in case the Council modifies the wording of the draft in such a way that it affects its substance[60]; this means that when the modifications which the Council unilaterally introduces in the original proposal of the Commission affect its substance, the decision of the Council is annulable on the ground of infringement of an essential procedural requirement,[61] since it could not be said that such decision was taken "on a proposal by the Commission."

The provision granting power to the Council to amend a Commission proposal being an exception to a general principle, it must be strictly interpreted.[62]

The Treaty explicitly provides that the Council shall exercise its power to take decisions "in accordance with the provisions of this Treaty,[63] thereby restating a basic principle underlying the transfer of sovereign powers from the Member States to the Community institutions. This principle can be found at the very beginning of all the European Treaties[64]: "Each institution shall act within the limits of the powers conferred upon it by this Treaty." The Council, therefore, is not endowed with a general regulatory competence, but may only take those decisions which are explicitly provided for by a provision of Community legislation[65]; it only has "conferred

[60] EEC, Art. 149, second para. Case 41/69 ACF *Chemiefarma* v. *Commission* [1970] E.C.R. 661 at 662 (3).

[61] EEC, Art. 173.

[62] An analogous question is whether, in order to avoid amendments to its proposal, the Commission may withdraw it. One may not deny the Council the right to amend the proposal within acceptable limits, and withdrawing a proposal each time the Council is going to do this, would empty Art. 149, first para. of its contents.

[63] EEC, Art. 145.

[64] ECSC, Art. 3; EEC, Art. 4 and Euratom, Art. 3.

[65] This explains why EEC, Art. 190 requires regulations, directives and decisions to state the reasons on which they are based; according to the Court of Justice, this means *inter alia* that the legal ground must be mentioned. So also the rules of procedure of the Council, Art. 11, which provides that a Council regulation must contain the indication of the provision by virtue of which the regulation is enacted. For further details see *infra*: Chap. 4; *Community Acts*. See Court of Justice, Case 22/70 *Commission* v. *Council* (AETR) [1971] E.C.R. 263 where the Court indicates that authority to act flows from the Treaty and from measures adopted within the framework of the Treaty provisions by the Community institutions.

powers." There are, however, cases where action by the Council appears necessary to attain one of the objectives of the Community, while the Treaty has not provided the necessary powers; in such a case the Council may, acting unanimously on a proposal from the Commission, and after consulting the European Parliament, take the appropriate measures.[66] This should not be considered as opening unlimited opportunity for the institutions to increase the powers of the Council, although it does constitute a way of supplementing the Treaty provisions without going through the cumbersome procedure of amending the Treaty.[67] Indeed, the appropriate measures may only be taken when action is necessary "to attain one of the objectives of the Community," which clearly indicates that the powers granted by this provision are purely complementary. Also, the required unanimous vote of the Council should provide the necessary guarantee, since the extension of the Community's powers, generally speaking, will reduce the powers of the Member States in the same proportion. Finally, the Commission's proposal and the opinion of the Assembly should assure that the Community's interests are taken into consideration.[68]

Related to this principle of "conferred powers" is the question of "implied powers." In several cases the Court of Justice has admitted that "rules established by international agreements or by law are considered to imply those rules without which the first either would have no sense or could not be reasonably or successfully applied."[69] This prudent approach to a very delicate question cannot be considered as opening the door to extensive treaty interpretation in regard to the powers of the Community institutions. The principle of "conferred powers" therefore remains.

[66] EEC, Art. 235; see also ECSC, Art. 95 and Euratom, Art. 203.

[67] See EEC, Art. 236.

[68] At the Paris Summit Meeting in October 1972 it was agreed that for the purpose of carrying out the tasks laid down in the different programmes of action "it was desirable to make the widest possible use of all the dispositions of the Treaties, including Art. 235 of the EEC Treaty" (Cmnd. 5109, para. 15). See also Case 8/73 *Hauptzollamt Bremerhaven* v. *Massey-Fergusson* [1973] E.C.R. 897, where the Court found that the authority for Reg. 803/68 on the value of goods for customs purposes was to be found in Art. 235.

[69] Case 8/55 *Fédération Charbonnière de Belgique* v. *High Authority* [1954 to 1956] E.C.R. 245 at p. 299 and Case 22/70 *Commission* v. *Council* [1971] E.C.R. 263 at p. 280 (72).

The decision-making powers of the Council are provided *inter alia* in the field of legislation, budget and international agreements.

When the Council enacts *legislation* through regulations, directives and decisions, it in fact continues, as was said, the work of the draftsmen of the treaties. This is particularly true for the EEC Treaty which, in many aspects, contains no more than general principles to guide the Community law-makers and the necessary rules of procedure.[70]

The *budgetary* powers have been examined in some detail in the previous section.[71]

As for *international agreements* to be entered into by the Communities, the powers to do so are based upon the fact that the Community was given legal personality[72] and the Treaty provides that agreements between the Community and one or more states or an international organisation shall be negotiated by the Commission and concluded by the Council.[73]

(2) *Co-ordination of economic policies*

Besides having the power to take decisions in all cases provided for by the treaties in order to ensure that the objectives set out therein are attained, the Council is more specifically entrusted with the task to "ensure co-ordination of the general economic policies of the Member States."[74] As will be seen, the provisions concerning the establishment and functioning of the Common Market are, generally speaking, of a rather technical character and consist of a set of more or less specific rules. These rules are intended to establish and guarantee the basic freedoms of movement of goods,

[70] See, *e.g.* Agricultural Policy: EEC, Art. 39 sets out the "objectives" while Art. 43 provides that "the Council shall on a proposal from the Commission and after consulting the Assembly, acting unanimously . . . make regulations, issue directives, or take decisions"; free movement of labour: EEC, Arts. 48, 49; the right of establishment: EEC, Art. 54; transport: EEC, Art. 75; the rules of competition: EEC, Art. 87; the approximation of laws: EEC, Art. 100. The EEC Treaty is therefore referred to as a "traité-cadre," as opposed to the ECSC Treaty which constitutes a "traité-loi."

[71] See under European Parliament: participation in budgetary procedure.

[72] EEC, Art. 210.

[73] EEC, Art. 228; it should be noted that those agreements are "binding upon the institutions of the Community and on the Member States."

[74] EEC, Art. 145.

persons, services, capital and related payments, the right of establishment and the rules governing agriculture and competition. Until now it is mainly in those domains that the Community institutions have exercised their law-making powers, by making regulations, issuing directives and taking decisions. But those freedoms alone do not make a single market.

The co-ordination of the general economic policies constitutes a necessary complement to those activities. The task of the Council in this field appears, on the other hand, less well defined; it is by its very nature a question of policy-making rather than law-making; it is not governed by precise timetables set out in the Treaty as it grows and varies with economic and political circumstances. This task is referred to in the EEC Treaty as "economic policy, conjunctural policy, balance of payments and commercial policy.[75] It should be noted that with regard to those fields of activity, the Treaty refers to the "application of procedures" and not to positive action in the form of legislation.[76] This explains the great variety of acts and the number of organs involved in defining these policies: declarations of the Council, resolutions of the Council, resolutions of the Council and of the representatives of the governments of the Member States, work programmes, etc. Out of this ill-defined situation grew, as was mentioned, the necessity to set up an organ with incontestable political power: the meetings of Heads of State and of Government, which became later the European Council.[77] It will also be observed that with regard to the above-mentioned policies, the Treaty either provides that the Member States shall regard them "as a matter of common concern,"[78] or that the Member States shall "pursue the needed economic policies"[79] or that the Member States shall "co-ordinate their economic policies [and] . . . shall provide for cooperation between their appropriate administrative departments"[80] or, finally, that the Member States shall "proceed by common action."[81]

[75] EEC, Pt. 3, Title II.

[76] EEC, Art. 2 (*g*); the other activities of the Community are described in a more precise way: elimination, establishment, abolition, adoption, institution.

[77] See *supra*, p. 42.

[78] EEC, Arts. 103 (1) and 107 (1).

[79] EEC, Art. 104.

[80] EEC, Art. 105 (1).

[81] EEC, Art. 116, first para.

Clearly, this task of co-ordinating economic policies is both essential for the development of the Community and ill-defined as regards its means and ultimate objectives.[82] Nevertheless the system works and considerable progress has been made, such as the setting-up of the European Monetary System for which neither powers nor procedures have been provided in the Treaty. This, however, does not mean that the actual situation is satisfactory, since the absence of procedures means that the delicate checks and balances of the institutional framework do not function. When Council decisions are not taken in the form of "regulations," "directives," or "decisions," there is no Commission proposal, no consultation of the European Parliament, and no judicial control by the Court of Justice. The same is true when decisions, often of vital importance to the Community, are taken by the European Council. It seems evident that some solutions will have to be found, if one wants to preserve a democratic approach to the exercise of those powers transferred by the Member States to the European institutions.

(3) *Political co-operation*

In the final communiqué of the Conference of Heads of State or Government on December 1 and 2, 1969 in The Hague, the Ministers of Foreign Affairs were instructed to study the best way of achieving progress in the matter of political unification within the context of enlargement.[83] At the request of the Ministers, the Davignon Report was submitted[84] and accepted by the Ministers of Foreign Affairs in 1970. The aim is to further political unification by

[82] It will be remembered that at one point the European Council sought to define the ultimate objective as "European Union," at the November 1976 meeting in The Hague. See statement published at that occasion, Bull. 11–1976, 93. The European Council invited the Foreign Ministers and the Commission to report to it, once a year, on the results obtained and the progress which could be achieved in the short-time in the various sectors of union, thus translating into reality the common concept of European union. These yearly reports are published; see Thirteenth General Report (1979), 23 and Bull. Suppl. 8–1977 and 1–1979. The concept of European union stems from the report on European union presented by Mr. Tindemans; see Bull. Suppl. 1–76. An intermediate stage is constituted by the Economic and Monetary Union, see Communiqué of the 1969 Summit meeting in The Hague, Bull. 1–1970, 11 and *infra*.

[83] Third General Report (1969) 489 (15).

[84] See Bull. 11–1979.

co-operating in the field of foreign affairs.[85] In 1974, the Heads of State or Government adopted a second report on European political co-operation[86] and approved, *inter alia*, the following measures: Foreign Ministers will meet four times a year; if the circumstances are sufficiently grave or the subject matter sufficiently important, a ministerial meeting may be replaced by a conference of Heads of State or Government. The Political Directors of the Foreign Ministries meet in the Political Committee with a view to preparing ministerial meetings and carrying out tasks entrusted to them by the Ministers.[87] The Commission is represented at all the meetings, and twice a year the Ministers meet with the Political Affairs Committee of the European Parliament.

It is important to note that the political co-operation machinery, which deals on the inter-governmental level with problems of international politics, is distinct, and additional to the activities of the institutions of the Community which are based on the commitments undertaken by the Member States in the EEC Treaty, although both sets of machinery have the aim of contributing to the development of European unification.

There exist, therefore, two parallel systems in connection with activities of the European Communities: one is "communautaire," the other is "inter-governmental." Obviously there is a danger of lack of co-ordination, if not of conflict. An attempt to prevent this is undertaken in the form of close contacts with the institutions of the Community.[88] The Commission thus plays an increasing role and is fully involved in almost all the political co-operation work being carried out. With regard to Parliament, it was agreed to associate it

[85] The objectives of that co-operation are:
- to ensure by means of regular consultations and exchanges of information, improved mutual understanding as regards the main problems of international relations;
- to strengthen solidarity between governments by promoting harmonisation of their views, and the alignment of their positions and, whenever it appears possible and desirable, joint action.

[86] See Seventh General Report (1973), 502.

[87] Other measures concern a "group of correspondents" with the task to follow the implementation of the political co-operation, working parties, medium and long term studies, the role of embassies in the nine capitals and in third countries.

[88] For further details, see Seventh General Report (1973), 508.

closely with the work of the President's office, *inter alia*, through replies to questions on political co-operation put by members.[89]

At the December 1974 Paris meeting of Heads of States or Governments, it was decided that the President of the Council would be the spokesman for the Nine and would set out their views in international diplomacy. The Community is getting more and more involved in several areas of international political co-operation, an area which strictly speaking does not come under the provisions of the European treaties.[90]

III. *The Commission of the European Communities*[91]

Although in many cases the Commission participates, as was seen, in the law-making process of the Community when it exercises its right of initiative through the submission of the required proposals to the Council, the latter must be considered as the Community legislator. The Commission, on the other hand, is responsible for the functioning and development of the Common Market and is the guardian of the Community legislation; it administers the Communities' finances, negotiates the international agreements and represents the Community both inside and in the international field; it also has its own powers of decision. In short, it should be seen as the executive branch of the Community. As such, it constitutes the moving power behind the Community's activities and its uninterrupted presence on the Brussels scene, its staff and its worldwide relations constitute the necessary conditions for it to play a major role within the institutional system of the European Communities.

[89] See, *e.g.* Thirteenth General Report (1979), 333, where a distinction is made between the Parliamentary questions addressed to the Commission, the Council and the "Conference of Ministers of Foreign Affairs (political co-operation)."

[90] The Final Act of the Conference on Security and Co-operation in Europe (Helsinki, on August 11, 1975) was signed by the President of the Council; The Community as such took part in the meeting of Belgrade (October 4, 1978–March 9, 1979). Twelfth General Report (1978), 264.
A section on political co-operation is to be found in the annual General Report of the Community and often in the monthly Bulletin.

[91] This is the official name of the institution which was established by the Merger Treaty (Art. 9) and which took the place of the High Authority of the European Coal and Steel Community, the Commission of the European Economic Community and the Commission of the European Atomic Energy Community. Hereinafter this institution will be referred to as "Commission."

Most important, however, is the fact that it embodies and represents the common or Community interest and is responsible for ensuring that this interest prevails as regards decisions taken by Member States, the Council and natural and legal persons alike.

1. The European Commissioners

The present Commission is composed of 13 members[92] but this will change on the accession of the Hellenic Republic (fixed for January 1, 1981), when a fourteenth member will be added.[93]

The requirements for designation as a European Commissioner are very broadly defined: apart from the fact that the members of the Commission must be nationals of one of the Member States[94] and that no more than two members from the same Member State are permitted,[95] the Treaty provides that members "shall be chosen on the grounds of their general competence" and that their "independence" must be "beyond doubt."[96]

This independence—which is the main characteristic of the Commission—is given a concrete meaning by the conditions required for the *performance of duties*.[97] This is particularly important since the Commission represents the Communities' general interest and must be in a position to take a stand against any government which tries to put national interests first. This function can only be accomplished when the members of the Commission are totally independent of national governments, especially their own.

[92] The High Authority of the ECSC was composed of nine members, as was the EEC Commission; the Euratom Commission had only five; a total of 23 Commissioners. This was reduced to 14 by the Merger Treaty. In 1970 this number was reduced to nine in accordance with Arts. 10 and 32 of the same Treaty. On January 1, 1973, when Denmark, Ireland and the U.K. joined the Community, this number was, once more, increased to 13 (Act of Accession, Art. 15 and Adaptation Decision, O.J. 1973, L 2/1). According to the Merger Treaty, Art. 10, second para., the number of members may be altered by the Council, acting unanimously.

[93] Act concerning Greek accession, Art. 15 (O.J. 1979, L 291/17).

[94] Merger Treaty, Art. 10 (1), last sub-para.; Art. 10 provides also that the Commission must include at least one national of each of the Member States.

[95] Merger Treaty, Art. 10 (1), fourth sub-para.

[96] Merger Treaty, Art. 10 (1), first sub-para.

[97] Merger Treaty, Art. 10 (2): "The members of the Commission shall in the general interest of the Communities, be completely independent in the performance of their duties."

It must be remembered that it is in connection with this independent position that the ECSC Treaty used the term "supranational."[98] Although the word did not reappear in the later European treaties, the substance of the concept remains. With regard to this independence, obligations are imposed both on the members of the Commission[99] and on the Member States.[1] If a Commissioner breaches these obligations he may be dismissed by the Court of Justice or, if no longer in office, deprived of his pension rights. It might seem odd, therefore, that the members of the Commission are appointed by the very governments of the Member States in relation to which this independence is so strongly stressed. Other methods of designation have been suggested in the Tindemans report to the European Council on European union.[2]

Members of the Commission are appointed for four years; the appointment is renewable.[3] The President, who is designated six months before taking office and the five Vice-Presidents on the other hand are appointed for two years only, also by common consent of the governments of the Member States; these appointments are renewable.[4]

2. The Commission's tasks and powers

The tasks and powers of the Commission are broadly described

[98] ECSC, Art. 9: "the Members of the High Authority will refrain from any action incompatible with the supranational character of their duties. Each Member State undertakes to respect this supranational character. . . ."

[99] Merger Treaty, Art. 10 (2) and (3): they may neither seek, nor take instructions from any government or any other body; they shall refrain from action incompatible with their duties; they may not engage in any other occupation, whether gainful or not, and they must give a solemn undertaking to behave with integrity and discretion as regards the acceptance, after they cease to hold office, of certain appointments and benefits.

[1] *Ibid.* The Member States undertake to respect this independence and not to seek to influence the Members of the Commission in the performance of their tasks.

[2] The report suggests that the President of the Commission be appointed by the European Council and that the President would appoint his colleagues in consultation with the Council, after having appeared before the Parliament to make a statement and have his appointment confirmed by vote; Bull. Suppl. 1/76, 31.

[3] Merger Treaty, Art. 11. See Arts. 12 and 13 for replacement and compulsory retirement.

[4] Merger Treaty, Art. 14. To date, the President and Vice-Presidents have always been reappointed at mid-term.

in EEC, Article 155 and in more precise form in various treaty provisions.

The main tasks of the Commission are the following:

- to enforce the application of Community law;
- to issue recommendations and opinions;
- to exercise its power of decision;
- to exercise the powers conferred upon it by the Council;
- to participate in the legislative procedure;
- to negotiate international agreements;
- to implement the Budget;
- to publish an annual General Report on the activities of the Communities.

(1) *Enforcement of Community law*

As the European treaties and the acts of the institutions under these treaties (secondary legislation) impose obligations on the Member States, the institutions and the natural and legal persons operating within the Community, the Commission was given certain powers with regard to all those who come under the jurisdiction of Community law. These powers concern the gathering of information and the institution of proceedings in case of failure to fulfil an obligation.

The power to gather information is generally provided for by EEC, Article 213 and more specifically by other provisions of the Treaty and of Community acts.[5] The Commission must be in a position to collect any information and carry out any checks required for the performance of the tasks entrusted to it. Although no general implementing provisions have been laid down by the Council, the obligation imposed upon the Member States to "facilitate the achievement of the Community's tasks"[6] should provide the necessary legal ground for the Commission to obtain all the required data.

When the Commission considers that a *Member State* has not fulfilled an obligation under a Community provision:

[5] See, *e.g.* EEC, Arts. 72, 73 (2), 93 (3), 109 (2) and 111 (5). EEC, Art. 213 provides that the Commission may collect information "within the limits and under conditions laid down by the Council in accordance with the provisions of this treaty"; although no general provisions have been laid down, there are several Community dirs. and regs. which provide the obligation for Member States and undertakings to supply the Commission with certain information. See, *e.g.* Reg. 17, Arts. 4 and 5, the first Reg. implementing EEC, Arts. 85 and 86 (J.O. 1962, 204).

[6] EEC, Art. 5.

(1) it shall[7] remind the Government in question of its duties and invite it to take the measures necessary to ensure conformity with Community law or submit its observations, all this within a time-limit of usually two months;
(2) if no action is taken by the Member State or no comment submitted, or if those comments do not convince the Commission, the latter shall deliver a reasoned opinion on the matter which will lay down a time-limit for the Member State to comply;
(3) if the Member State does not comply, the Commission may[8] bring the matter before the Court of Justice;
(4) if the Court of Justice finds that the Member State has failed to fulfil its obligation, "the State shall be required to take the necessary steps to comply with the judgment."[9]

Since the EEC Treaty[10] does not provide for legal coercive ways where Member States are concerned, further compliance is left to

[7] EEC, Art. 169. The terms used by this provision indicate that once the Commission has determined that a Member State has not fulfilled an obligation (and with regard to this determination the Commission has discretionary power) there is an obligation for the commission to act. The existence of this obligation is essential in a system where the plea of *non-ad impletus contractus* is not admissible (see Cases 90 and 91/63 *Commission* v. *Luxembourg* and *Belgium* [1964] E.C.R. 625 at p. 631); the other Member States must have the assurance that violation of an obligation under the Treaty will be prosecuted, although they could either initiate action themselves against the culprit in accordance with EEC, Art. 170 or against the Commission for failure to prosecute the infringement, EEC, Art. 175, although the Commission is not likely to publicly announce that a failure exists on the part of a Member State; furthermore one might wonder whether the existence of Art. 170 does not preclude for a Member State the use of Art. 175 in this case.

[8] At this point the Commission's power is entirely discretionary; there is no legal obligation to go to Court, but the considerations developed in the preceding footnote apply all the same.

[9] EEC, Art. 171. Interesting is the fact that the whole procedure starts because the Member State did not comply with an obligation under the Treaty; the Commission requires the State to "comply with the opinion" (EEC, Art. 169, second para.) delivered by the Commission; the consequence of a finding by the Court that the State has failed to fulfil an obligation, is that the latter must "comply with the judgment." This means that both reasoned opinion and judgment contain indications on how the obligation must be fulfilled: this gives those two institutions wide discretionary powers as regards the manner in which the consequences of violations have to be dealt with.

[10] The ECSC Treaty provides for some kind of coercive measures (see Art. 88) but they were never applied.

the Member State. The only other step the Commission can take in case the Member State does not comply with the judgment of the Court, is to start the procedure all over on the ground that by not complying with the judicial decision, the Member State has failed to fulfil an obligation under the Treaty.[11]

On the other hand, the more advanced the economic integration of the Member States, the more difficult it becomes for one of them to break the rules, since each Member State is in some way or another dependent on the goodwill of its partners for implementing the various common policies. The Court of Justice refers to a "failure in the duty of solidarity" accepted by Member States by the fact of their adherence to the Community and adds that such a failure strikes at the fundamental basis of the Community legal order[12]; furthermore it seems clear that if the violation were to cause damage to other Member States, the Community or private parties, it might engage the responsibility of the Member State in question.

The majority of infringements by Member States concern quantitative restrictions on the free movement of goods, and more particularly, measures having equivalent effect.[13] It should be noted, on the other hand, that violations by Member States are the object of contacts and discussions between the Commission and the government concerned and are often settled outside Court.

With regard to other *institutions*—the only one concerned here is the Council—the Commission can initiate a Court action both when it is of the opinion that an action by the Council violates the Community provisions[14] or when a failure of the Council to act is considered by the Commission as an infringement of Community legislation.[15] No legal recourse exists against the European Parlia-

[11] This happened in the case of Italy, see Case 48/71 *Commission* v. *Italy* [1972] E.C.R. 527, and in the case of France, see Case 232/78 *Commission* v. *France* (not yet published)—import of sheepmeat and Commission appeal of January 14, 1980.

[12] See Case 39/72 *Commission* v. *Italy* [1973] E.C.R. 101 at 112 and Case 128/78 *Commission* v. *U.K.* [1979] E.C.R. at 429 (12).

[13] A list of infringements is to be found since 1968 in the Bull. See also the General Report, *e.g.* Tenth General Report, 295; Eleventh General Report, 282, Twelfth General Report, 310 and Thirteenth General Report, 279.

[14] EEC, Art. 173; this action will be examined in detail *infra*. See, *e.g.* Case 22/70 *AETR* [1971] E.C.R. 263.

[15] EEC, Art. 175. To date, no such actions were undertaken by the Commission against the Council.

ment since its powers to take binding decisions are extremely limited.

With regard to *undertakings* (and natural persons) the Commission has been endowed in certain cases with the power to impose penalties. It is generally admitted that the EEC Treaty empowers the Council to provide for penalties in case of non-compliance by natural and legal persons in the regulation it makes pursuant to the Treaty.[16] Penalties have been provided in several cases, the most important ones being in the field of competition.[17] It should be noted also that decisions of the Commission imposing such fines are enforceable in the Member States.[18]

(2) *Recommendations and opinions*

The Commission shall formulate recommendations and deliver opinions on matters dealt within the Treaty, if the latter expressly so provides or if the Commission considers it necessary.[19] It should be remembered that recommendations and opinions have no binding force[20] so that in fulfilling this task the Commission exercises a purely advisory task.

The EEC Treaty provides for several cases where a recommendation or opinions from the Commission is required,[21] other cases where it is simply provided as a possibility.[22] According to the Treaty, the Commission can also issue recommendations and

[16] EEC, Art. 172.

[17] EEC, Art. 87 (2), see Reg. 17, Art. 15, first Regulation implementing EEC, Arts. 85 and 86 (J.O. 1962, 204); see also Reg. 11, Art. 18, concerning the abolition of discrimination in transport rates and conditions in implementation of EEC, Art. 79 (3) (J.O. 1960, 1121) and Reg. 1017/68, Art. 22, applying rules of competition to transport by rail, road and inland waterway (J.O. 1968, L 175/1). The ECSC Treaty has conferred the power to impose penalties in several instances: Arts. 47 (refusal to furnish information), 54 (use of outside funds for investment), 58 (violation of production quotas), 59 (allocation of resources), 64 (prices), 65–66 (competition rules) and 68 (wages).
The Euratom Treaty provides for penalties in Arts. 83 (safeguard) and 145 (other infringements).

[18] EEC, Art. 192; see also Chap. 4, 4.

[19] EEC, Art. 155.

[20] EEC, Art. 189.

[21] A Commission recommendation is required by EEC, Art. 111 (2) (tariff negotiations with third countries); an opinion is required by EEC, Art. 237 (accession of new Member States).

[22] See, *e.g.* EEC, Art. 93 (1) although the term used is "propose," but legally speaking it has the same value as a recommendation.

opinions when this is not expressly provided for but then it must be "on matters dealt with in this treaty."[23] The term treaty must be interpreted as including the whole of the Community legislation: from the moment the Council has acted in a given field, for instance on the basis of EEC, Article 235, this field comes under the provisions of the Treaty and the Commission may formulate recommendations and deliver opinions.[24]

(3) *Exercise of power of decision*

The Treaty does not confer upon the Commission a general power to take decisions: the basic principle of "conferred powers" also applies here,[25] as is made clear by the words "in the manner provided for in this treaty." Since, as was seen, the Council must be considered as the Community law-maker, the fact that the Commission also has the power of decision might create the impression that the legislative power within the Community is shared by two institutions. However, a distinction must be made between the power of decision in the sense of "legislation" and the power of decision in the sense of "execution." Both the legislator and the executive have the power to make regulations, issue directives and take decisions,[26] but they do not operate quite on the same level, although it must be recognised that no clear-cut distinction exists between the two.[27]

The power of decision directly entrusted by the Treaty to the Commission is mainly situated in the field of the "functioning and development of the common market,"[28] *i.e.* administration of the

[23] That limitation necessarily applies only to recommendations and opinions not provided for in the Treaty; from the moment they are provided for, the matter they refer to necessarily is dealt with in the Treaty.

[24] See, *e.g.* the Commission's opinion and recommendation to the Member States on the regional development programmes (O.J. 1979, L 143/7 and 9); these programmes are provided for in Reg. 724/75 (O.J. 1975, L 73/1).

[25] So does the principle of "implied powers" (see *supra* under Council, power of decision).

[26] See EEC, Art. 189, first para., which makes no distinction between Council and Commission.

[27] The most that can be said is that the Council decisions lay down general rules which often complete the Treaty provisions in important matters of overall policies and are therefore of a rather legislative nature, while the Commission decisions in general apply Community legislation to concrete situations or concern matters of less overriding importance and are therefore situated in the administrative sphere.

[28] EEC, Art. 155.

customs union,[29] the safeguard clauses,[30] the competition rules,[31] the Community budget,[32] and to some extent the external relations.[33] Other, more extensive powers of decision for the Commission have been provided by the Council through Community secondary legislation.[34]

In certain cases, when exercising its right to act, the Commission has a choice as to the form of the measure,[35] in other instances no form is prescribed,[36] sometimes a given act is required.[37]

Decisions of the Commission are taken by the majority of its members[38]; and when at least seven members are present[39]; the Commission may not delegate its power of decision to any one of its members or to its civil servants[40]; neither can the Commission delegate such powers to autonomous organs.[41]

[29] See EEC, Arts. 10 (2), 13 (2), 22, 33 (6) and (7).
[30] See EEC, Arts. 17 (4), 25 (2) and (3), 26, 37 (3), 46, 73 (1) and (2), 107 (2), 108 (3), 115, first and second paras., 226, Act of Accession, Art. 135 (2).
[31] See EEC, Arts. 89 (2), 90 (3), 91 (2), 93 (2), 97, second para.
[32] The Commission is responsible for implementing the budget and administering the various Community Funds, such as the Social Fund (EEC, Art. 124).
[33] See *infra*, 199. [34] In accordance with EEC, Art. 155, last indent; see *infra*, 61.
[35] See EEC, Art. 90 (3): the Commission shall address "appropriate directives or decisions."
[36] *e.g.* EEC, Art. 10 (2) "the Commission shall determine the methods of administrative co-operation."
[37] *e.g.* EEC, Art. 45 (2): ". . . directives issued by the Commission."
[38] Merger Treaty, Art. 17, first para. At present the Commission consists of 13 members, the majority being 7; after Greek accession the numbers become 14 and 8.
[39] Rules of Procedure, Art. 6; after Greek accession this will be 8.
[40] See, however, Dec. 68/183 authorising certain management measures to be taken within the framework of the common organisation of agricultural markets (J.O. 1968, L 89/13). This decision is based upon Art. 27 of the Rules of Procedure of the Commission: "The Commission may empower its members and officials to take on its responsibility, all or any of the measures, in particular financial measures, required for the preparation and implementation of acts adopted by the Commission within the scope of their duties" (J.O. 1963, 181). See Case 8/72 *Vereniging van Cementhandelaren* v. *Commission* [1972] E.C.R. 977, concerning the legality of a document signed by a Director-General rather than by a member of the Commission. According to the Court the official acted "not under a delegation of powers but merely under an authorisation to sign" and such an authorisation constitutes "a measure concerning internal organisation of the services of the Commission in accordance with Article 27 of the Provisional Rules of Procedure adopted under Article 7 of the Treaty of 8 April 1965, establishing a single Council and a single Commission." *Ibid.* 989 (12) and (13).
[41] See Case 9/56 *Meroni* v. *High Authority* [1957 and 1958] E.C.R. 133.

The Rules of Procedure of the Commission, amended several times, have been published in the *Official Journal of the European Communities*.[42]

(4) *Exercise of powers conferred by the Council*

Most of the Commission's decisions are based on powers provided for in the acts of the Council; the Treaty empowers the latter to confer powers on the Commission for the implementation of the rules the Council lays down.[43] The necessity of such delegation was felt very early when the first decisions were taken regarding the common agricultural policy. This common policy required an impressive number of administrative decisions to be taken on a day-by-day basis and for which the Council was definitely not equipped. On the other hand, the Treaty clearly indicates that the basic rules must be decided upon by the Council and that it is only the implementation of those rules which may be delegated to the Commission. The Community practice shows, however, that even in the field of implementation the Council seldom delegates to the Commission without retaining some sort of control.[44]

In most cases, the Commission must consult either the national authorities or a Committee.[45] The rule is that after consultation the

[42] O.J. 1974 (2nd) vii; for amendments, *ibid.* 22; O.J. 1973, L 7/1, O.J. 1975, L 199/43.

[43] EEC, Art. 155, last indent. See Case 34/78 *Yoshida* v. *Kamer van Koophandel en Fabrieken voor Friesland* [1979] E.C.R. 115 where the Court found that the Commission had exceeded the powers conferred upon it by the Council and consequently annulled Art. 1 of the Commission Regulation.

[44] See, *e.g.* Reg. 2727/75 on the common organisation of the market in cereals, Art. 14 (4).

[45] There are 3 kinds of such committees: advisory, management and regulatory committees.

Advisory committee: see, *e.g.* Reg. 724/75 as amended by Reg. 214/79 (see updated version O.J. 1979, C 36/12) establishing a European Regional Development Fund, Art. 5 (2): consultation of the Regional Policy Committee. Such consultation has no further legal consequence.

Management committee: see, *e.g.* Reg. 2727/75 (see n. 52), Arts. 25 and 26. Such committees are composed of representatives of the Member States and presided over by a representative of the Commission. The votes are weighted in accordance with EEC, Art. 148 (2). The Committee delivers an opinion by a majority of 41 votes on the draft of the measure to be taken which is submitted to it by the Commission. The Commission adopts measures which apply immediately; if the measures are not in accordance with the opinion they are communicated to the Council, which may take a different decision within one month with a qualified majority.

Commission decides—even if the opinion received is negative—but the matter goes to the Council which within a certain time-limit may reverse the Commission's decision. This system allows the Member States to follow closely the implementation of the common policy and puts the Council in a position to decide itself in the event of a disagreement between the Commission and the Committee. This procedure has been used mainly in the field of agriculture.[46]

(5) *Participation in the legislative procedure*

As was described,[47] the Council in many instances, may act only on a proposal from the Commission; by submitting draft regulations, directives and decisions, the Commission participates, as the Treaty calls it "in the shaping of measures taken by the Council."[48] When such proposals are required by the Treaty,[49] the Commission exercises its exclusive right of initiative in the law-making process. There are cases where the Commission is bound to make proposals and to do so within a given time limit[50]; there are other cases where the Commission must use its own judgment as to the

Regulatory or rule-making committee: the procedure is the same as for the management committee except that the Commission may not take the measure if it is not in conformity with the committee's opinion. The Council has three months to adopt another measure after which the Commission is free to act. See, *e.g.* the committee on the origin of goods (Reg. 802/68, J.O. 1968, L 148/1), the Committee on customs values (Reg. 803/68, J.O. 1968 L 148/6) and the Standing Veterinary committee (Dec. 68/361, J.O. 1968, L 255/23). See also Third General Report (1969), 458.

With regard to the implementation and interpretation of the rules governing these committees see Court of Justice, *e.g.* Case 25/70 *Einfuhr- und Vorratsstelle* v. *Kšter* [1970] E.C.R. at 1170, where the Court bases the legality of the "management committee" procedure on Art. 155; Case 23/75 *Rey Soda* v. *Cassa Conguaglio Zucchero* [1975] E.C.R. 1279 and Case 35/78 *Schouten* v. *Hoofdproduktschap voor Akkerbouwprodukten* [1978] E.C.R. 2543, where the Court stated that the absence of an opinion by a "management committee" in no way affects the validity of the measures adopted by the Commission.

46 See also Reg. 724/75, Art. 16 establishing a Regional Development Fund.

47 See *European Parliament*, Tasks and Powers; participation in the legislative procedure and Council, Tasks and Powers, Power of Decision.

48 EEC, Art. 155, third indent.

49 See list in n. 23, 37 *supra*.

50 *e.g.* EEC, Art. 21 (2). Were the Commission not to act, a Member State or an institution (Council or Parliament) could report the matter to the Court of Justice to have the infringement established (EEC, Art. 175).

opportuneness of making a proposal.[51] The Council may, however, request the Commission to submit to it any appropriate proposal.[52]

The Commission's proposal constitutes the basis for the consultation of the European Parliament by the Council. This proposal may be altered by the Commission as long as the Council has not acted[53]; and it constitutes the basis for the Council's decision, and if the Council wishes to adopt an act constituting an amendment to that proposal, it may only do so unanimously.[54]

When required by the Treaty, the Commission consults the Economic and Social Committee[55] before submitting its proposal to the Council; unlike consultation of the European Parliament, which only the Council can do, consultation of the Economic and Social Committee may also be initiated by the Commission.

In preparing its proposals to be submitted to the Council, the Commission usually consults with representatives of the Member States[56] on an informal basis. The main discussions, however, take place after the proposal has been received by the Council either with the Committee of Permanent Representatives or with working groups set up by the latter. Following these discussions the Commission has in several cases modified its original proposal; but it also happens that the Commission insists that, notwithstanding disagreement in the working groups or in the Committee, the

[51] *e.g.* EEC, Art. 94. If the Commission decides not to act there is no recourse to the Court of Justice.

[52] EEC, Art. 152. It is of course debatable whether or not in such a case the Commission is legally bound to make a proposal, which might seem in contradiction with the much heralded "right of initiative" of the Commission. It seems however that when such a request is made it becomes extremely difficult, politically speaking, for the Commission to refuse.

[53] This could *inter alia* be the case where the Assembly having been consulted has delivered a diverging opinion. EEC, Art. 149, second para.

[54] EEC, Art. 149, first para.; see further *supra* under Council, Tasks and Powers, Power of Decision.

[55] See *infra* for more details on this Committee. An example of prescribed consultation can be found in EEC, Art. 43 (2).

[56] See arrangement adopted by the Council on January 28 and 29, 1966, in Luxembourg (Bull. 3–1966, 5), point 1: "Before adopting any particularly important proposal, it is desirable that the Commission should take up the appropriate contacts with the governments of the Member States, through the Permanent Representative, without this procedure compromising the right of initiative which the Commission derives from the Treaty."

proposal be discussed by the Council itself in the hope that an acceptable situation might be found at the political level.

It must be noted that the Commission might be called upon to justify the proposals it makes to the Council, not only before the European Parliament[57] but also before the Court of Justice, since the latter recognised the right of applicants, in an action concerning the legality of a Council decision to bring proceedings not only against the Council for having legislated, but also against the Commission for having made the proposal.[58] The Commission's proposals are usually published in the *Official Journal of the European Communities*.[59]

(6) *External relations*

The Commission's tasks are not limited to the internal activities of the Community; the Commission is also responsible for maintaining all appropriate relations with all international organisations, in particular with the organs of the United Nations, of its specialised agencies and of the General Agreement on Tariffs and Trade.[60]

The Commission is also in charge of negotiating the agreements to be concluded between the Community and one or more states or an international organisation; since such agreements are concluded by the Council, the Commission must obtain a mandate from the Council before opening such negotiations. The Commission may obtain beforehand the opinion of the Court of Justice as to whether the envisaged agreement is compatible with the provisions of the Treaty.[61]

(7) *Implementation of the Community budget*

In the budgetary procedure the role of the Commission is limited to consolidating the estimates of all the institutions in a preliminary

[57] *e.g.* in answer to parliamentary questions.
[58] Cases 63–69/72 *Hansamühle* v. *Council* [1973] E.C.R. 1229 at 1247 (8).
[59] In this respect see also point (a) (2) of the Luxembourg Arrangement (Bull. 3–1966, 8).
[60] EEC, Art. 229. For more details see *infra*, the European Economic Community, pt. 17, External relations. See also point (a) (5) of the Luxembourg Arrangement (Bull. 3–1966, 9).
[61] EEC, Art. 228 (1). The right to obtain an opinion of the Court also belongs to the Council and the Member States. See, *e.g.* Opinion 1/76 [1977] E.C.R. 741 and Opinion 1/78 [1978] E.C.R. 2151.

draft budget to be placed before the Council before September 1[62] and to declare, after consulting the Economic Policy Committee, what the maximum rate of increase is for the "non-compulsory" expenditures.[63]

Once the budget is adopted, it falls to the Commission to implement it in accordance with the provisions of the regulations laid down by the Council.[64] Consequently, the Commission must seek discharge in respect of this implementation. To this end the Commission submits, annually to the Council and to the Assembly the accounts of the preceding financial year together with a financial statement of the assets and liabilities of the Communities.[65] In exercising their powers of control over the implementation of the budget, the Council and the Assembly are assisted by the Court of Auditors, which forwards to them an annual report after the close of each financial year.[66] The Council and the Assembly in turn examine the accounts, the financial statement and the report, and discharge is given by Parliament on a recommendation of the Council.[67]

As part of the Community budget financed by the Communities' own resources[68] the Commission administers the European Agricultural Guidance and Guarantee Fund, the Social Fund and the European Regional Development Fund. The Commission is also responsible for administering the European Development Fund for the African, Caribbean and Pacific States, financed by direct Member State contributions and for the "banking activities" of the European Coal and Steel Community.[69]

The Commission is also empowered to raise loans in order to finance atomic energy projects[70] and to finance industrial and

[62] EEC, Art. 203 (2) and (3). For more details on the budgetary procedure see *supra* under European Parliament, 29.

[63] *Ibid.* at (9).

[64] See, *e.g.* O.J. 1976, L 362/52.

[65] EEC, Art. 205a; this provision was added by Art. 14 of the Treaty amending certain financial provisions.

[66] EEC, Art. 206a (4), fourth sub-para. For the Court of Auditors see *infra*. See Final Report, 1978 (O.J. 1979, C 326/1).

[67] EEC, Art. 206b.

[68] See *infra* 218.

[69] See ECSC, Arts. 54 and 56.

[70] See Euratom, Art. 172 (4) and O.J. 1977, L 88/9.

infrastructure projects[71]; the Commission has delegated the administration of these resources to the European Investment Bank.

(8) *Publication of General Report*

The Commission publishes every year in February—*i.e.* one month before the opening of the sessions of the Assembly[72]—a general report on the activities of the Communities. This report covers all the activities of all the institutions and organs of the Communities and as such it is an invaluable source of information. However, several activities are covered very summarily because they are the object of separate reports; this is the case, *inter alia*, for the European Investment Bank, the Agricultural Situation in the Community, Competition Policy, the Development of the Social Situation in the Community, the European Regional Development Fund and Consumer Interests. The General Report is discussed by Parliament which closes the debates by the adoption of a resolution.

3. The Commission's staff

The Treaty provides that the Commission shall adopt its rules of procedure so as to ensure that both it and its departments operate in accordance with the provisions of the treaties.[73] Consequently, the staff is divided into units—Directorates-General, Services or Groups which more or less correspond to the main sub-division of the three basic European treaties.[74]

[71] See O.J. 1978, L 298/9; generally referred to as the "Ortoli" facilities and officially known as New Community Instrument.

[72] See *supra* under Assembly (European Parliament), the General Report, 28.

[73] Merger Treaty, Art. 16.

[74] At the beginning of 1980 the Commission had the following units: Legal Service, Statistical Office, Customs Union Service, Environment and Consumer Protection Service, DG I—External Relations, DG II—Economic and Financial Affairs, DG III—Internal Market and Industrial Affairs, DG IV—Competition, DG V—Employment and Social Affairs, DG VI—Agriculture, DG VII—Transport, DG VIII—Development, DG IX—Personnel and Administration, DG X—Spokesman's Group and Directorate-General for Information, DG XII—Research, Science and Education, DG XIII—Scientific and Technical Information and Information Management, DG XIV—Fisheries, DG XV—Financial Institutions and Taxation, DG XVI—Regional Policy, DG XVII—Energy, DG XVIII—Credit and Investments, DG XIX—Budgets, DG XX—Financial Control, Joint Research Centre, Euratom Supply Agency, Security Office.

As regards the Communities' staff two texts must be mentioned: the *Protocol on the Privileges and Immunities of the European Communities*[75] and the *Staff Regulations of Officials and the Conditions of Employment of other servants of the European Community.*[76] Officials are recruited directly by the various institutions and organs of the Communities[77]; in other words the Communities' staff is not composed of national civil servants seconded by the Administrations of the Member States[78]; the obligations concerning the independence of the members of the Commission described above, applies *mutatis mutandis* to the officials.

IV. *The Court of Justice*

As was pointed out at the beginning of this Chapter, the Convention on certain institutions common to the European Communities, provides that the jurisdiction conferred by the three basic European Treaties to a Court of Justice shall be exercised in accordance with those Treaties by a single Court of Justice.[79]

The three European Treaties contain an identical provision to describe the task of the Court: it shall ensure that in the implementation and application of the Treaty the law is observed. This short

[75] See Protocol annexed to the Merger Treaty. This Protocol replaced the Protocols on Privileges of the ECSC, Euratom and EEC Treaties. Art. 12 of the Protocol provides that officials shall be immune from proceedings in respect of acts performed by them in their official capacity, including their words spoken or written. Art. 13 provides that officials shall be exempt from national taxes on salaries, wages and emoluments paid by the Communities but that they shall be liable to a tax for the benefit of the Communities (see J.O. 1962, 1461).

[76] A consolidated version in English was published as a supplement to O.J. 1973, C 12.

[77] Conflicts between officials and those bodies come within the jurisdiction of the Court of Justice, the Community being represented in each case by the relevant organ, including the Social and Economic Committee. One hundred such cases have been introduced in Court.

[78] It goes without saying that the nationality of the officials must be taken into account and although "no post may be reserved for a given nationality" (Staff Reg., Art. 27) a geographical equilibrium must exist based on the size of the population of the respective Member States. For the exact number of civil servants and their repartition among the various Commission departments, categories and nationalities, see answer to Parliamentary question No. 392/79 (O.J. 1979, C 275/5). There were about 8,300 officials at the end of 1979, including those working in the research centres located in various Member States.

[79] Signed together with the EEC and Euratom Treaties, in Rome, on March 25, 1957; see Arts. 3 and 4.

and sibylline text covers an extremely varied series of activities since the Court acts in several capacities: administrative court (legality of Community measures, compensation for damages caused by wrongful Community acts, unlimited jurisdiction in regard to penalties), penal court (dismissal of Commissioners), internal administrative tribunal (conflicts between officials and their employer), international court (conflicts between Member States), constitutional court (conflicts between the institutions, conformity of international agreements with the Treaties) and civil jurisdiction (when competent in contracts concluded by the Community with third parties).[80]

The Court's task is complicated by the fact that Community law is basically economic law which by definition is essentially evolutive and in constant need of adaptation as far as implementation of the general rules is concerned. It was out of the question to try to regulate the economic policies of the Member States in a document of no more than 250 Articles. Furthermore, only part of the EEC Treaty is drafted with some precision.[81]

Consequently, when called upon to state what the Community law is in a given field, it is by reference to the objectives of the Community that the Court interprets the existing rules and formulates new ones. The task of the Court is not only to interpret, but also to state what the law is when the existing legislation does not explicitly provide for it.[82] This, of course, is not unique to the Court

[80] See the General Report for a cumulative list of all the cases submitted to the Court analysed by subject matter and by type; *e.g.* Thirteenth General Report (1979), 340.

[81] It has been pointed out before that by and large the EEC Treaty contains two sets of rules: the first pertains to the establishment and functioning of the common market and more particularly of the Customs Union; the second concerns the approximation of the economic policies of the Member States. For this second category, the Treaty only contains some very general principles and entrusts the institutions with the task of finishing the legislative work started by the Treaty draftsmen. The only guidelines in those cases are the objectives of the Community as specified in EEC, Arts. 2 and 3 and procedures.

[82] The Court has been well aware of this fundamental obligation to create Community law; in Cases 7/56, 3–7/57 *Algera et al.* v. *Assembly* [1957] E.C.R. 39 at 55, the Court held in regard to the possibility of revoking an individual administrative act, that this is "a problem of administrative law which is familiar in the case-law and learned writings of all the countries of the Community, but for the solution of which the Treaty does not contain any rules. Unless the Court is to deny justice it is therefore obliged to solve the problem by reference to the rules acknowledged by the legislation, the learned writings and the case-law of the Member States."

of Justice: "wherever there are courts, the law grows in the hands of the judges,"[83] but for the reasons just indicated it is particularly appropriate in the case of the European Community.

This is the main reason why it is so important for the judges to be totally independent,[84] the more so since, as was explained above, the Council tends to act as an intergovernmental conference where every member fights for his country's interests, the European Parliament has none of the powers required for exercising a democratic control and the Commission, which besides its overwhelming administrative task must fulfil a political function, is bound to accept compromises in the implementation of Community Legislation by the Member States.

The Court can only express itself in judgments[85] and when called upon to do so; nevertheless, over the years it was able to build up a set of rules which were of prime importance in shaping the evolution of the Communities themselves; this happened not so much when the Court was called upon to control the legality of Community acts[86] but mainly when giving rulings concerning the interpretation of Community legislation[87] at the request of national tribunals which were confronted with questions of interpretation of Community law applicable in cases pending before them. These rulings enabled the Court over the years to develop an impressive number of basic principles which now guide institutions, Member States and individuals of the Community alike when implementing the European treaties.

1. The members of the Court

The Court consists of nine Judges[88] and is assisted by four

[83] Schwarzenberger, *Internal Law*, p. 24.

[84] See EEC, Art. 167: judges shall be chosen from persons whose independence is beyond doubt.

[85] And exceptionally also in "opinions," see EEC, Art. 228 (1), second sub-para.

[86] See EEC, Art. 173 and *infra*.

[87] See EEC, Art. 177; it will be noticed that when secondary legislation is concerned the Court's jurisdiction is not limited to interpretation but also includes the validity; cases concerning the latter are in practice rather exceptional.

[88] EEC, Art. 165, first para., as amended by Art. 17 of the Act of Accession. Article 16 of the Act concerning Greek accession provides that upon accession of the Hellenic Republic the Council acting unanimously shall decide on the adjustment to be made to this provision in order to increase by one the number of judges constituting the Court. See also EEC, Art. 165, fourth para., which empowers the Council to increase the number of judges.

Advocates-General,[89] the latter, however, are not "members" of the Court. The Judges and Advocates-General are to be chosen from persons whose independence is beyond doubt and who have the qualifications for appointment to the highest judicial offices in their respective countries[90] or "who are jurisconsults of recognised competence."[91] At first sight, this might mean that Judges have to possess a legal degree, but it appears that the reference to jurisconsults was added precisely to allow others to sit on the European bench[92]; it seems indeed that the presence of people with other expertise might add the necessary competence to a court which interprets and applies provisions of economic and social law.

Judges and Advocates-General are appointed for a term of six years by common accord of the governments of the Member States[93]; they are eligible for reappointment.

The nine Judges are grouped in three Chambers of three Judges each; cases brought before the Court are normally heard by one of

[89] The Act concerning the accession of Greece does not contain provisions with regard to an increase in the number of Advocates-General. However, when at the beginning of August the Council approved the new Rules of Procedure of the Court of Justice (O.J. 1979, L 238/1) the Council also indicated that it would examine without delay the Court's request to increase the number of Advocates-General in accordance with EEC, Art. 166, third para. For the implementation of the new Rules see O.J. 1979, C 265/8.

[90] EEC, Art. 167, first para.; this means that qualifications are determined in accordance with national law and that, therefore there are no uniform requirements, the more so since certain Member States have different categories in their judicial system including commercial tribunals for which no legal training is required.

[91] EEC, Art. 167, first para.

[92] In the ECSC Court two of the six judges had no law degree: one was an economist, the other was versed in the social sciences.

[93] The Treaty does not specify that Judges or Advocates-General must be nationals of one of the Member States, nor that at least one national of each Member State must be on the bench.

To date only nationals were appointed, and except for the Court of Justice of the ECSC which, consisting of seven members of six Member States, counted two judges of Dutch nationality, the Member States have always appointed one national of each Member States. The situation is different for the Advocates-General of which there are now four: they have always been chosen from the four large Member States: Germany, France, Italy and the U.K.

Further provisions concerning the Judges and the Advocates-General are to be found in the Statute of the Court of Justice annexed as a Protocol to the Treaty and in the Rules of Procedure.

the Chambers[94]; only cases for which there exist particular circumstances can be heard in plenary session.

The position of the Advocates-General is a particularly interesting one: their independent position—they do not participate in the discussions that lead to the Court's decision—allow them to carry out their own personal examination of the case and express personal opinions—which the Judges cannot; they are also free to examine any related question even when it was not brought forward by the parties. Although the reasoned submissions they make in open court do not of course, reflect the Court's views, they often contain precious indications in regard to the reasoning which led to the decisions.

2. The Court's jurisdiction

As was pointed out at the beginning of this section, the Court fulfils many different tasks: in the order of the Treaty provisions the Court's jurisdiction consists mainly of the following:

- finding whether a Member State has failed to fulfil an obligation under the Treaty: actions can be brought either by the Commission or by another Member State (Articles 169, 170 and 171);
- unlimited jurisdiction with regard to penalties, actions can be brought by natural or legal persons (Article 172);
- review of the legality of an act or a failure to act of the Council and the Commission at the request of Member States, the Council or the Commission and under certain circumstances natural or legal persons (Articles 173–176);
- preliminary rulings at the request of a national court or tribunal (Article 177);
- compensation for damages caused by the institutions; actions can be brought against the Community by Member States and natural or legal persons (Articles 178 and 215);
- disputes between the Community and its servants (Article 179).

[94] EEC, Art. 165 provides that the Court shall sit in plenary session but that the Chambers may adjudicate on particular categories of cases. It also provides that cases brought before it either by a Member State or by an institution of the Community and in principle also preliminary rulings must be heard by the Court sitting in plenary session. This rule was modified by the Court with the approval of the Council on August 3, 1979 (O.J. 1979, L 238/1) with the result that presently all cases may be referred to one of the Chambers except when a Member State or an institution of the community requests that a case be heard in plenary session.

(1) *The finding of a failure by a Member State to fulfil its treaty obligations*

When the Commission or a Member State considers that a Member State has failed to fulfil an obligation under the Treaty, they may bring the matter before the Court. The possibility of the Commission initiating an action of this kind constitutes the main instrument at its disposal for fulfilling its task as guardian of Community law. The procedure to be followed by the Commission has been explained in some detail above.[95]

As regards the procedure initiated by other Member States, the Treaty provides for an intermediate phase corresponding to an internal administrative procedure.[96]

The Court's jurisdiction in cases brought against a Member State consists merely in "finding"[97] that the State has failed to fulfil an obligation under the Treaty. If such finding is made, the Member State "shall be required to take the necessary measures to comply with the judgment of the Court."[98] With respect to cases brought by a Member State against another State attention must be drawn to the obligation undertaken by the Member States "not to submit a dispute concerning the interpretation or application of the Treaty

[95] See *supra* p. 55. Up to December 31, 1979, the Commission has introduced 87 cases on the basis of EEC, Art. 169.

[96] See EEC, Art. 170. The first time this procedure was used was in 1977, Case 58/77 *Ireland* v. *France* (O.J. 1977, C 142/8); the case was later withdrawn (O.J. 1978, C 76/8); however, the subject of the quarrel became the basis for Case 232/78 *Commission* v. *France* (not yet published). See also Case 141/78 *France* v. *United Kingdom* [1980] 1 C.M.L.R. 6.

[97] EEC, Art. 171. The "finding" must be seen in contradistinction to the "unlimited jurisdiction" in the case for instance of penalties (EEC, Art. 172; see *infra*) and the power to declare an act void in the case of a review of the legality of the act of an institution (EEC, Art. 174; see *infra*).

[98] EEC, Art. 171. It follows that the obligation to take measures results not from a Court order but from Art. 171.

Noteworthy are the words "comply with the judgment" rather than "fulfil the obligation under the Treaty." It could be argued that these terms do give the Court a much larger jurisdiction than would appear at first sight; if this text were taken literally the Court could determine what has to be done by the Member State once the failure has been ascertained; this seems rather logical when one takes into account the fact that the failure to act might have caused damages to other Member States, and those should be taken into account, or also that simple compliance with obligations resulting from Community law might no longer be possible. Anyway, to date the Court of Justice has limited itself to stating that the Member State had failed to fulfil an obligation under Community law.

to any method of settlement[99] other than those provided for therein."[1] The principal method being the Court, this provision guarantees uniformity in the interpretation of Community law. The exclusion of outside international tribunals, however, does not exclude entirely the application of the rules of international law to which the Court has several times referred.[2]

(2) *Unlimited jurisdiction with regard to penalties*

In order to ensure compliance with the obligations laid down in its regulations, the Council may make provisions for penalties to be imposed on natural or legal persons.[3] The right of those persons to ask the Court to review the legality of a decision taken by an institution under such provision is provided under the general jurisdiction of the Court to review the legality of Community acts, with the result that if the action is founded the Court may annul the act in question.[4] In case the Council wants to grant unlimited jurisdiction to the Court this must be explicitly done.[5] In that case not only may the Court squash the fine but it may decide also to increase or decrease it.[6]

The Court's unlimited jurisdiction also applies in two other areas: claims for damages resulting from non-contractual liability

[99] Other methods of settlement could have been the International Court of Justice whose compulsory arbitration was accepted by several Member States, or the Benelux Court of Arbitration where Belgium, the Netherlands and Luxembourg are concerned.

[1] EEC, Art. 219.

[2] For the application of international law to the Community, see *infra* Chap. 7.

[3] Penalties can only be imposed upon natural or legal persons not on Member States. Some sort of penalties was provided for in the ECSC Treaty with regard to Member States (ECSC, Art. 88 (*a*)), but they were never applied and this possibility does not exist in the EEC Treaty.

The Council's competence to provide for penalties results from EEC, Arts. 79 (3) discrimination by carriers and 87 (2) rules of competition. It is debatable whether or not EEC, Art. 172 besides attributing unlimited jurisdiction to the Court also confers upon the Council a general competence to provide for fines in its regulations. If the answer were to be negative the power to provide for fines could be found in EEC, Art. 235.

[4] EEC, Arts. 173–174.

[5] See Reg. 11, Art. 18 (J.O. 1960, 1121) and Reg. 17 (J.O. 1962, 204).

[6] See, *e.g.* Case 27/76 *United Brand* v. *Commission* [1978] E.C.R. 207 where a fine was reduced from 1,000,000 units of account to 850,000. There are not examples of the Court increasing a penalty.

of the Community[7] and disputes between the Community and its servants.[8]

(3) *Review of the legality of an act or failure to act of an institution*

The procedure directed at a Community act is also referred to as an appeal for annulment since the object is to have the Court declare the act concerned to be void; actions brought because of inactivity of the Community institutions can be referred to as appeals against failure to act.

(a) APPEAL FOR ANNULMENT[9]

In supervising the legality of Community acts[10] the Court protects all those who are subject to Community law against arbitrary action of the institution (in which case it acts as an administrative court), but it also restrains the Community activities within the boundaries laid down by the European Treaties and ensures that the institutions respect the balance of powers within the Community and thus acts as a constitutional court.

Who may lodge an appeal for an annulment? With regard to the admissibility of court actions, all Member States apply a general rule well coined in French as 'pas d'intérêt, pas d'action"; the same principle applies within the Communities: the Member States[11]

[7] EEC, Arts. 178 and 215; see *infra*.

[8] Such Court cases are very numerous indeed but only rarely involve questions of general interest for Community law.

[9] EEC, Art. 173. It should be noted from the onset that the proceedings for annulment must be instituted within two months of the publication or notification of the measure.

[10] The Treaty refers to "acts of the Council and the Commission other than recommendations or opinions" (EEC, Art. 173, first para.); these other acts are mainly the regulations, directives and decisions provided in EEC, Art. 189, but are by no means limited to those. They include also agreement and generally speaking any measures which binds (some of) those who are subject to Community law. See Case 22/70 *Commission* v. *Council* [1971] E.C.R. 263 at 277 (42): "an action for annulment must therefore be available in the case of all measures adopted by the institutions whatever their nature or form, which are intended to have legal effects."

[11] All Member States have at one time or another appealed for annulment of a Commission act; rarer are appeals against Council acts; see Case 151/73 *Ireland* v. *Council* [1974] E.C.R. 285.

and the institutions[12] are considered to have an overall interest in the correct implementation of the Community law and have therefore, subject to a two months time-limit, an unlimited right to initiate proceedings aimed at controlling the legality of Community acts. Natural and legal persons on the other hand must prove their interest in such a control.[13] In this respect it is assumed that acts having a general application concern everybody, but nobody in particular and therefore cannot be challenged in Court by individuals unless those acts contain provisions which in reality have an "individual"[14] rather than a "general" application. This can be the case notwithstanding the fact that the act in question was taken in the form of a "general" act, *i.e.* a regulation[15] or of an individual act but addressed to another person.[16]

The interpretation of the Treaty provisions is of course essential in determining the extent of the legal protection enjoyed by individuals within the European Communities; hence the importance of the case law of the Court of Justice in this field: the Court without resorting to "extensive interpretation" has always given the texts a

[12] Appeals by the Council or the Commission for annulment of each other's acts are very rare: see Case 22/70 *Commission* v. *Council* [1971] E.C.R. 263.

[13] Case 77/77 *BP* v. *Commission* [1978] E.C.R. 1513 at 1525 (13).

[14] The treaty refers to an act which "is of direct and individual concern" to a person; this according to the case law of the Court of Justice is the case only "if that decision affects them by reason of certain attributes which are peculiar to them or by reason of circumstances in which they are differentiated from all other persons and by virtue of these factors distinguishes them individually just as in the case of the person addressed"; Case 25/62 *Plaumann* v. *Commission* [1963] E.C.R. 95 at 107. This would not be the case if the plaintiff is affected by the act because he belongs to a category designated abstractly and as a whole; Case 42/71 *Nordgetreide* v. *Commission* [1972] E.C.R. 110; see also Case 72/74 *Union Syndicale* v. *Council* [1975] E.C.R. 401 at 410 (17), where the Court found that an organisation formed for the protection of the collective interests of a category of persons was not "directly and individually concerned by a measure affecting the general interest of that category."

[15] Cases 41 and 44/70 *International Fruit Company* v. *Commission*. The Court held that Art. 1 of Reg. 983/70 "is not a provision with a general application but must be analysed as a bundle of individual decisions" [1971] E.C.R. 411 at 422 (21).

[16] According to the Court of Justice "another person" in EEC, Art. 173, second para. can include Member States since no limitation as to the meaning of these words are to be found in the Treaty. Persons can therefore appeal against acts of the institutions addressed to a Member State when they are directly concerned; Case 25/62 *Plaumann* v. *Commission* [1973] E.C.R. 95; see also Case 26/76 *Metro SB-Grossmärkte* v. *Commission* [1977] E.C.R. 1875.

meaning which allowed a wide access to review of the legality of Community acts,[17] although the Court explicitly recognised that the EEC Treaty "lays down more restrictive conditions than the ECSC Treaty for the admissibility of application for annulment by private individuals."[18]

Nonetheless, the opportunities for private parties to appeal directly for annulment are much more limited than for the Member States and the Community institutions. However, other means exist whereby persons and enterprises may obtain a Court ruling, if not on the legality at least on the applicability of Community acts, which, for the applicant has identical consequences if the action is well founded.[19]

[17] See, *e.g.* Case 20/58 *Phoenix-Rheinrohr* v. *High Authority* [1959] E.C.R. 75 at 82: "the nature of an administrative measure depends above all on its subject matter and its content" and not on its form"; in other words, in determining the admissibility of a private party in an appeal for annulment "the Court cannot restrict itself to considering the official title of the measure." Cases 16, 17–62 *Confédération nationale des producteurs de fruits et légumes et al.* v. *Council* [1962] E.C.R. 471 at 478. However, the Court added in Cases 53, 54/63 *Lemmerz-Werker GmbH et al.* v. *High Authority* [1963] E.C.R. 239 at 248, that "it is necessary for the legal protection of all those affected that they should be able to identify by its very form a decision which involves such serious legal consequences." Also in Case 16 and 17/62, the Court found that a given act can contain provisions of differing nature: a measure entitled by its author a regulation can contain provisions which are capable of being not only of direct but also of individual concern to certain natural or legal persons without prejudice to the question whether the measure considered in its entirety is indeed a regulation; Case 26/76 *Metro* v. *Commission* [1977] E.C.R. at 1901 where the Court found that it is in the interest of a satisfactory administration of justice that natural or legal persons who are entitled to request the Commission to find an infringement of Arts. 55 and 86 should be able, if their request is not complied with, to institute proceedings in order to protect their legitimate interests; Cases 103 to 109/78 *Société des Usines de Beaufort* v. *Council* [1979] E.C.R. at 25 (20) where the Court concluded that a contested regulation was not of direct and individual concern to the applicants (note that the English text of the judgment mentions "is not of direct or individual concern"; Art. 173 (2) of the Treaty reads "is of direct and individual concern"; the original text of the judgment is French and literally translated it would read: "is neither of direct nor of individual concern"; obviously the English text contains a translation error since both criteria have to be fulfilled) and Case 123/77 *UNICME* v. *Council* [1978] E.C.R. at 852 (16): "the possibility of determining more or less precisely the number or even the identity of the persons to whom a measure applies by no means implies that it must be regarded as being of individual concern to them" and Case 101/76 *Koninklijk Scholten Honig* v. *Council and Commission* [1977] E.C.R. 797.

[18] Cases 16 and 17–62, *supra*, at 478.

[19] See *infra*, preliminary ruling, compensation for damages and the exception of illegality.

Grounds for annulment. The European Treaty provides for four grounds for annulment[20] which have their origin in French administrative law.

(i) *Lack of competence*: this is the expression in juridical terms of the general principle according to which the Community institutions only have the powers that have explicitly been attributed to them by the Community law[21]; as mentioned before, the Community has no general legislative power. The review by the Court of the competence of the institution to issue binding acts must be seen in relation with the requirement that Community acts must "state the reasons on which they are based,"[22] *i.e.* thus "to give an opportunity to the parties of defending their rights, to the Court of exercising its supervisory functions and to Member States and to all interested nationals of ascertaining the circumstances in which the Commission has applied the Treaty."[23]

[20] EEC, Art. 173; the same grounds are provided by the ECSC and Euratom Treaties: respectively Arts. 33 and 146.

[21] Since appeals for annulment must be lodged within two months after publication or notification it could happen that a Community act without legal ground continues to be implemented (see however the exception of illegality, *infra*). The question was raised by the French Government in a procedure before the Court. See Cases 6, 11–69 *Commission* v. *France* [1969] E.C.R. 523 at 539 (11–13). The Court first found that since no proceedings for annulment were brought within the prescribed period the decision must be considered as definitive. It then states that the French Government on the one hand refers to public policy within the Community and on the other hand takes the view that too exclusive an attachment to forms is incompatible with the true Community spirit and that the decision was taken in a sphere which belongs exclusively to the jurisdiction of Member States.

The Court concluded that "if this allegation were valid, the above-mentioned decision would lack all legal basis in the Community legal system and that in an Art. 169 procedure, it is a fundamental requirement of the legal system that the Court should investigate whether this is the case. What the Court did not state is what the consequences would have been with regard to the decision had the Court accepted the French contention (which it declined to do). The Court could not have declared the decision to be void since it stated that the decision was definitive, *i.e.* no longer voidable. Could the Court then have considered that the decision was null and void from the outset thereby introducing the new concepts of lack of legal basis in the Community legal system and of conflict with public policy within the Community (ordre public Communautaire). In this writer's view the Court, in this case, went too far and should have refused to consider the French allegation.

[22] EEC, Art. 190; see *infra* under Community Acts, 97.

[23] Case 24–62 *Germany* v. *Commission* [1963] E.C.R. 63 at 69.

(ii) *Infringement of an essential procedural requirement*: as was mentioned before, if the Council were to take a decision without a proposal from the Commission or without consulting the European Parliament (when these are required under the Treaty) it would infringe an essential procedural requirement and therefore an appeal for annulment of the decision in question could be lodged. The same would apply if the Commission were to make a proposal to the Council without requesting the opinion of the Economic and Social Committee, when required by Community law to do so. The absence of sufficient reasons in a Community act must also be considered as a ground for annulment under this heading.

(iii) *Infringement of the Treaty or of any rule of law relating to its application*: it could of course be argued that the above-mentioned grounds also constitute infringements of the Treaty and that this last ground in fact covers all possible illegalities.[24] However, the Treaty refers to four grounds and accordingly they must be examined here.

In the expression "infringement of the Treaty," the word treaty must be understood as referring also to secondary legislation, *i.e.* the acts of the institutions issued in accordance with the treaty provisions,[25] the treaties modifying the three basic European treaties, such as the Treaty of Accession, and the Protocols.[26]

[24] The four grounds for annulment mentioned in the Treaty are four different aspects of what in French administrative law is referred to as "*excès de pouvoir*"; furthermore, the distinction between various grounds has a special significance under the ECSC Treaty, since general binding decisions can only be challenged by enterprises and individuals when they can invoke a "détournement de pouvoir" (one of the four grounds). But under the EEC Treaty, where the admissibility of an appeal for annulment depends on the nature of the act and the standing of the plaintiff, the distinction between the four grounds seems rather senseless.

[25] These acts are not only the regulations, directives and decisions, but also the agreements concluded by the Community with international organisations and third countries. (See, *e.g.* Case 181/73 *Haegeman* v. *Belgium* [1974] E.C.R., 449 in which the Court was called upon to interpret provisions of the EEC-Greece Association Agreement) and conventions between Member States such as those concluded pursuant to Art. 220 to facilitate economic integration: Convention of February 29, 1968, on the mutual recognition of companies and bodies corporate (Bull. E.C. Supp. 1969/2) and Convention of September 27, 1968, on jurisdiction and the enforcement of civil and commercial judgments (O.J. 1975, L 204/28) amended by the convention of Accession of October 9, 1978 (O.J. 1978, L 304/1).

[26] See EEC, Art. 239.

As to the expression "rules of law relating to its application" it refers to international law[27] and to the general principles of law.[28] The latter include, besides the principles universally recognised,

[27] See Cases 21–24/72 *International Fruit Company* v. *Produktschap vooz Groenten en Fruit*: "before the incompatibility of a Community measure with a provision of international law can affect the validity of that measure, the Community must first of all be bound by that provision," [1972] E.C.R. 1219 at 1226 (7); see also Case 41/74 *Van Duyn* v. *Home Office* "it is a principle of international law which the EEC Treaty cannot be assumed to disregard in the relations between Member States, that a State is precluded from refusing its own nationals the right of entry or residence" [1974] E.C.R. 1337 at 1351 (22). In other cases, the Court however did not accept arguments based on international law; see, *e.g.* Cases 90 and 91/63 *Commission* v. *Belgium and Luxembourg*, "international law allows a party, injured by the failure of another party to perform its obligations, to withhold performance of its own," "however, this relationship between the obligations of parties cannot be recognised under Community law" [1964] E.C.R. 625 at 631.

[28] See, *e.g.* Case 8/55 *Fédération Charbonnière de Belgique* v. *High Authority* [1954 to 1956] E.C.R. 245 at 299; Case 92/71 *Interfood* v. *Hauptzollamt Hamburg-Ericus* [1972] E.C.R. 231 at 242. This was again confirmed by the Case 112/77 *Töpfer* v. *Commission* [1978] E.C.R. 1019 at 1033 (19) "the submission that there has been a breach of this principle (protection of legitimate expectation) is admissible in the context of proceedings instituted under Art. 173, since the principle in question forms part of the Community legal order with the result that any failure to comply with it is an "infringement of this treaty or of any rule of law relating to its application" within the meaning of the article quoted." Other principles of law recognised by the Court are:
- the right to be heard: Case 17/74 *Transocean Marine Paint Association* v. *Commission* [1974] E.C.R. 1063 at 1080;
- respect for fundamental rights: Case 11/70 *Internationale Handelsgesellschaft* v. *EVSt* [1970] E.C.R. 1125 at 1134 (4) and Case 36/75 *Rutili* v. *Minister for the Interior* [1975] E.C.R. 1219; see *infra*, Chap. 4 under sources of Community law.
- freedom of trade union activity, Case 175/73 *Union Syndicale et al.* v. *Council* [1974] E.C.R. 917 at 925;
- legal certainty: Case 13/61 *de Geus* v. *Bosch* [1962] E.C.R. 45 at 52; Case 41/69 *ACF Chemiefarma* v. *Commission* [1970] E.C.R. 661 at 683; (19–21); Case 77/71, *Gervais-Danone* v. *Hauptzollamt München* [1971] E.C.R. 1127 at 1138 (11) and Case 43/75 *Defrenne* v. *Sabena* [1976] E.C.R. 455 at 481 (74);
- equality: Case 8/57 *Groupement des Hauts Fourneaux et Aciéries Belges* v. *High Authority* [1957 and 1958] E.C.R. 245 at 256; Cases 14, etc., *Meroni et al.* v. *High Authority* [1961] E.C.R. 161 at 169; Case 148/73 [1974] E.C.R. 81 at 89 (12);
- contractual certainty: Case 48/72 *Brasserie de Haecht* v. *Wilkin-Janssen* [1973] E.C.R. 77 at 86 (9).
- protection of the legal expectation: Case 97/76 *Merkur* v. *Commission* [1977] E.C.R. 1063 at 1078 (7).
- principle of proportionality between the means employed and the end in view, Cases 119 and 120/76 *Ölmühle and Becher* v. *Hauptzollamt Hamburg and Hauptzollamt Bremen-Nord* [1977] E.C.R. 1286 (5).

those principles which are particular to the Member States and which the Court formulates on the basis of the wording, the contents and the system of the treaties or also on the basis of a comparative study of the nine legal systems.[29]

(iv) *Misuse of power*[30] There is misuse of power when a public authority uses its lawful powers to attain an objective for which the powers were not intended. Although this ground has been invoked many times, the Court has not yet based an annulment on misuse of power.[31]

Consequences of annulment. When reviewing the legality of a binding Community act the Court limits itself, in case the action is well founded, to declare the act void; after that, it is up to the institution which issued the act to "take the necessary measures to comply with the judgment of the Court of Justice"[32]; indeed, "if the Court entertains the application, it may not dictate . . . the decision which should be consequent upon the judgment annulling the decision but the Court must confine itself to referring the matter back"[33] to the institution.

Since annulment means that the act in question is to be considered as having never existed—the Court's declaration has effect *ex tunc* and *erga omnes*—the institution must endeavour to recreate

[29] See EEC, Art. 215, second para. which refers to the "general principles common to the laws of the Member States"; such principles will allow the Court to formulate Community law in the absence of explicit rules; see, *e.g.* Cases 7/56, 3/57–7/57 *Algera et al.* v. *Assembly* [1957 and 1958] E.C.R. 39 at 55.

[30] Probably better known by its French equivalent "*détournement de pouvoir*." As was pointed out *supra* in n. 24 this ground plays a major role under the ECSC Treaty since in accordance with Art. 33 undertakings may institute proceedings against general decisions (= regulations in the EEC Treaty) which they consider to involve a misuse of powers affecting them. The Court of Justice held it to be sufficient for the admissibility of an appeal that the plaintiff formally alleges a misuse of power concerning him and specifies the reasons for which the applicant considers that there has been a misuse of power; see Case 3/54 *ASSIDER* v. *High Authority* [1954 to 1956] E.C.R. 63 at 69.

For more details as to the meaning of *détournement de pouvoir* see the comparative study of the law of the original six Member States made by the Advocate-General in his opinion in the above-mentioned case, *ibid.* at 75.

[31] See, however, Cases 18, 35/65 *Guttmann* v. *Commission* [1966] E.C.R. 103 at 118 where according to some authors the Court did annul a decision on this ground.

[32] EEC, Art. 176.

[33] Case 30/59 *Steenkolenmijnen* v. *High Authority* [1961] E.C.R. 1 at 17.

the situation which would have existed had the act not been issued. This might be impossible, especially when the nullity affects a regulation; this is the reason why the Treaty provides that in the case of annulment of a regulation, the Court may state which effects shall be considered definitive.[34]

It should also be noted that annulment of an act does not mean that the whole act must be declared void: if the nullity concerns only certain provisions, the others are not affected as long as they can remain operative independently of the annulled ones. The same applies to the implementing acts.

(b) APPEAL AGAINST FAILURE TO ACT[35]

In the case of *failure to act*[36] the Court may be called upon to declare that this failure constitutes an infringement of Community law[37]; the term "treaty" must be interpreted also as including secondary legislation.[38] Although in the case of the review of the legality of an act the Court may declare the act void while in the case of a failure to act the Court can only declare this to be an infringement, "both provisions merely prescribe one and the same method of recourse."[39]

One important difference with the annulment proceedings is that an action for failure to act can also be brought by the European Parliament.

[34] EEC, Art. 174, second para.

[35] EEC, Art. 175. Such an appeal is admissible only when plaintiff has first called upon the institution to act and the latter has not defined its position within two months; plaintiff then has another two months to bring his action.

[36] To date mainly actions by natural or legal persons have been brought under this provision against the Commission.

[37] Art. 175 provides for only one ground on which to base a claim, contrary to the action for annulment under Art. 173. Obviously, this does not constitute a limitation: besides the fact that, *e.g.* the first ground logically cannot apply, it was pointed out *supra* that *de jure* all four grounds constitute a violation of Community law; the formal distinction between the four grounds is irrelevant under the EEC Treaty, contrary to the ECSC Treaty where one of the grounds, misuse of power, must be alleged by private parties in order to be admissible in an annulment action.

[38] Whether in the absence of the words "of any rule of law relating to its application" a failure to act could be challenged in Court for infringement of a general principle of law has not as yet been tested. It seems however that if an act violating such principles is to be considered illegal, the same applies to failures to act.

[39] Case 15/70 *Chevalley* v. *Commission* [1970] E.C.R. 975 at 979 (6).

Actions for failure to act initiated by an institution or a Member State, are not limited to cases when the Council or Commission were supposed to take a binding decision; also when the Commission, *e.g.* fails to send a proposal to the Council where this is required by the Treaty, the Council, the Assembly or a Member State can bring an action.

Natural or legal persons may only bring proceedings when an institution fails to issue[40] a binding act of which they would have been the addressee.[41]

(4) *Preliminary ruling*[42]

The preliminary ruling which pre-supposes direct effect of Community law (*i.e.* possibility to invoke Community rules before national courts) constitutes with the action for compensation for damages, the best means of protection for the Community citizens against illegal activities of the institution; it is also the ideal instrument in the hands of the Court to define and develop Community law. When the Court interprets a provision of Community law, this interpretation must be accepted and applied by the national courts[43] when called upon to ensure the application of said provision. On the other hand, parties will not contest lightly such an interpretation although they remain free to do so. In other words,

[40] Failure to act must be distinguished from refusal to act; in the latter case such refusal which constitutes a decision, can only be challenged under Art. 173, annulment, see Case 8/71 *Komponistenverband* v. *Commission* [1971] E.C.R. 705 at 710 (2). See also Cases 10 and 18/68 *Eridania* v. *Commission* [1969] E.C.R. 459 at 483 (17), where the Court stated that no action could be brought against an institution, when the latter has failed to comply with a request to revoke an act considered by the plaintiff to be illegal; here again the normal way is an appeal for annulment of said act.

[41] Case 15/71 *Mackprang* v. *Commission* [1971] E.C.R. 797 at 804 (4).

[42] EEC, Art. 177.

[43] See 1972 European Communities Act, s. 3 (1) and Case 33/76 *Rewe* v. *Landwirtschafts kammer Saarland* [1976] E.C.R. 1989 at 1979 (5) where the Court based this obligation on EEC, Art. 5. With regard to Community law the Treaty provides for a "division of labour" between the Court of Justice and the national courts. (The Court refers to "juridical co-operation: Cases 110, 111–78 *Ministère Public* v. *Van Wesemael* [1979] E.C.R. 35 at 51 (21)). By and large the national courts are responsible for applying community law while the Court of Justice has exclusive competence to interpret its provisions. The respective tasks and powers have been specified by the case-law of the Court:

(a) the Court has no jurisdiction under Art. 177 to apply the Treaty to a specific case; Case 6/64 *Costa* v. *ENEL* [1964] E.C.R. 425 at 592; nevertheless it may furnish the national court with the interpretative criteria necessary to enable it to dispose of the dispute: Case 49/76 *Gesellschaft für Uberseehandel* v. *Handelskammer Hamburg* [1977] E.C.R. 41 at 52 (4);

(b) the considerations which may have led a national court or tribunal to its choice of questions as well as the relevance which it attributes to such questions in the context of a case before it are excluded from review by the Court; Case 26/62 *Van Gend en Loos* v. *Nederlandse Administratie der Belastingen* [1963] E.C.R. 1 at 11;

(c) the Treaty does not prescribe a particular form in which a national court must present its request for a ruling; it is up to the Court to render a decision on that request only in so far as it has jurisdiction to do so; Case 13/61 *De Geus* v. *Bosch* [1962] E.C.R. 45 at 50; the Court must derive from the wording of the request the questions which relate exclusively to the interpretation of the Community provision; Case 5/69 *Völk* v. *Vervaecke* [1969] E.C.R. 295 at 301 (2/4);

(d) the Court cannot involve itself in assessing the reasons for which the national court or tribunal has considered a decision on the question necessary to enable it to give judgment; Case 56/65 *L.T.M.* v. *Maschinenbau Ulm* [1966] E.C.R. 235 at 247 and Case 52/76 *Benedetti* v. *Munari* [1977] E.C.R. 163 at 180 (12);

(e) when it gives an interpretation of the Treaty in a specific action pending before a national court, the Court limits itself to deducing the meaning of the Community rules from the wording and spirit of the Treaty it being left to the national court to apply in the particular case the rules which are thus interpreted; Cases 28–30/62 *Da Costa et al.* v. *Nederlandse Belastingadministratie* [1963] E.C.R. 31 at 38;

(f) the Court when giving a preliminary ruling cannot give judgment on the propriety of a measure of domestic character; Case 100/63 *Kalsbeek* v. *Sociale Verzekeringsbank* [1964] E.C.R. 565 at 572;

(g) it is not for the Court to appropriate to itself an assessment of the jurisdiction of the national court to refer the question or of the presence of a legal interest requiring protection on the part of the applicant in the main action. Once the Court of Justice is validly seized of a request for a preliminary ruling it is obliged to give judgment; Case 19/68 *De Cicco* v. *Landesversicherungsanstalt Schwaben* [1968] E.C.R. 473 at 478;

(h) the Court may not on the basis of Art. 177, give judgment on the interpretation of a provision of national law; Case 78/70 *Deutsche Grammophon* v. *Metro* [1971] E.C.R. 487 at 498 (3);

(i) the Court in applying Art. 177 is not competent to decide on the compatibility of a national provision with Community law; Case 10/71 *Ministère public Luxembourgeois* v. *Muller* [1971] E.C.R. 723 at 729 (7); nevertheless, the Court has the power to provide the national court with aids to interpretation based on Community law which may guide the said court in its assessment of the effects of this law; Case 1/72 *Frilli* v. *Belgium* [1972] E.C.R. 457 at 465 (10);

(j) the preliminary ruling of the Court is binding on the national court as to the interpretation of the Community provision; Case 52/76 *Benedetti* v. *Munari* [1977] E.C.R. 163 at 184 (3);

(k) the jurisdiction of the Court to give rulings on the validity of measures adopted by the institutions cannot be limited by the grounds on which the validity of those measures may be contested. It therefore extends to all the grounds capable of invalidating those measures, including the fact that they

if the Court's interpretation is limited *de jure* to the case under review, *de facto* it has effect *erga omnes*.

The object of the Court's competence in this field is to ensure uniform interpretation and application, within all the Member States, of the provisions of Community law; such uniformity constitutes an essential requirement for the existence and functioning of a common market.[44]

Requests for preliminary rulings must emanate from national courts or tribunals[45]; this can occur when having to apply a Community rule, they find themselves confronted with a question concerning this rule. The national court then suspends the proceedings before it and asks the European Court to solve the question. The national court or tribunal may, when there is no judicial remedy against its decision, request such a ruling each time it considers that in order to give judgment in a case pending before it, it needs a decision on the question. A distinction must be made between primary Community law in which case only interpretation can be requested, and secondary Community law, in which case the Court also has jurisdiction to give a ruling on the validity.

As to the precise meaning of the words "where such a question is raised," it seems that this condition is fulfilled as soon as a

are contrary to a rule of international law; Cases 21–24/72 *International Fruit Company* v. *Produktschap voor Groenten en Fruit* [1972] E.C.R. 1226 (6);

(l) a question relating to the application of the second para. of Art. 215 (non-contractual liability of the Community) cannot be determined in proceedings for a preliminary ruling; Case 101/78 *Granaria* v. *Hoofdproduktschap voor Akkerbouw produkten* [1979] E.C.R. 623 at 638 (10).

[44] See Case 6/64 *Costa* v. *ENEL* [1964] E.C.R. at 594: the executive fate of Community law cannot vary from one State to another without jeopardising the attainment of the objectives of the Treaty. See also Case 28/67 *Molkerei-Zentrale* v. *Hauptzollamt Paderborn* [1968] E.C.R. 143 at 153 where the Court pointed out that proceedings by an individual are intended to protect individual rights in a specific case, while intervention by Community authorities has as its object the general and uniform observance of Community law.

[45] Whether or not a national organ which refers a question to the Court of Justice is a court of law must be determined in accordance with national law. See, *e.g.* Case 61/65 *Vaassen* v. *Beamtenfonds Mijnbedrijf* [1966] E.C.R. 261 at 272 where the Court examined Dutch law in order to determine that a given court of arbiters was indeed a court or tribunal within the meaning of Art. 177. In another case also concerning a Dutch body: the section for Administrative Litigation of the Raad van Staten (Council of State) the Court did not go into the matter at all; Case 36/73 *Nederlandse Spoorwegen* v. *Minister van Verkeer en Waterstraat* [1973] E.C.R. 1299 at 1308.

difference of opinion arises concerning the interpretation (and in the case of acts also the validity) of a provision of Community law. This, however, does not mean that as soon as one of the parties in a case before a national court claims that a given Community rule does apply and expresses a view concerning its meaning which differs from that of the other party, the national judge must immediately suspend proceedings and refer the matter to the Court. The obligation to refer a question only exists when the national judge considers that a decision on the question is necessary to enable him to give judgment; in other words, it is his decision. Furthermore, it is also within the discretionary powers of the national judge to decide whether a question is raised in good faith or whether it is a purely procedural move initiated by a party for instance to delay judgment.[46] There is therefore nothing automatic in the procedure of the preliminary ruling: it lies entirely within the discretionary powers of the national judge and neither the Court,[47] national law[48] nor a Community rule[49] can deprive him of this right.

It should be noted also that the summary and urgent character of a procedure in the national court does not prevent the Court from regarding itself as validly seized to give a preliminary ruling[50]; however, a national court or tribunal is not required to refer to the Court, even when no judicial remedy is available against the decision, when the question is raised in interlocutory proceedings for an interim order, provided that each of the parties is entitled to institute proceedings or to require proceedings to be instituted on the substance of the case and that during such proceedings the question provisionally decided in the summary proceedings may be re-examined and may be the subject of a reference to the Court of Justice.[51]

[46] See opinion of the Advocate-General in the Case 6/64 *Costa* v. *ENEL* [1964] E.C.R. 585 at 607 where mention is made of a "preliminary inquiry of legality" concerning the relevance of the question to the solution of the dispute. It is also up to the national judge to decide at which stage of the procedure he will refer the question for a preliminary ruling: High Court of Justice of England [1974] C.M.L.R. 347.

[47] Case 5/77 *Tedeschi* v. *Denkavit* [1977] E.C.R. 1555 at 1574 (17).

[48] Case 166/73 *Rheinmühlen* v. *EVST* [1974] E.C.R. 33 at 38 (4).

[49] Case 127/73 *BRT* v. *Sabam* [1974] E.C.R. 51 at 63 (23).

[50] Case 107/76 *Hoffman-La Roche* v. *Centrafarm* [1977] E.C.R. 957 at 973.

[51] *Ibid.* 974. In a decision in summary proceeding, the President of the Arrondissementsrechtbank of Utrecht gave an interim order which was subject to the

It is clear from the abundance of requests for preliminary rulings that here lies an essential function, not only in regard to the development of Community law, but also as an instrument at the disposal of natural or legal persons confronted with Community measures whose legality thay cannot directly challenge in the Court. Indeed when an act is declared by the Court to be invalid in the course of a proceeding for a preliminary ruling, the act becomes inapplicable.

(5) *Compensation for damages caused by institutions*

In case of non-contractual liability the Community, in accordance with the general principles common to the laws of the Member States, shall make good any damage caused by its institutions or by its servants in the performance of their duties.[52]

In one of its first judgments concerning a claim for redress, the Court held that an administrative measure which has not been annulled cannot in itself constitute a wrongful act on the part of the administration, inflicting damage upon those whom it affects.[53] In more recent judgments, however, the Court has reversed its position, indicating that actions for annulment and claims for damages were different proceedings and that the Treaty in providing for an appeal for damages introduced an autonomous form of action, with a particular purpose to fulfil within the system of actions, and subject to conditions on its use dictated by its specific nature. Indeed it differs from an application for annulment in that its end is not the abolition of a particular measure, but compensation for damage caused by an institution in the performance of its duties.[54]

However, the Court maintained that non-contractual liability of the Community pre-supposes at the very least the unlawful nature of the act alleged to be the cause of the damage. On the other hand, the unlawful nature does not in itself make the Community

proviso that the plaintiff initiate proceedings in the same court within a period of six weeks so as to request that Court to make a preliminary ruling which indeed was done: Case 36/74 *Walrave and Koch* v. *Union Cycliste Internationale* [1974] E.C.R. 1405.

[52] EEC, Art. 178 and 215.

[53] Case 25/62, *Plaumann* v. *Commission* [1963] E.C.R. 95 at 108. See also Cases 35/62 and 16/63, *Leroy* v. *High Authority* [1963] E.C.R. 197 at 207 and Case 93/63, *Minot* v. *Commission* [1964] E.C.R. 489 at 511.

[54] Case 5/71 *Zuckerfabrik Schöppenstedt* v. *Council* [1971] E.C.R. 975 at 983 (3).

responsible for compensation in case of damage.[55] Where legislative action involving measures of economic policy is concerned, the Community does not incur non-contractual liability unless a sufficiently flagrant violation of a superior rule of law for the protection of the damaged party has occurred.[56]

The damage for which compensation is sought must of course be certain and have been assessed or assessable; the Court has, however, admitted the admissibility of an action in which the Court is asked to declare the Community liable for imminent damage foreseeable with sufficient certainty even if the damage cannot yet be precisely assessed.[57]

The Court has stated that it has no jurisdiction in cases in which the application for compensation is in fact directed against measures adopted by the national authorities for the purpose of applying provisions of Community law; but when the damage caused by the national implementing measures finds its origin in the underlying Community rule the latter can incur the liability of the Community.[58]

[55] Cases 83 and 94/76, 4, 15 and 40/77 *HNL* v. *Council and Commission* [1978] E.C.R. 1209 at 1224 (4) where the Court held that the Community does not incur non-contractual liability for damage caused to individuals through the effects of a legislative measure which involves choices of economic policy unless a sufficiently serious breach of a rule of law for the protection of the individual has occurred. Therefore the finding that a legislative measure is null and void is insufficient by itself for the Community to incur liability; *id* in Case 101/78 *Granaria* v. *Hoofdproduktschap voor Akkerbouwprodukten* [1979] E.C.R. 623, Case 238/78 *Ineks Azkady* v. *Council and Commission* (not yet reported).

[56] See Case 5/71 (n. 54) at *Ibid.* 984 (11); 63–69/72, *Werhahn et al.* v. *Council* [1973] E.C.R. 1229 at 1248 (10) and 74/74 *CNTA* v. *Commission* [1975] E.C.R. 533 at 546 (16).

The Court held in Case 9/75 *Meyer-Burckhardt* v. *Commission* [1975] E.C.R. 1171 was answerable concerning compensation for damages lies outside the sphere of EEC, Arts. 178 and 205.

[57] Case 44/76 *Eier-Kontor* v. *Council and Commission* [1977], E.C.R. 393 at 407 (8).

[58] Case 126/76 *Dietz* v. *Commission* [1977] E.C.R. 2431 and Case 101/78 *Granaria* v. *Hoofdproduktschap voor Akkerbouwprodukten* [1979] E.C.R. 640 where the Court held that "the question of compensation by a national agency for damage caused to private individuals by the agencies and servants of Member States, either by reason of an infringement of Community law or by an act or omission contrary to national law, in the application of Community law, does not fall within the second paragraph of Article 215 of the Treaty and must be determined by the national courts in accordance with the national law of the Member State concerned."

When the Court allocates compensation for damages caused by a Community act, the latter becomes virtually inapplicable, in the same way as an act declared invalid in a proceeding for a preliminary ruling. The action for compensation of damages, therefore, constitutes another instrument put at the disposal of natural and legal persons confronted with Community measures whose legality they cannot directly challenge in the Court.

(6) *Other cases within the Court's jurisdiction*

The *exception of illegality*[59] gives, according to the Court of Justice,[60] "expression to a general principle conferring upon any party to proceedings the right to challenge, for the purpose of obtaining the annulment of a decision of direct and individual concern to that party, the validity of previous acts of the institutions which form the legal basis of the decision which is being attacked, if that party was not entitled under Article 173 of the Treaty to bring a direct action challenging those acts by which it was thus affected without having been in a position to ask that they be declared void." Although the Treaty refers explicitly to "a regulation," the Court refers to "acts" in general.[61] For the Court it is clear, from the wording and the general scheme of Article 184, that although this is not specified, a declaration of inapplicability is only contemplated in proceedings brought before the Court itself under some other provisions of the Treaty and that the plea may be used only against a regulation which is the basis of the act in dispute; the intention of said Article is not to "allow a party to contest at will the applicability of any regulation in support of an application. The regulation of which the legality is called in question must be applicable, directly or indirectly, to the issue with which the appli-

[59] EEC, Art. 184.

[60] Case 15/57 *Compagnie des Hants Fournaux de Chasse* v. *High Authority* [1957 and 1958] E.C.R. 211 and Case 9/56, *Meroni* v. *High Authority* [1957 and 1958] G.C.R., 133.

[61] Case 92/78 *Simmenthal* v. *Commission* [1979] E.C.R. 777 at 800 (39). The Court added that "the field of application of said article must therefore include acts of the institution which, although they are not in the form of a regulation, nevertheless produce similar effects and which for those reasons cannot be challenged under Art. 173 by natural or legal persons other than Community institutions and Member States."

cation is concerned."[62] A typical case would be when an undertaking would be fined by the Commission for violation of a regulation which the undertaking considers illegal; the undertaking would then appeal to the Court for annulment of the decision imposing the fine, alleging that the regulation itself is inapplicable on the basis of one of the four grounds specified in Article 173. This exception of illegality, therefore constitutes another way for natural or legal persons to challenge a measure whose illegality they cannot directly ask the Court to review. However, this kind of action was very seldom brought to the Court.

Disputes between the Community and its servants[63] come under the exclusive jurisdiction of the Court; with some rare exceptions[64] actions brought by Community servants present little interest for Community law as such. Many hundreds of actions have been brought under Article 179 thereby clogging the Court's register. On several occasions it was proposed to create a special tribunal for those disputes giving the Court more time to develop Community law.

Reference must also be made to the possibility provided for in the Treaty of *attributing jurisdiction* to the Court in contracts concluded by or on behalf of the Community whether those contracts are governed by public or private law.[65] An explicit attribution of jurisdiction to the Court is necessary the more so since the Treaty also provides that disputes to which the Community is a party shall not on that ground be excluded from the jurisdiction of the courts or tribunals of the Member States.[66]

In this context the attributions of jurisdiction in the Protocol on the interpretation by the Court of Justice of the Convention on

[62] Case 32/65 *Italy* v. *Council and Commission* [1966] E.C.R. 409, and Cases 31–33/62 *Wöhrmann* v. *Commission* [1962] E.C.R. 507.

[63] EEC, Art. 179 and Staff Regulations, Art. 91.

[64] See, *e.g.* Cases 7/56, 3–7/57 *Algera et al.* v. *Common Assembly* [1957 and 1958] E.C.R. 39 at 55 and Case 6/60 *Humblet* v. *Belgium* [1960] E.C.R. 559, which in fact concerned a dispute between a servant and a Member State.

[65] EEC, Art. 181. Such clauses are to be found in practically all the procurement contracts concluded by the EEC and in the research contracts concluded under Euratom, Art. 10.

[66] EEC, Art. 183.

Jurisdiction and the enforcement of judgments in civil and commercial matters[67] concluded between the Member States[68] should also be mentioned.

The Court in cases before it may also prescribe the necessary *interim measures* including suspension of application of the contested act and suspension of the enforcement measures.[69] With regard to suspension of application it must be noted that actions brought before the Court do not have suspensory effect.[70] An application to suspend the operation of any measure adopted by an institution shall be admissible only if the applicant is challenging that measure in proceedings before the Court.[71]

It is of great interest to note that the Court can prescribe interim measures applicable to a Member State[72] although it has no such powers in the dispute itself.[73] There is no limit as to the kind of interim measures the Court may prescribe; besides the suspension of the application of a measure, the Court has ordered parties to start negotiations to agree upon an alternative solution,[74] authorised another to adopt temporary measures with the consent of the Commission,[75] and suspended the application of a measure on condition that a party continues to provide security.[76]

[67] See the Protocol of June 3, 1971, Art. 3 (O.J. 1975, L 204/28), as amended by the Convention of Association of October 9, 1978, to the "Judgments" or "Brussels" Convention of September 27, 1968 (O.J. 1978, L 304/77). See, *e.g.* Cases 9, 10/77 *Bavaria Fluggesellschaft* v. *Eurocontrol* [1977] E.C.R. 1517.

[68] This Protocol does not constitute a special agreement to submit disputes between Member States to the Court of Justice in the sense of EEC, Art. 182; indeed the Convention does not concern a "subject matter of the Treaty."

[69] EEC, Arts. 185, 186 and 192; Chap. I of Title III of the Rules of Procedure of the Court of Justice (O.J. 1974, L 300 and O.J. 1975 L 102) refers to "suspension of operation or enforcement and other interim measures."

[70] EEC, Art. 185.

[71] Rules of Procedure of the Court of Justice, Art. 83 (1).

[72] See, *e.g.* Cases 31/77 R and 53–77 R, *Commission* v. *U.K.* [1977] E.C.R. at 925, where the U.K. was ordered to forthwith cease applying the aid measure which it had been operating since January 31, 1977.

[73] As pointed out *supra* in "the finding of a failure by a Member State to fulfil its treaty obligations" the Court of Justice may only "find" that a Member State has "failed," but it is up to the State to take the "necessary measures to comply with the judgment of the Court of Justice," EEC, Art. 171.

[74] Case 61/77 R *Commission* v. *Ireland* [1977] E.C.R. 937 at 943 (34).

[75] Case 61/77 R *Commission* v. *Ireland* [1977] E.C.R. 1411 at 1415.

[76] Cases 113 and 118-121 R/77, *NTN TOYO and Others* v. *Council*, [1977] E.C.R. 1721 at 1726.

(7) *Judicial remedies: a summary*

As was pointed out, the Member States, the Council and the Commission have, subject to time-limits, unlimited access to the Court of Justice; the access is rather limited for natural and legal persons, although they have several actions at their disposal.

To summarise, proceedings in the Court of Justice can be initiated by:

- a Member State, against another Member State for failure to fulfil an obligation;
  against the Council for annulment, failure to act or give compensation,
  against the Commission for annulment, failure to act or give compensation,
- the Council, against the Commission for annulment or failure to act;
- the Commission, against a Member State for failure to fulfil an obligation,
  against the Council for annulment or failure to act;
- the Assembly, against the Council for failure to act;
  against the Commission for failure to act;
- a person, against the Council for annulment, failure to act or give compensation;
  against the Commission for annulment, failure to act or give compensation,

  furthermore a person may:
  ask a national court to request a preliminary ruling,
  in a case before the Court of Justice, plead inapplicability of underlying regulation
- servants, against the Council, the Commission, the Assembly, the Court of Justice and the Social and Economic Committee.

3. The procedure

The rules concerning the procedure before the Court of Justice are laid down in a Protocol on the Statute of the Court of Justice of the European Communities annexed to the EEC Treaty and in the Rules of Procedure which the Court adopts after having received the unanimous approval of the Council.[77] These rules contain,

[77] EEC, Art. 188.

apart from those "contemplated" by the Statute, any other provisions necessary for applying and when necessary, for supplementing it.[78]

The procedure before the Court consists of two parts: written and oral; as for the language of the proceedings, it must be one of the official languages of the Community and is determined by the applicant.[79]

(1) *The written procedure*[80]

This procedure starts with the submission to the Court of a written application addressed to the Registrar. The Statute and the Rules of Procedure contain various requirements as to form, content and accompanying documents of the application.[81] The Member States and the institutions are represented by an agent appointed for each case; other parties must be represented by a lawyer entitled to practise before a court of a Member State.[82] It is important that the application must state the grounds on which it is based, since parties may not in the course of proceedings raise fresh issues, unless they are based on matters of law or of fact which come to light in the course of the written procedure.[83] The time-limit within which the application must be filed is also essential: appeals for annulment must be instituted within two months of the publication of the measure or of its notification to the

[78] Statute, Art. 44. The Court and the Council have given this provision a very extensive interpretation since the last revision (O.J. 1979, L 238/1) allows the Court to let the Chambers adjudicate any cases brought before the Court, although EEC, Art. 165, second para., limits the jurisdiction of the Chambers to "particular categories of cases."

[79] At present there are six official languages: Danish, German, English, French, Italian and Dutch. Irish is also an official language but the Irish Government agreed to limit its use to the text of the European Treaties and other basic Acts. The right of the applicant to determine the language of the proceedings is provided in the Rules of Procedure, Art. 29 (2).

[80] See Statute, Arts. 18 *et seq.* and Rules Title II, Chap. I.

[81] See Statute, Art. 19 and Rules, Arts. 38 *et seq.*

[82] Statute, Art. 17. The application must also state an address for service at the place where the Court has its seat. It shall also give the name of a person who is authorised and has expressed willingness to accept service; Rules, Art. 38 (2).

[83] Rules, Art. 42 (2).

plaintiff.[84] This time-limit was slightly extended by the Rules of Procedure for all parties living outside Luxembourg.[85]

The application is notified by the Court's registrar to the defendant who then has one month to file a *defence.*[86] Plaintiff's *application* and the defendant's *defence* may be supplemented by a *reply* from the applicant and by a *rejoinder* from the defendant. The time-limit within which these pleadings have to be lodged shall be fixed by the President of the Court. Before formally closing the written part of the procedure, the Court, at the suggestion of the Judge-Rapporteur[87] or the Advocate-General, may decide to prescribe measures of inquiry[88] for the case, *i.e.* interrogation of parties, request for information, hearing of witnesses,[89] etc.

In the case of a preliminary ruling, the parties, the Member States, the Commission and, where appropriate, the Council, shall be entitled to submit statements of case or written observations to the Court.[90] Finally, it should be noted that the Member States and the institutions may always intervene in cases before the Court; other persons have the same right in certain cases when they establish an interest in the result of a case.[91]

(2) *The oral procedure*

The oral procedure[92] consists of the reading of the report presented by the Judge-Rapporteur, the hearing by the Court of

[84] EEC, Art. 173, third para. See Case 232/78 *Commission* v. *France* (not yet published) where the Court did not allow the plaintiff to modify his application to take account of the Court's judgment in a similar case, *i.e.* Case 231/78 *Commission* v. *United Kingdom* [1979] E.C.R. 1447.

[85] O.J. 1974, L 350/1.

[86] Rules, Art. 40 (1).

[87] See Rules, Art. 9 (2): as soon as an application originating proceedings has been lodged, the President of the Court assigns the case to one of the Chambers and designates from the Chamber a Judge to act as Rapporteur and the Advocate-General.

[88] For details see Rules, Arts. 45–54.

[89] The Rules contain several provisions concerning witnesses: the Court may impose penalties in case of default (Statute, Art. 24), the Court may have a witness heard by the judicial authorities of the place of his permanent residence (Statute, Art. 26), Member States must treat any violation of an oath by a witness in the same manner as if the offence had been committed before one of its courts with jurisdiction in civil procedure and prosecute the offender before its competent court at the instance of the Court of Justice (Statute, Art. 27).

[90] Statute, Art. 20. [91] *Ibid.* Art. 37.

[92] See Statute, Art. 18, fourth para. and Rules. Arts. 55–62.

agents, legal advisers or council and of the opinion of the Advocate-General, as well as the hearing, if any, of witnesses and experts. The opinion of the Advocate-General is usually read during a separate Court session which indicates the end of the oral part of the procedure.[93] The judgment[94] is in turn read in open court at a later date.

(3) *Special form of procedure*

The Statute of the Court of Justice and the Rules of Procedure contain provisions for various special forms of procedure such as the adoption of interim measures, judgments by default, third party proceedings, revision.[95]

V. *Other Bodies of the European Communities*

1. The Court of Auditors

The Court of Auditors was set up by the Treaty amending certain financial provisions of the European Treaties and of the Merger Treaty.[96] Generally speaking, the provisions concerning the members of the Court of Auditors are similar to those concerning the Judges of the Court of Justice.[97] The members, however, are appointed by the Council after consulting the Assembly.

The Court of Auditors examines the accounts of all revenue and expenditure of the Community and of any body created by the Community,[98] not only to determine whether all revenue has been received and expenditure incurred in a lawful manner, but also whether the financial management has been sound. Since a vast

[93] Rules, Art. 59.

[94] For the prescribed contents of the judgment see Rules, Art. 63; *e.g.* the judgment always contains a decision regarding the costs which are normally paid by the losing party; see Rules, Art. 69 *et seq.*

[95] See Statute, Art. 36 *et seq.* and Rules, Arts. 83 *et seq.*

[96] Art. 15 modifying EEC, Art. 206.
The Treaty was signed at Brussels on July 22, 1975, but only entered into force on June 1, 1977 (O.J. 1977, L 359).

[97] See EEC, Art. 206 (2)–(10).

[98] EEC, Art. 206a (1); *e.g.* the European Centre for the Development of Vocational Training (O.J. 1975, L 39/1) and the European Foundation for the improvement of living and working conditions (O.J. 1975, L 139/1). An Annex to the Treaty provides that the Court of Auditors also has jurisdiction to audit the European Development Fund.

proportion of the Community revenue is collected and made available by the Member States, on-the-spot checks by the Court of Auditors are provided, not only in the institutions of the Community, but also in the Member States.

The Court of Auditors draws up an annual report which is forwarded to all the institutions of the Community and published in the *Official Journal* together with the replies of the institutions to the observations of the Court of Auditors.[99]

The Court of Auditors may also submit observations on specific questions on its own initiative and deliver opinions at the request of one of the institutions.[1]

2. The Economic and Social Committee[2]

The Economic and Social Committee plays a consultative role mainly within the decision-making process of the Community. When consultation is provided for by the Treaty, it must necessarily take place lest decisions be annulled by the Court for infringement of an essential procedural requirement; the required consultation must also be referred to in the relevant Community measure.

The Committee may also be consulted either by the Council or by the Commission, in all cases in which they consider it appropriate; however, the Heads of State or of Government decided at their 1972 Paris Summit meeting to invite "the Community institutions to recognise the right of the Economic and Social Committee in future to advise on its own initiative on all questions affecting the Community."[3]

The Committee is composed of 144 members appointed for four years by the Council in their personal capacity; they may not be bound by mandatory instructions. The members are representatives of the various categories of economic and social activity, in particular producers, farmers, carriers, workers, tradesmen, craftsmen, members of the professions and the general public.[4]

[99] See, *e.g.* Report for the year 1978 (O.J. 1979, C 326).
[1] See, *e.g.* Opinion (O.J. 1979, C 225/3 and C 221/1).
[2] EEC, Arts. 193–198.
[3] Declaration of the Summit, pt. 15, Bull. 10–1972, 23.
[4] For further information on the Committee's composition and activities, see its annual report and the accounts published in the Bulletin under "Economic and Social Committee."

3. The Consultative Committee of the ECSC

The ECSC Treaty provides for the creation of a Consultative Committee[5] attached to the High Authority and consisting of between 60 and 84 members made up of an equal number of producers, workers, consumers and dealers. They are appointed for two years in their personal capacity by the Council from lists drawn up by representative organisations also designated by the Council. The functions of the Consultative Committee are comparable in all points to those of the Economic and Social Committee.

4. The Scientific and Technical Committee of Euratom

This Committee, set up by the Euratom Treaty, is attached to the Commission[6]; it consists of 27 members appointed for five years by the Council after consultation of the Commission. The Committee has a consultative status.

[5] ECSC, Arts. 18 and 19.
[6] Euratom, Art. 134.

CHAPTER 4

COMMUNITY ACTS

THE main lines of the decision-making process within the European Community were outlined briefly in Chapter 3 in respect of the role played by the Commission, the European Parliament and the Council; reference was made also to the various forms which the Community rules can take. As was pointed out, the actual practice does differ from what the Treaty provisions indicate; at first sight the procedure appears extremely simple: the Commission drafts a proposal, where required after consulting the Economic and Social Committee, transmits its proposal to the Council, which decides after consulting the European Parliament when the Treaty so prescribes. This description does not take into account the preparatory work carried out by the Commission as requested by the Council at its extraordinary session of January 28 and 29, 1966,[1] the effective participation of the European Parliament in the procedure for preparing and adopting decisions which give rise to important expenditure and revenue,[2] the role of the Committee of Permanent Representatives,[3] the abandonment of majority voting and the increasing role played by the European Council.

These new developments have not modified the respective tasks of the various institutions, *i.e.* the right of initiative of the Commission, the advisory function of the European Parliament and the legislative powers of the Council; they have, however, somewhat blunted the lines of separation and thereby the system of check and balance which characterised the original institutional set-up.

[1] Also referred to as the "Luxembourg Agreement"; Sweet and Maxwell, *European Community Treaties* (3rd ed., 1977), at p. 235 (*a*), 1.

[2] Joint Declaration of the European Parliament, the Council and the Commission of March 4, 1975 (O.J. 1975, C 89/1).

[3] Merger Treaty, Art. 4.

The one aspect which to date has remained unaltered is the judicial control exercised by the Court of Justice and consequently the protection which the various proceedings offer to Member States, institutions and persons. Hence the increasing importance of the nature of the Community measures since only binding acts of the Council and the Commission can be submitted to the Court's review; the tendency, however, is to multiply the forms of the decisions and the bodies issuing them. Besides the "communiqués," "declarations" and "conclusions" of the Summits and the European Council, there are now "programmes," "resolutions," and "declarations" not only of the Council, but also of the governments of the Member States, of the representatives of the Member States in Council and the representatives of the governments. None of those constitutes acts whose legality the Court can review or for which a Commission proposal is required or the Assembly's opinion requested; nonetheless those measures shape essential Community policies and therefore the future development of the Community itself. It sometimes appears that the more important the decision, the less formal the procedure and the measure.

Nevertheless the binding acts provided for by the Treaty still play an essential role and the conditions laid down for the decision-making process and for the contents of those acts must be seen as so many guarantees for lawfulness and judicial control and protection.

The above-mentioned developments seem to run counter to the Treaty provisions which invest the Council and the Commission with the responsibility to achieve the purposes of the Community and to carry out this task by making regulations, issuing directives, taking decisions, making recommendations and delivering opinions, all in accordance with the provisions of the Treaty. Each one of these acts fulfils a specific function in the development of Community law and the Treaty therefore explicitly provides in several cases, which kind of act must be adopted. Different procedural rules apply to the various categories and, more important, the extent of legal protection afforded individuals under the treaties varies widely from one category to another.[4]

[4] It should be noted that it is not the name given to a measure which classifies it in one of the above-mentioned categories, but rather the contents and objective of its provisions; Case 20/58 *Phoenix-Rheinrohr* v. *High Authority* [1959] E.C.R. 75 at 82;

1. Acts provided in Article 189

A *regulation* has general application, is binding in its entirety and is directly applicable in all Member States. The criterion for the distinction between a regulation and other acts, especially decisions, must be sought in the general "application." Being essentially of a "legislative nature a regulation is applicable not to a limited number of persons, defined or identifiable, but to categories of persons viewed abstractly and in their entirety."[5]

Secondly, a regulation is binding in its entirety; this distinguishes it from a directive which only binds the Member State to which it is addressed to achieve the specified results. Since a regulation "has general application and is binding in its entirety, Member States may not, in the absence of a provision of Community law to the contrary, have recourse to national measures capable of modifying its application."[6] The Court has also considered that since a regulation is binding in its entirety, it cannot be accepted that a Member State should apply in an incomplete or selective manner provisions of a Community regulation so as to render abortive certain aspects of Community legislation."[7]

Finally, a regulation is directly applicable in all Member States: a regulation therefore promotes the unity of the common market by creating uniform conditions in the whole Community. Direct applicability means that a regulation does not require a national measure to become binding upon the citizens of a given country and also that national authorities and national measures cannot prevent their application.[8] Nevertheless provisions contained in a regulation might need national implementing measures to become

see also Case 15/70 *Chevalley* v. *Commission* [1970] E.C.R. 975 at 980 (10). The Court has also admitted that the same act can contain provisions pertaining to different categories: a regulation for instance can contain provisions which by their very nature constitute individual decisions: Cases 16 and 17/62 *Producteurs de fruits* v. *Council* [1962] E.C.R. 471 at 479. In Cases 41–44/70 *International Fruit Co.* v. *Commission* [1971] E.C.R. 411 at 422 (21), the Court found that Art. 1 of Regulation 983/70 is not a provision of general application within the meaning of EEC, Art. 189, second para. but must be regarded as a conglomeration of individual decisions.

[5] Cases 16 and 17/62, *supra*.

[6] Case 18/72 *Granaria* v. *Produktschap voor Veevoeder* [1972] E.C.R. 1163 at 1171 (16).

[7] Case 39/72 *Commission* v. *Italy* [1973] E.C.R. 101 at 115 (20).

[8] See Case 34/73 *Variola* v. *Administrazione Italiana delle Finanze* [1973] E.C.R. 981 at 990 (10) and Case 230/78 *Enidania* v. *Ministry of Agriculture* (not yet published).

applicable, but the regulation itself does not have to be "transformed into national law by a national measure."[9]

Direct applicability must not be confused with "direct effect." A Community measure has direct effect when it creates rights for the citizens of the Community which they can invoke in national courts and which the latter must uphold even when they conflict with national measures whether anterior or posterior.[10] And indeed, as was pointed out before, the European treaties are more than agreements which merely create mutual obligations between the contracting states. The Community constitutes a new legal order for the benefit of which the states have limited their sovereign rights albeit within limited fields and the subjects of which comprise not only the Member States but also their nationals. Independently of the legislation of the Member States, Community law therefore not only imposes obligations on individuals, but is also intended to confer upon them rights which become part of their legal heritage. These rights arise not only where they are expressly granted by the Treaty, but also by reason of obligations which Community rules impose in a clearly defined way upon individuals as well as upon Member States and upon the institutions of the Community.[11]

Not all the provisions of Community law have direct effect. To have this effect it is necessary and sufficient that the provision by its very nature is capable of producing this effect, *i.e.* that the obligation does not leave anything to the discretion of the Member State, is not qualified by any condition, or subject, in its implementation or effects, to the taking of any measure either by the institutions of the Community or by the Member States. If not all Community provisions have direct effect, the Court of Justice is of the opinion that a regulation, by reason of its very nature and its function in the system of sources of Community Law, has direct effect, *i.e.* is "capable of creating individual rights which national courts must protect." It is for the national legal system to determine which court or tribunal has jurisdiction to give this protection

[9] For instance, many regulations in the field of agriculture require implementing national measures.

[10] For further discussion of direct effect, see *infra*, Chap. 7.

[11] Case 28/67 *Molkerei-Zentrale Westfalen* v. *Hauptzollamt Paderborn* [1968] E.C.R. 143 at 152–153; see also Case 13/68 *Salgoil* v. *Italy* [1968] E.C.R. 453 at 461. For a more detailed discussion of direct effect, see *infra*, Chap. 7.

and, for this purpose, to decide how the individual position thus protected is to be classified.[12]

Directives can be issued by the Council and the Commission and constitute the appropriate measure when existing national legislation must be modified or national provisions must be enacted: the Member States for instance are free to decide whether those provisions will be legislative or administrative in nature.

Although directives are not directly applicable, since they normally require implementing measures, their provisions can nevertheless have direct effect, but in each case it must be ascertained whether by their nature, background and wording the provisions are capable of producing direct effects in the legal relationships between the addressee of the act and third parties.[13]

As for a *decision*, it is binding in its entirety upon those to whom it is addressed. The addressee can be Member State or a legal or natural person and decisions can be taken by the Council and by the Commission. Decisions are generally of an administrative nature implementing other Community rules, *e.g.* granting of exceptions or authorisations or imposition of fines.

There are no requirements as to the form of a decision, so that it can be doubtful whether a given act constitutes a binding decision or not. Obviously, the institutions must ensure that a decision is

[12] Case 43/71 *Politi* v. *Italy* [1971] E.C.R. 1039 at 1048 (9) and Case 13/68 *Salgoil* v. *Italy* [1968] E.C.R. 453 at 463. See also Case 39/71 *Leonesio* v. *Italian Ministry for Agriculture and Forestry* [1972] E.C.R. 287 at 295 (22–23) where the Court held that "so as to apply with equal force with regard to nationals of all the Member States, Community regulations become part of the legal system applicable within the national territory, which must permit the direct effect provided for in Art. 189 to operate in such a way that reliance thereon by individuals may not be frustrated by domestic provisions or practices."

[13] Case 9/70 *Grad* v. *Finanzamt Traunstein* [1970] E.C.R. 825 at 837 (5): "although it is true that by virtue of Article 189, regulations are directly applicable and therefore by virtue of their nature capable of producing direct effects, it does not follow from this that other categories of legal measures mentioned in that article can never produce similar effects." The Court used as an argument the fact that Art. 177 empowers the national courts to refer to the Court of Justice all questions regarding the validity and interpretation of all acts of the institutions without distinction, which implies that individuals may invoke such acts before the national courts.

See also Case 79/72 *Commission* v. *Italy* [1973] E.C.R. 667 at 672 (7) Case 41/74 *Van Duyn* v. *Home Office* [1974] E.C.R. 1337 at 1352 and Case 51/76 *VNO* v. *Inspecteur der invoerrechten en accijnzen* [1977] E.C.R. 113 at 127 (23).

recognisable as a binding act by its very form.[14] Being binding in its entirety a decision can have direct effect.[15]

Finally, the Treaty provides for *recommendations* and *opinions* which have no binding force. Generally speaking, recommendations aim at obtaining a given action or behaviour from the addressee, while the opinions express a point of view, in most cases at the request of a third party. Having no binding effect, the legality of recommendations and opinions cannot be reviewed by the Court, neither submitted for a preliminary ruling concerning their validity or interpretation.

2. Regulations, directives and decisions must be reasoned

Regulations, directives and decisions must state the reasons on which they are based and must refer to the proposals and opinions which were required to be obtained pursuant to the Treaty.[16]

"Reasons" must be understood as referring both to the legal provision which entitles the institution to take the measure and the reasons which motivated the institution to act. The mention of the provision is particularly important since, as was mentioned before, the institutions of the Community can only exercise those powers which are explicitly provided for by Community law.

As for the motives which prompted the institution to act, they must be mentioned in order to make it possible for the interested parties and for the Court to reconstruct the essential elements of the institution's reasoning,[17] thereby permitting the parties to defend their rights, the Court to exercise its control and the Member States, and in the same way all interested citizens, to know the conditions under which the institution has applied the Treaty.[18]

To attain these objectives it is sufficient for the act to set out, in a concise but clear and relevant manner, the principal issues of law and fact upon which it is based and which are necessary in order that the reasoning which has led the institution to its decision may

[14] Case 28/63 *Hoogovens* v. *High Authority* [1963] E.C.R. 231 at 235.
[15] Case 9/70 *Grad* v. *Finanzamt Traunstein* [1970] E.C.R. at 837 (5).
[16] EEC, Art. 190.
[17] Case 14/61 *Hoogovens* v. *High Authority* [1962] E.C.R. 253 at 275.
[18] Case 24/62 *Germany* v. *Commission* [1963] E.C.R. 63 at 69.

be understood.[19] The extent of this requirement depends on the nature of the measure in question. The condition can also be considered as fulfilled when reference[20] is made to the reasons developed in an earlier act.[21]

If an act is not sufficiently "reasoned," this constitutes a ground for annulment: infringement of an essential procedural requirement which can be invoked in an action for review of the legality of the act concerned by the Court of Justice. The Court can and must of its own motion take exception to any deficiencies in the reasons which would make such review more difficult.[22]

As for the reference to the required proposals and opinions, a simple mention is considered sufficient; the institutions are not required to indicate whether or not the opinion was favourable[23] still less to refute dissenting opinions expressed by the consultative bodies.[24]

3. Publication and entry into force[25]

Since regulations are of a legislative nature and therefore concern an unidentifiable group to whom they apply, they must be published in the *Official Journal of the European Communities* which is published in the six official languages[26] of the Community. They

[19] *Ibid.* See also Cases 36, 37, 38 and 40/59 *Präsident et al.* v. *High Authority* [1960] E.C.R. 423 at 439, where the Court indicated that the mention of the reasons is especially required when the institution exercises discretionary powers, since in such cases the judicial control of the Court is limited and the decision to act is based upon the institution's findings.

[20] Case 75/77 *Mollet* v. *Commission* [1978] E.C.R. 897 at 906 (12); Case 34/77 *Oslizlok* v. *Commission* [1978] E.C.R. 1099 at 1114 (22); Case 87/78 *Welding* v. *Hauptzollamt Hamburg-Waltershof* [1978] E.C.R. 2457 at 2468 (11).

[21] Case 1/69 *Italy* v. *Commission* [1969] E.C.R. 277 at 285 (9). See, however, Case 73/74 *Papiers peints* v. *Commission* [1975] E.C.R. 1514.

[22] EEC, Art. 173. Case 18/57 *Nold* v. *High Authority* [1959] E.C.R. 41 at 52.

[23] This, however, is no secret since both the Commission's proposals and the Parliament's opinions are published in the *Official Journal.*

[24] Case 4/54 *I.S.A.* v. *High Authority* [1954 to 1956], E.C.R. 91 at 100 (6).

[25] EEC, Art. 191.

[26] The official languages and working languages of the institutions of the Community are Danish, German, English, French, Italian and Dutch: see Council Reg. 1 (J.O. 1958, 385) as modified in pursuance of Art. 29 of the Act of accession together with Point XIV (1) of Annex 1 of said Act, which in turn was amended by the Adaptation Decision (O.J. 1973, L 2/1). See also Reg. 857/72 concerning the establishment of special editions of the *Official Journal* (J.O. 1972, L 101/1).

enter into force on the day specified in them or, in the absence thereof, on the twentieth day following their publication.[27]

Directives and decisions on the other hand concern only a limited number of persons—Member States or natural or legal persons—and must therefore be notified directly to those to whom they are addressed. However, since the Court may review the legality of decisions at the request of parties which are not addressees of said acts, when the latter are of "direct and individual concern"[28] to them, it is important that they be informed of the contents of all such decisions. The same applies to directives; as was seen, the citizens may invoke them in the national courts and request the latter to ask the Court of Justice for a preliminary ruling on their validity or interpretation. Consequently directives are always published in the *Official Journal* as are decisions which may affect the rights of third parties.[29]

4. Enforcement[30]

Decisions of the Council and the Commission which impose a pecuniary obligation[31] on persons other than Member States and judgments of the Court of Justice[32] are enforceable.

Enforcement of Community acts is governed by the rules of civil procedure in force within the Member State where it is carried out. The following steps must be taken. The institution, for instance, which wants to enforce a decision, presents it for verification of

[27] A typical example is Reg. 17 giving effect to the principles of competition: the regulation was adopted by the Council on February 6, 1962, published in the *Official Journal* on February 21, 1962 and, since it did not mention the date of entry into force, it became effective on March 13, 1962.

There is an interesting case of a regulation which was to enter into force on the basis of a date indicated therein but the date was anterior to the actual date of publication; the Court of Justice decided that if evidence is produced that the date on which an issue of the *Official Journal* is in fact available does not correspond to the date which appears on the issue, regard must be had to the date of actual publication; Case 98/78 *Racke* v. *Hauptzollamt Mainz* [1979] E.C.R. 69 at 89 (15). See also Case 99/78 *Decker* v. *Hauptzollamt Landau* [1979], E.C.R. 101 at 109 (3).

[28] EEC, Art. 173, second para.

[29] See in this respect Cases 73–74/63 *Handelsvereniging Rotterdam et al.* v. *Minister van Landbouw* [1964] E.C.R. 1 at 14 and Case 130/78 *Salumificio* v. *Ministry of Finance* [1979] E.C.R. 867.

[30] EEC, Art. 192.

[31] For instance decisions of the Commission imposing fines pursuant to Art. 15 of Reg. 17, for violation of the competition rules (O.J. 1959–1962, 87).

[32] EEC, Art. 189.

authenticity to the national authority which the Government of each Member State has designated for this purpose[33] and made known to the Commission and the Court of Justice. This authority then appends to the decision an order for its enforcement.[34] The institution can then proceed to enforcement in accordance with national law, by bringing the matter directly before the competent national authorities. From that moment on, the national rules of civil procedure apply with the exception that suspension of the enforcement may only be decided by the Court.

An action brought before the Court against the decision which is being enforced has no suspensory effect.[35]

5. Binding acts not provided under Article 189

Community acts are not limited to regulations, directives and decisions. As was pointed out, judgments of the Court are also binding upon the parties and can be enforced. The same applies to agreements concluded by the Community with third countries or

[33] The Netherlands: Law of February 24, 1955, Stb 73, modified by Law of January 13, 1960, Stb 15: Minister of Justice is addressee of request; Greffier of Hoge Raad implements. Belgium: Law of August 6, 1967: Greffier en Chef of the Court of Appeal at Brussels. France: Décret No. 57/321 of March 13, 1957, *Journal Officiel*, March 19, 1957, 2885, designates (1) persons who have received delegation from the Prime Minister and (2) Secrétariat Général du Comité Interministériel. Germany: Bundesgesetzblatt, February 3, 1961, II, 50: Minister of Justice. Italy: Decree of December 2, 1960, Official Gazetta, February 21, 1961, No. 46, 738: Minister of Foreign Affairs. Luxembourg: Reg. of October 17, 1962, Memorial of October 31, 1962, No. 58, 1028: verification by Minister of Foreign Affairs, and order for enforcement appended by Minister of Justice. United Kingdom: European Communities (Enforcement of Community Judgments) Order 1972, S.I. 1972, No. 1590, which provides for the registration in the High Court of England and Northern Ireland and the Court of Session in Scotland of Community judgments and orders to which the Secretary of State has duly appended an order for enforcement. Ireland: S.I. No. 331 of 1972: enforcement order appended by the Master of the High Court, Denmark: by the Minister of Justice.

[34] The way in which this order is appended varies from state to state. In the Netherlands, for instance, the formula "in the Queen's name" is written on the document itself, which thereby acquires the same legal force as a national Court or administrative order. In the United Kingdom "order for enforcement" means an order by or under the authority of the Secretary of State that the Community judgment to which it is appended is to be registered for enforcement in the United Kingdom (S.I. 1972, No. 1590) 2.

[35] When the Commission takes a decision imposing fines on a person, it usually does not seek enforcement in case an appeal has been lodged against the decision.

international organisations; they are binding upon the institutions of the Community and on the Member States.[36]

The same applies to agreements concluded by the Member States among themselves regarding matters connected with the Treaty.[37] Somewhat different is the position of international agreements concluded by the Member States with third countries: in so far as, under the Treaty, the Community has assumed the powers previously exercised by Member States in the area governed by such international agreement, the provisions of that agreement have the effect of binding the Community.[38] These agreements can be submitted to the control of legality exercised by the Court when the Community is a party[39] to them and they constitute rules of law relating to the application of the Treaty[40] with the result that regulations, directives and decisions can be annulled in case of infringement of these rules.

Finally there are the decisions of the representatives of the governments of the Member States in Council; these cannot be submitted to the Court, since they do not emanate from the Council or the Commission, but they can be binding within the whole Community.[41] But it will have to be established on a case by case basis whether those decisions are binding only for the Member States or also for the institutions of the Community and even for natural or legal persons. Although those "decisions," not provided for under the Treaty, constitute a flexible instrument to solve a number of questions within the scope of the treaties, they are not without danger for the institutional equilibrium provided by the Treaty. Besides immunity from the Court's control these acts do not require a Commission proposal or an opinion of Parliament. Of

[36] EEC, Art. 228 (2).

[37] See, *e.g.* EEC, Arts. 50 and 220.

[38] Cases 21–24/72 *International Fruit Company et al.* v. *Produkschap voor Groenten en Fruit*, [1972] E.C.R. 1219 at 1227 (18).

[39] See, *e.g.* Case 22/70 *Commission* v. *Council* [1971] E.C.R. 263.

[40] EEC, Art. 173.

[41] See, *e.g.* the "acceleration" decisions by which the Member States agreed to establish the customs union within a shorter time-limit than provided for under the Treaty (J.O. 1960, 1217 and 1962, 1284).

These decisions are not to be confused with decisions of the Member States such as the appointment of the Members of the Commission (Merger Treaty, Art. 11) or of the Judges of the Court of Justice (EEC, Art. 167).

course, nothing can prevent the latter from trying to exercise its political control over these acts anyway.

Binding acts not provided for under Article 189 can have "direct effect"; this applies in the first place to international agreements.[42]

6. Other forms of Community measures

A form often used is the *resolution*, either of the Council,[43] or of the Council and of the representatives of the governments of the Member States.[44] These resolutions are not to be confused with the decisions of the representatives of the governments of the Member States in Council; in the first place the decisions of the representatives of the Member States are legally binding upon the latter while resolutions only constitute a political commitment; secondly, the fact that they act within the institutional framework is intended to indicate that the matter directly concerns the implementation of the Treaty; resolutions, generally speaking, concern matters directly connected with the Community, but not explicitly provided for under the Treaty.

There is also the *programme* or programmes of action, which intend to lay down general principles for future action both by the Member States and by the institutions of the Community. Such programmes are generally adopted by the Council and by the representatives of the governments of the Member States meeting

[42] See Case 65/77 *Razanatsimba* [1977] E.C.R. 2229 concerning the Convention of Lome; Case 91/78 *Firma Hansen* v. *Hauptzollamt Flensburg* [1979] E.C.R. 935, concerning association of overseas countries and territories and Cases 21–24/72 *International Fruit Company* v. *Produktschap voor Groenten en Fruit* [1972] E.C.R. 1219, concerning direct effect of GATT rules.

[43] See, *e.g.* Council Resolution of February 6, 1979 concerning the guidelines for Community Regional Policy (O.J. 1979, C 36/10).

In one case, the Court was asked to interpret a Council resolution in a request for preliminary ruling: Case 9/73 *Schlüter* v. *Hauptzollamt Lörrach* [1973] E.C.R. 1135 at 1162. It is remarkable that a resolution should be submitted for interpretation to the Court, since the words "acts of the institutions of the Community" must be interpreted as referring to binding acts: only those can be invoked and can be relevant in a national court case. It must be admitted however that resolutions can clarify the meaning of other related binding acts and should therefore also be susceptible for reference to the Court of Justice under EEC, Art. 177.

[44] See, *e.g.* Resolution of the Council and of the representatives of the governments of the Member States of March 21, 1972 concerning the implementation of the Resolution of March 22, 1972 concerning the establishment by stages of an economic and monetary union (J.O. 1972, C 38/3).

within the Council, either by a decision,[45] a *declaration*[46] or a resolution.[47]

Other matters are decided upon by *decisions* which are not formal binding acts[48] in the sense of EEC, Article 189, since they are not provided for under the Treaty; they are used to settle questions related to Community affairs but which do not impose rights or obligations upon the institutions of the Community neither on the natural or legal persons.[49] Once again, these "decisions" are not to be confused with the decisions taken by the governments of the Member States in pursuance of the Treaty provisions such as the appointment of the Judges and Advocates-General of the Court of Justice and the members of the Commission. These acts are binding in certain ways, are Community acts, but do not constitute acts of the institutions of the Community and do not therefore come under the jurisdiction of the Court of Justice.[50]

What characterises those resolutions, declarations and decisions, is the absence of procedural requirements and of political and judicial control. This proliferation of forms of Community measures is certainly not conducive to legal certainty; furthermore, there is the risk that matters which should be acted upon through one of the measures provided for under Article 189, with the resulting procedural requirements, will be settled in a manner

[45] See, *e.g.* Decision of the Council and of the representatives of the governments of the Member States of March 14, 1977, adopting the fourth medium-term economic policy programme (O.J. 1977, L 101/1).

[46] See, *e.g.* Declaration of the Council and of the representatives of the governments of the Member States of November 22, 1973 concerning the implementation of a European Communities programme of action on the environment (O.J. 1973, C 112/1).

[47] See, *e.g.* Resolution of the Council and of the Representatives of May 17, 1977 on the continuation and implementation of a European Community policy and action programme on the environment (O.J. 1977, C 139/1).

[48] Other languages such as Dutch and German use a word ("Besluit; Beschlus") which clearly distinguishes this act from an Art. 189 decision ("Beschikking; Entscheidung").

[49] See, *e.g.* Decision of the Representatives of the Member States of July 24, 1973, on the provisional location of the European Monetary Cooperation Fund (O.J. 1973, L 207/46). The Fund itself was established by Reg. 907/73, based on Art. 235 (O.J. 1973, L 89/2).

[50] The Court could indirectly be involved in the implementation of the corresponding treaty provisions in case the Commission for instance instituted proceedings under Art. 169.

which is not in accordance with the provisions of the Treaty. On the other hand, it must be recognised that the various forms, briefly described in this paragraph, create the necessary flexibility without which agreement among the Member States could often not have been reached.

CHAPTER 5

THE SECTORAL TREATIES: ECSC AND EURATOM

I. *The European Coal and Steel Community*

IN a White Paper presented to the United Kingdom Parliament in July 1971 it is stated that the Coal and Steel Community "is designed to ensure an orderly supply of coal and steel to the Community, whilst at the same time taking account of the needs of third countries; to promote the orderly expansion and modernisation of production; and to provide better conditions of living and employment for the workers in the industries."[1] Even allowing for the brevity of this statement, it hardly does justice to the objectives pursued by the founders of this Community; it fails completely to mention that, as provided by Article 1 of the Paris Treaty, the Coal and Steel Community is "based on a common market, common objectives and common institutions."

1. The common market

The establishment and functioning of this common market for coal and steel products[2] was of essential interest for the six countries, since it gave to their heavy industries a production and distribution basis comparable to that of the United States or the U.S.S.R.; by allowing the European enterprises to lower their production cost through economies of scale, they had a chance of becoming competitive on the world market. The powers attributed to the common institutions of the Community must be interpreted in relation to the necessities of setting up and maintaining this common market. The legal implications thereof are defined in

[1] Cmnd. 4715, 37–38.

[2] The terms coal and steel are defined in Annex 1 to the Treaty; for instance steel tubes (seamless or welded), cold rolled strips less than 500 mm. in width are not included.

Article 4; this provision specifies what existing measures in the field of trade, administration, finance or commerce are thereby abolished and prohibited within the Community.[3]

First, import and export duties or taxes having equivalent effect[4] are abolished and as a result Member States have no longer the power to impose new ones: the same applies to quantitative restrictions on the movement of coal and steel.

Secondly, all measures or practices—whether public or private—which discriminate among producers, buyers or consumers—especially with regard to prices, delivery terms and transport rates—are similarly considered to be "incompatible with the Common Market for coal and steel and are therefore abolished and prohibited." Consequently, the price-lists and conditions of sale applied by enterprises within the common market must be made public (Art. 60)[5]; the High Authority may, under certain circumstances, fix for one or more products maximum and minimum prices (Art. 61)[5a] and the High Authority is empowered to impose fines upon enterprises which violate those provisions (Art. 64).[5b] In regard to transport, the aim of the ECSC Treaty is to ensure that the transport industry will not jeopardise the fulfilment of the Treaty objectives; it therefore provides for two specific rules: the prohibition of "discriminatory prices, delivery terms and transport rates" (ECSC, Art. 4 (2)) and the obligation "to apply to the carriage of coal and steel to and from another country of the Community, the scales, rates and all other tariff rules of every kind which are applicable to the internal carriage of the same goods on the same route" (ECSC, Art. 70). The High Authority may however give a temporary or conditional agreement to the application of special domestic tariff measures in the interest of one or several enterprises. In 1958 the High Authority authorised a special tariff in favour of German undertakings situated near the demarcation line between East and West Germany because these undertakings,

[3] See EEC Treaty, Chap. 6, p. 125.

[4] In Case 24/68 *Commission* v. *Italy* the Court of Justice stated that "any pecuniary charge, however small and whatever its designation and mode of application, which is imposed unilaterally on domestic or foreign goods by reason of the fact that they cross a frontier, and which is not a customs duty in the strict sense, constitutes a charge having equivalent effect" [1969] E.C.R. at 201 (9).

[5] See Dec. 30/53 (as amended) on practices prohibited by Art. 60 (1) of the Treaty, in the common market for coal and steel.

[5a] See Dec. 962/77 (O.J. 1977, L 114/1).

[5b] See Cases 26 & 86/79.

having lost their natural markets, were in need of aid either to adapt themselves to the new situation or simply to survive. This decision was upheld by the Court of Justice. By another decision, the High Authority requested the French Government to abolish special rates in favour of undertakings located in the South of France. This decision was also upheld by the Court of Justice.[6]

Article 70 also provides that in order to ensure that comparable[7] price conditions are applied to consumers in comparable positions, the rates, prices and all other tariff rules applied to the carriage of coal and steel within each Member State and between the Member States shall be published or brought to the knowledge of the High Authority. In February 1959, the Commission issued Decision 18–59[8] concerning publication or notification of rates, prices and tariff provisions of all sorts for coal and steel road transport. This decision was annulled by the Court of Justice[9] which specified in its judgment what powers the High Authority possesses in regard to the implementation of ECSC, Article 70, since this provision is not directly applicable but requires implementation measures. The Court of Justice held that the Community does not have the power to enact binding measures with regard to transport conditions; it is up to Member States to implement them. Consequently, the High Authority sent the Member States a recommendation (which is the equivalent of an EEC Directive)[10] enjoining them to take all necessary measures to ensure that scales, rates and all other tariff rules of every kind applied to the carriage of coal and steel shall be published or brought to the knowledge of the High Authority. This recommendation concerns all means of transport; so far, it has not been implemented.

[6] Cases 27–29/58 *Hauts Fournaux de Givors et al.* v. *High Authority* [1960] E.C.R. 241.

[7] The concept of comparability was clarified in several decisions of the Court of Justice; see Cases 3/58, etc., *Barbara Erzbergbau et al.* v. *High Authority* [1960] E.C.R. 173 at 191: comparability in Art. 70 must be appreciated solely "from a point of view of transport." The Court also held that "discrimination" does not imply "direct injury" (*ibid.* at 192); in other words, if there is injury, this might be considered proof for the existence of discrimination, but the absence of injury does not mean there is no discrimination.

[8] J.O. 1959, 287.

[9] Case 20/59 *Italy* v. *High Authority* [1960] E.C.R. 325; see also Case 25/59 *Netherlands* v. *High Authority* [1960] E.C.R. 355.

[10] O.J. 1959–1962, 69; J.O. 1961, 469.

Thirdly, the common market entails the prohibition and abolition of subsidies or state assistance or special charges imposed by the State, in any form whatsoever. To ensure the implementation of this provision "any action by a Member State which is liable to have appreciable repercussions on the conditions of competition . . . shall be brought to the knowledge of the High Authority by the Government concerned" (Art. 67).[11]

Fourthly, the common market implies the maintenance and the observance of normal conditions of competition. This in practice means the absence of restrictive practices tending towards the division or improper exploitation of the market. This principle applies exclusively to enterprises and therefore all agreement among enterprises tending to distort the normal operation of competition are forbidden (Art. 65)[12]; concentrations of enterprises must be submitted to a prior authorisation of the High Authority[13] (Art. 66).[14] By the decision of March 14, 1974, the Commission authorised the acquisition by Guest Keen and Nettlefolds Ltd. of Miles Druce and Co. Ltd. Miles Druce applied to the Court of Justice for annulment of the said decision: but this application was later withdrawn.

Finally it must be mentioned that within this common market workers have access to employment in other Member States under the same conditions as nationals of those States (the limitations of ECSC, Article 69 were superseded by EEC, Article 49 and Regulation 1612/68[15]) and that the Community has at its disposal con-

[11] See Case 30/59 *Gezamenlijke Steenkolenmijnen* v. *High Authority* [1961] E.C.R. 1. Cases 27, 28, 29/58 *Hauts Fourneaux et Fonderies de Givors et al.* v. *High Authority* [1960] E.C.R. 241 and Case 59/70 *Netherlands* v. *Commission* [1971] E.C.R. 639.

[12] See Dec. 1–65 of the High Authority concerning notification of decisions on information to be obtained from or checks to be made on associations of undertakings for the purpose of the application of Art. 65 of the Treaty (J.O. 1965, 438).

[13] See Dec. 24–54 of the High Authority laying down in implementation of Art. 66 (1) of the Treaty a regulation on what constitutes control of an undertaking (J.O. 1954, 345). For Art. 66 (3) see O.J. 1978, L 300/21.

[14] Several such authorisations have been given in recent years: see for instance: Ruhrkohle A.G., decision of November 27, 1969, third General Report, 68; Cockrill-Ougree-Providence and Esperance-Longdoz, July 11, 1969, Bull. Nos. 9, 10, 1969; Salzgitter and Peine, July 5, 1970, Bull. No. 8, 1970; Pompey, October 30, 1970, Bull. No. 12, 1970; Creuzot and Loire, October 27, 1970, Bull. No. 12, 1970; Arbed and Rocchling, June 11, 1971, Bull. No. 8, 1971; *BSC*, O.J. 1979, L 245/30. See also Cases 160, 161, 170/73 R II *Miles Druce* v. *Commission* [1974] E.C.R. 281.

[15] J.O. 1968, L 257/2.

siderable funds which derive from levies on the coal and steel production of Community undertakings. As stated in the White Paper 1972, "these funds help the development of the industries, provide cheap loans for workers' houses and help finance new employment opportunities and retraining schemes for any coal and steel employees who become redundant. They also provide grants for coal and steel research."[16] The total amount made available for readaptation aid to workers in ECSC industries within the Community in the 1979 budget was just over 67 million European units of account.[17] Research aid amounted to 44 million, interest relief grants on loans for investment and conversion, 66 million and coking coal aid, 6 million.[17]

Loan funds for financing investments in the coal and steel industry taken up during 1979, totalled 957 million EUA.[18]

2. Common objectives

The main objective of the Coal and Steel Community is to "bring about conditions which will of themselves ensure the most rational distribution of production at the highest possible level of productivity" (Art. 2). In real terms this means for instance the closing down of unproductive coal mines and the concentration of production in those basins which can compete with imported coal.

Other objectives are the expansion of the economy, the development of employment (not necessarily in the coal and steel industries), the improvement of the standard of living, the retraining of workers and the restructuring of the coal and steel industry.

In order to attain those objectives, the institutions of the Community must among others

(a) ensure that the common market is regularly supplied,
(b) assure to all consumers equal access to the sources of production,
(c) seek the establishment of the lowest possible prices while at the same time permitting necessary amortisation and normal returns on investments,

[16] Cmnd. 4715, 154.

[17] For the U.K. alone this amounted to 21 million EUA for 13,000 workers. For further details see Thirteenth General Report (1969), 49 and 114.

[18] The breakdown is 615 million for industrial projects, 159 for conversion programme and 20 for low-cost housing. See Thirteenth General Report (1979), 63.

(d) maintain conditions which will encourage enterprises to expand and improve their ability to produce and
(e) promote the regular expansion and the modernisation of production (Art. 3).

Even the Court of Justice has implicitly recognised that some of those objectives are contradictory and may therefore conflict, when it stated that "it goes without saying that in practice it will be necessary to keep a balance between the various objectives of Article 3, since it is obviously impossible to implement them all together and each one of them to the full, since these objectives are general principles and that their realisation and harmonisation must be pursued as far as possible."[19]

3. Common institutions

The institutions of the Coal and Steel Community are:

- a High Authority, which was the equivalent of the EEC Commission; it was merged with the latter, together with the Euratom Commission, as of July 1, 1967, under the so-called Merger Treaty;
- a Common Assembly; this institution was replaced by the Assembly provided for in the Rome Treaties (EEC and Euratom), on January 1, 1958, in conformity with Article 2 of the Convention on to certain institutions common to the European Communities signed in Rome on March 25, 1957;
- a Special Council of Ministers; although in theory this institution existed until it was merged in 1967, it ceased for all practical purposes to function as an independent organ when the Council (of Ministers) for the Economic Community was set up on January 1, 1958;
- a Court of Justice which was replaced in 1958 by the single Court set up for the Economic Community and Euratom (Convention on to certain institutions, Arts. 3 and 4).

The institutions have been discussed in more detail in Chapter 3.

4. Recent developments

The difficulties facing the steel industry led the Commission to decide on December 20, 1976, to implement the first anti-crisis measures of the Community steel policy; they entered into force on

[19] Case 8–57 *Hauts Fourneaux et Aciéries Belges* v. *High Authority* [1958] E.C.R. L 45.

January 1, 1977. The measures, known as the "Davignon Plan," were based on voluntary undertakings by steel firms to comply with supply targets on the domestic market for certain products, *i.e.* not a limitation of production since, in theory, the supply outside the Community was not involved.

A Community steel policy was presented to the European Council in Rome on March 1977, and consequently measures were adopted to redress the market situation consisting of the introduction of guidance prices for rolled products and compulsory minimum prices for certain products.[20] Towards the end of 1977 it was found that the resulting rise in internal market prices—on which the profitability of steel firms depends—was being compromised by the pressure exerted by imports. Previously the Commission had addressed these recommendations to the Member States[21] but now an anti-dumping scheme based on the GATT rules was brought into operation on January 1, 1980.[22] In order to preserve the traditional patterns of trade, agreements were signed with the EFTA countries and a large number of other non-member countries, including certain state-trading countries.[23]

II. *The European Atomic Energy Community (Euratom)*[24]

1. Euratom's objective

The essential objective of Euratom is to create "conditions necessary for the speedy establishment and growth of nuclear industries" (Art. 1). After nearly 20 years the Community has not succeeded in achieving this aim. It might be useful briefly to explain at this point the reasons for this failure. In the first place, the expectations placed in nuclear energy in the fifties were much

[20] O.J. 1977, L 114/1 and C 174/2. See Thirteenth General Report (1979), 85.

[21] Recommendations relating to protection against imports which constitute or threaten to constitute a serious danger to production in the common market of similar or directly competitive products (O.J. 1977, L 114/4).
Recommendation on protection against dumping on the granting of bounties or subsidies by countries which are not members of the ECSC (*ibid.* at 6).
Recommendation establishing Community surveillance in respect of the importation in the Community of certain iron and steel products covered by the ECSC, originating in third countries (*ibid.* at 15).

[22] O.J. 1977, L 352/8. For further details see Eleventh General Report (1977), 85 *et seq.*

[23] See Thirteenth General Report (1979), 226.

[24] See P. Mathijsen, "Some Legal Aspects of Euratom," C.M.L. Rev. 1965–1966, 326.

too high, also the expected need for this supplementary source of energy did not materialise until 1973, partly because of the availability at reasonable prices of oil and of the seemingly unlimited discoveries of natural gas. On the other hand, the need for joint fundamental research disappeared as soon as the industrial applications appeared to promise rich commercial rewards, which seems to have been the case towards the mid-sixties. Finally, inside the Community itself the disparity between the partners was much too great to make fruitful co-operation possible: France was far ahead of the other countries at the start and (understandably) was suspicious of anything that could jeopardise its lead: it went its own way, trying to develop new techniques, whilst the others, particularly Germany, successfully adopted and adapted proven American or British technology. Consequently, France's advance rapidly disappeared creating bitterness and frustration and leaving Europe, in this field, more divided than ever. The recent oil crisis followed by enormous price increases has renewed the interest in nuclear energy; the question remains, however, whether Euratom can still play a role in this field.

2. Euratom's means

To achieve the above mentioned objective the Community

(i) develops research and disseminates the results; this research is carried out either through research contracts[25] with individuals, laboratories, universities or industries or in the Community's Joint Nuclear Research Centre which was set up under Euratom, Article 8. This research centre at present has four branch establishments in the territories of the Member States: Ispra in Italy, Petten in The Netherlands, the Central Nuclear Measurement Bureau at Geel,

[25] Thermonuclear fusion constitutes one of the main Community programmes; it includes the construction of a major experimental facility: JET (Joint European Torus) at Culham in the U.K. Part of the programme is being implemented on the basis of association contracts between the Commission and specialised bodies in the Member States. For the period 1976–80 this part of the programme provides for a Community contribution of 124 million EUA towards total expenditure of 500 million. A new programme covering 1979–83 and including participation to construction of the JET (1981–83) provides for an expenditure by the Community of 222.3 million EUA.
The JET project was established as a joint undertaking, see *infra* under (iii).
The Commission is also active in the field of nuclear fusion energy; see Thirteenth General Report (1979), 190.
Over 600 research contracts were concluded in 1978.

Belgium, and the European Transuranium Institute at Karlsruhe, Germany. The implementation of the Community's research programme has thus imposed upon the European Commission a great variety of tasks ranging all the way from planning and building reactors and laboratories of the most elaborate kind, the acquisition of great quantities of scientific instrumentation and the training of personnel in the management of large research establishments to the actual operation of reactors. All these activities are carried out directly by the European Commission, unlike agencies elsewhere, which (like the United States Atomic Energy Commission) have entrusted most of this work, by contract, to private organisations.

According to Euratom, Article 10 the Commission may "by contract, entrust the carrying out of certain parts of the Community research programme." This has been done on a very large scale.

The technical and scientific information obtained through the implementation of the Community's research programme, is disseminated on a non-discriminatory basis. Articles 12 and 13 of the Euratom Treaty provide that Member States, persons and enterprises have, under certain conditions, the right to receive all information acquired and to obtain a licence on all patents owned by the Community[26];

(ii) has established by directive basic standards for the protection of the health of workers and of the general public from the dangers arising from ionising radiation.[27] Member States have enacted the legislative or administrative provisions required to ensure compliance;

(iii) has constituted the following joint undertakings in order to encourage the construction of basic facilities required for the development of nuclear energy: Société d'Energie Nucléaire franco-belge des Ardennes (SENA), Kernkraftwerk Rheinisch-Westfälisches Elektrizitätswerk Bayernwerk G.m.b.H., Kernkraftwerk Lingen G.m.b.H., Kernkraftwerk Obrigheim G.m.b.H., and Hochtemperatur-Kernkraftwerk G.m.b.H.[28]; JET

[26] See Announcement of the Commission concerning the communication of information to persons and enterprises of the Community (J.O. 1963, 2569).

[27] O.J. 1959–1962, 7; J.O. 221/59—modifications in O.J. 1959–1962, 229; J.O. 1633/62 and O.J. 1965–1966, 265; J.O. 3693/66. See latest proposal O.J. 1979, C 140.

[28] See for SENA, J.O. 1173/61; for K.R.B., J.O. 1745/63; for Lingen, J.O. 3642/64 for Obrigheim, J.O. 2681/66 and for Hocktemperatur-Kernkraftwerk, O.J. L 165, 1974.

at Culham in the United Kingdom[29]; the Commission also expresses its views on all the investment projects in the nuclear field; all projects must therefore be communicated to the Commission (Euratom, Art. 41)[30];

(iv) has constituted a Supply Agency having a right of option on all ores, source materials and special fissile materials produced in the territories of Member States and having the exclusive right of concluding contracts relating to supply of ores, source materials and special fissile materials coming from inside or outside the Community (Euratom, Art. 52 (2) (*b*)). The applicability of these provisions was challenged by the French Government and the Commission appealed to the Court of Justice, which in its judgment in Case 7/71 *Commission* v. *France*, confirmed the applicability of chapter VI of Title II of the Euratom Treaty concerning "Supplies."[31] The statutes of the Agency were laid down by the Council[32] and various regulations have specified the conditions under which nuclear materials can be required, sold and transferred.[33]

The Community also concluded agreements with the U.S.,[34] Great Britain,[35] Canada,[35a] Brazil[35b] and Argentina[35c] to secure a regular supply of nuclear materials, especially enriched uranium;

(v) guarantees, by appropriate measures of control, that nuclear materials are not diverted for purposes other than those for which they are intended; Euratom in other words does not guarantee

[29] The Council Dec. was taken in October 1977 (Bull. 10–1977, 34); see also Council Dec. of May 30, 1978 (O.J. 1978, L 151/10 and 1979, L 213/9) relating to its construction. A JET Council, the highest authority in the joint undertaking was established and assigned the task of administering the 128 million EUA allocated to the JET project up to the end of 1980 by the Community (80 per cent.), the U.K. (10 per cent.) and other participants (10 per cent.): Thirteenth General Report (1979), 191.

communicated to the Commission, J.O. 417/58 and Regulation of the Commission, J.O. 511/58 and 571/59.

[31] [1971] E.C.R. 1003. For new developments see Thirteenth General Report (1979), 185.

[32] See J.O. 534/58.

[33] See O.J. 1959–1962, 46; J.O. 777/60 (Rules of the Agency determining the manner in which demand is to be balanced against supply); J.O. 116/62 and O.J. 1965–1966, 297; J.O. 4057/66 (regulations of the Commission concerning the implementation of the supply provisions) and J.O. 1460/60 and 240/64 (Communications of the Agency).

[34] See J.O. 312/59; 53/61; 2038/62; 2045/62 and O.J. 1974, L 139. [35] J.O. 331/59.

[35a] J.O. 1165/59. [35b] J.O. 1969, L 79/7. [35c] J.O. 2966/63.

peaceful use unless materials have been intended for such purpose by their supplier or consumer. The control system which was set up under Euratom, Articles 78, 79 provides mainly for declarations, inspections and production of operating records[36];

(vi) has created a common market for specialised materials and equipment[37] and guarantees free movement of capital for nuclear investment (Euratom, Arts. 99, 100) and freedom of employment for specialists within the Community[38];

(vii) enjoys wide powers in the field of external relations (Euratom, Arts. 101–106) to conclude agreements or contracts; Member States wishing to conclude with a third state, an international organisation or a national of a third state agreements or contracts which concern matters within the purview of the Treaty must communicate the draft to the Commission; if the latter raises objections the Court of Justice can be asked to give a ruling.[39]

This general survey of Euratom's means would not be complete without the mention of the vesting in the Community of property in all special fissionable materials (Euratom, Art. 86). This ownership is limited to materials subject to Euratom's safeguards control; this control does not, according to Euratom, Article 84 extend to "materials intended to meet defence requirements. . . ."

3. Euratom's institutions

Two of the institutions of the European Atomic Energy Community were from the beginning institutions common to the three Communities: the Assembly and the Court of Justice.

The Council, composed of ministers was, for all practical purposes, the same as the Council of the Economic Community.

The Commission ceased to exist in 1957 and was replaced, under the Merger Treaty, by the European Commission.

The four institutions have been examined in more detail in Chapter 3, *supra*.

[36] See Regs. Nos. 2, 8 and 9 (O.J. 1959–1962, 23, J.O. 298/59; O.J. 1959–1962, 27, J.O. 651/59, and O.J. 1959–1962, 43, J.O. 482/60).

[37] The Member States concluded two agreements establishing a common customs tariff for the products mentioned in lists A_1 and A_2 of Annex IV to the Euratom Treaty (J.O. 406/59 and 410/59).

[38] See Directive of the Council concerning freedom of access to qualified employment in the nuclear field (O.J. 1959–1962, 245; J.O. 1650/62).

[39] See Court of Justice, Ruling 1/78 on Draft Convention of the International Atomic Energy Agency on the Physical Protection of Nuclear Materials, Facilities and Transports [1978] E.C.R. 2151.

CHAPTER 6

THE EUROPEAN ECONOMIC COMMUNITY

THE EEC Treaty is by far the most important of the three basic European treaties. While the ECSC and Euratom Treaties provide for "sectoral integration," the EEC Treaty, touching upon most aspects of the economy, constitutes the basis for general economic integration.[1]

The importance of the EEC Treaty also derives from the fact that the full implementation of its objectives requires a common policy of the Member States or even a Community policy[2] in fields not explicitly mentioned in the Treaty itself, or for which no specific powers have been provided. This is for instance the case with regional development, industrial policy, scientific and technological research, energy, monetary policy, environment and political co-operation.[3] That all these aspects of general economic policy are closely interrelated, both with each other and with European economic integration, goes without saying; however, no specific provisions concerning them were included in the Treaty. Faced with the necessity to organise concerted action in those fields, the institutions of the Community and the Member States had to improvise procedures, and especially new forms of measures since it is not always possible to create policies by way of legislation: consensus is more important than legal obligations, and consequently the role of governments and therefore of politicians has

[1] The EEC Treaty also applies to all the subjects covered by the ECSC and Euratom Treaties in so far as specific rules are not provided by the latter, *e.g.* ECSC competition rules: these constitute *leges speciales* in regard to the EEC Treaty, see EEC, Art. 232.

[2] In the case of common policies of the Member States the responsibility and therefore powers of decisions lay with the national authorities; in the case of Community policies, jurisdiction is transferred to the Community institutions.

[3] In each one of those fields some powers have been assumed by the Community institutions; they will be examined in some detail, *infra*.

increased at the expense of that of the Community institutions. But the absence of binding rules and procedures may also endanger the exercise of the political control by the European Parliament and of the judicial control by the Court of Justice, which are essential guarantees for the safeguard of democracy within the European Communities.

I. *Objectives of the EEC*

The premable to the EEC Treaty lists very broadly formulated objectives[4]; however these cannot be considered as practical guidelines for Community action: more specific aims[5] are set out in Articles 2 and 3. Article 2 summarises in a few words not only the basic objectives but also the means by which those objectives have to be attained. The objectives are nothing particularly new since they correspond to the goals of practically any public policy in the economic field. They are: to promote throughout the Community[6]

- harmonious development of economic activities;
- continuous and balanced expansion[7];
- increase in stability[8];

[4] Those objectives include the establishment of "the foundations of an ever closer union among the peoples of Europe," the furtherance of "economic and social progress by common action in eliminating the barriers which divide Europe," improvement of "living and working conditions," concerted action to guarantee "steady expansion, balanced trade and fair competition," reduction of "the differences existing between various regions," abolition of "restrictions in international trade and development of the prosperity of associated overseas countries."

[5] EEC, Art. 2 refers to the "tasks" of the Community and Art. 3 to the "activities"; however, the Court refers to the "principles and . . . objectives set out in Articles 2 and 3 of the Treaty," Case 6/72 *Europemballage and Continental Can* v. *Commission* [1973] E.C.R. 215 at 244 (25).

[6] By using this terminology the draftsmen of the Treaty intended to indicate that all the regions of the Community should participate in the economic development and that, in case this could not be achieved by the operation of the common market and the co-ordination of national economic policies, a deliberate regional policy would be required. This was formally recognised by the Heads of State or of Government of the enlarged Community at their Paris 1972 Summit Meeting. See *infra*: Regional Policy.

[7] This refers to the necessity to avoid accentuated cyclical ups and downs.

[8] Reference here is made *inter alia* to monetary stability; this objective is at the origin of the European Monetary System; see *infra*: Economic and Monetary Policy.

– accelerated raising of the standard of living[9];
– closer relations between the Member States.[10]

To achieve these objectives, the Community institutions have been provided with two means: the establishment of the Common Market and the progressive approximation of the economic policies of the Member States. These two means are rather different in nature, but essentially complementary; they correspond to two major phases in the development of the European Community, *i.e.* the so-called "negative and the positive integration." The first corresponds to the abolition of all obstacles to free movement of goods, persons, services, capital and payments, although that phase is also characterised by the adoption of a common policy in the sphere of agriculture and of transport, the institution of a system ensuring that competition is not distorted and the establishment of special relations with the overseas countries and territories.

The rules provided in the Treaty for this first phase are of a rather legal-technical nature: they constitute a set of more or less specific provisions which apply to industrial and agriculture production and to transport. It is mainly in these areas that the Community institutions have exercised their law-making powers.

The second instrument, *i.e.* progressive "convergence" of national economic policies, corresponds to a more constructive stage, but concerns policy rather than law-making, it is therefore much less defined. If it has been designated as "positive integration," it is nevertheless dependent upon economic and political circumstances,while the development of the first stage is determined by time-limits prescribed by the Treaty itself.

The policies referred to in the EEC Treaty[11] are those relating to economic trends, balance of payments, rates of exchange and commercial policy; clearly this list is too limiting, and overall economic and monetary policies including budgetary matters, taxation, regional development and industrial policies have to be included if the co-ordination of economic policies[12] is really to take

[9] On this aim is based *inter alia* the Community's Social Policy; see *infra*.

[10] Of course, this relates not only to commercial actions, but also to political co-operation; see *supra*: Council of the European Communties.

[11] Each one of those policies is examined in some detail, *infra*.

[12] Co-ordination of economic policies is referred to in Art. 2 (as one of the instruments to achieve the general objectives of the Community), in Art. 6 (obligation

place. It is clear also that none of those policies will have a chance to succeed if tackled individually; an overall approach is needed. This was attempted in 1971 by the decision concerning the phased establishment of economic and monetary union[13]; it failed due mainly to the deterioration of the overall economic conditions aggravated by the oil crisis; it was revived recently in the form of the European Monetary System.[14]

Contrary to the first instrument, the EEC Treaty does not provide the necessary powers for the establishment of the above-mentioned policies. This probably largely explains the emergence of the European Council where the required political decisions are taken by the heads of government, leaving it to the Community institution to devise the necessary legal instruments for their implementation.[15]

After the broad formulation of the objectives of the EEC in the Preamble and in Article 2, Article 3 provides a more concrete description of the main[16] activities of the Community. To each activity correspond several provisions in Parts Two, Three and Four of the Treaty, which define in more detail their content and the procedures to be followed for enacting the required implementing legislation. The provisions of Article 3 should not be considered as a mere enumeration having no legal force on its own: the Court of Justice rejected that view because it ignores the fact

imposed upon the Member States to co-ordinate their respective economic policies to the extent necessary to attain the objectives of the Treaty) and Art. 145 (as the main task of the Council).

[13] Resolution of the Council and of the Representatives of the Governments of the Member States of March 22, 1971 (J.O. 1972, C 28); see *infra*.

[14] See *infra*: Economic and Monetary Policy.

[15] It was via that procedure that the European Monetary System, the new Community borrowing and lending instrument, the European Institute for Economic and Social Policy Research, the Community financing of structural changes and conversion, the Regional Policy, the Environment Policy, measures in the field of energy, enlargement, etc., were established. All these aspects of the Community activity are examined *infra*.

[16] The word "main" is not used here to indicate a hierarchy between the activities enumerated in Art. 3 and all the other tasks assumed by the institutions. In the first place, Art. 3 itself mentions that "the activity of the Community shall include" those which are listed in the following sub-paragraphs. It will be noticed, for instance, that relations with third countries come under the common commercial policy as a complement to the establishment of a common customs tariff.

that Article 3 considers the pursuit of the objectives it lays down as indispensable for the achievement of the Community's tasks.[17]

The activities of the Community, including those not mentioned in the Treaty, will be examined *infra* together with the corresponding Community law.

II. *Activities of the EEC*

1. **Free movement of goods**

(1) *Elimination of customs duties and quotas*

An essential element of the Common market[18] is the series of freedoms which constitute, with the common transport policy, the "foundations of the Community." Of these freedoms the most important is the free movement of goods which also, in principle, includes the agricultural products.[19] This free movement requires the prohibition, and, therefore, also the elimination between Member States of customs duties on imports and exports and of all charges having equivalent effect and of quantitative restrictions (quotas) and all measures having equivalent effect.[20]

[17] Case 6–72 *Europemballage and Continental Can* v. *Commission* [1973] E.C.R. at 244 (23, 24): the Court rejected the applicant's argument that this provision (*i.e.* EEC, Art. 3 (*f*)) merely contains a general programme devoid of legal effect.

[18] The Treaty does not provide a definition of the concept "common market." In Art. 9 it states that the Community shall be based upon a *customs union* which shall cover all trade in goods and which shall involve the prohibition of all internal customs duties and charges having an equivalent effect, and the adoption of an external common customs tariff. The latter differentiates between a customs union and a *free trade area*; having no common customs tariff, the free trade area is necessarily limited to free movement of products originating in states belonging to the trade area. On the other hand, the common market is more than a customs union, it also provides for free movement of workers, of services, of capital, of payments, freedom of establishment, free competition, a social and transport policy and, generally speaking, the prohibition of any discrimination on grounds of nationality. The common market cannot be defined, only described by its contents. Art. 8 provides that it will be established during a transitional period of 12 years. This period ended on Dec. 31, 1969 when all the rules and measures required for establishing the common market were to have been implemented.

[19] EEC, Art. 38; "the common market shall extend to agriculture and trade in agricultural products." Exceptions are to be found in Arts. 39–49; see *infra*, Agricultural Policy.

[20] EEC, Arts. 12 *et seq.* for the customs duties and Arts. 30 *et seq.* for the quotas.

The addition of the words charges or measures "having equivalent effect"[21] is essential to guarantee full freedom of movement: it includes in the prohibition all charges not formally designated as customs tariffs or quantitative restrictions, but which in fact have the same effect. This is the case, *e.g.* for any charge imposed upon an imported product and not on a similar national product, whatever the reason for this imposition; in other words it enables the prohibition to be made effective.

Free movement, and therefore the prohibition to apply customs duties, quotas or measures having equivalent effect, also applies to products coming from third states which are in free circulation in Member States.[22] Products from third countries are in free circulation if the import formalities have been complied with and any customs duties and charges which are payable have been levied in a Member State, and if they have not benefited from a total or partial repayment of such duties or charges. Since the introduction of the common customs tariff, goods entering the Community from third countries pay the same duties wherever they enter: as far as customs formalities are concerned, those goods must be able to circulate freely within the whole Community as within an internal market.[23]

[21] The Court has always given a very wide interpretation to this notion: see, *e.g.* Cases 2 and 3–62 *Commission* v. *Luxembourg and Belgium* [1962] E.C.R. 425 at 432; Case 24–68 *Commission* v. *Italy* [1969] E.C.R. 193 at 199 (3); Case 8–70 *Commission* v. *Italy* [1970] E.C.R. 961 at 965 (3); Cases 37 and 38–73 *Sociaal Fonds Diamantarbeiders* v. *Indiamex et al.* [1973] E.C.R. 1609 at 1622 (3); Case 63–74 *Cadsky* v. *Instituto Nazionale per il commercio estero* [1975] E.C.R. 281 at 291 (12) and Case 52–77 *Cayrol* v. *Rivorra* [1977] E.C.R. 2261 at 2284, where the Court states once again that the requirement of an import licence for the introduction into a Member State of goods put into free circulation in another Member State is incompatible with the provisions of the Treaty.

[22] EEC, Art. 9 (2).

[23] Such free circulation does not mean, however, that internal borders are no longer necessary: as long as internal taxes, such as VAT, have not been harmonised within the Community, the differences in tax levels make it necessary to check goods at the border to collect possible differences in taxation. Internal taxes, which are part of the national fiscal policies, and come under the Arts. 95 *et seq.* of the Treaty (see *infra*) must not be confused with levies charged at the border solely on imported products and also called sometimes "taxes" but referred to in the treaty as "charges" (see, *e.g.* Art. 13 (2)). The latter when they have an effect equivalent to that of a customs duty are prohibited by the Treaty. See, *e.g.* Court of Justice, Cases 80 and 81/77 *Commissionnaires réunis* v. *Receveur des douanes* [1978] E.C.R. 927 where the Court declared a Reg. invalid in so far as it authorised a levy

Within the original Community the duties, charges, restrictions and equivalent measures were abolished over a period of $10\frac{1}{2}$ years: January 1, 1958, to July 1, 1968, although the Treaty provided for a minimum of 12 years.[24] An analogous elimination took place for the new Member States under the Brussels Treaty of January 22, 1972, over a period extending from April 1, 1973, to July 1, 1977.[25]

It goes without saying that the prohibitions of Articles 12 and 30 do not only apply to duties and quotas existing at the time of entry into force of the said provisions, they also prevent Member States from introducing new duties or charges and from increasing existing ones.[26]

(2) *Common customs tariff and commercial policy*

As was pointed out in the preceeding section, the elimination of internal customs duties and quantitative restrictions also applies to products coming from third countries which are in free circulation in Member States. This is made possible by the adoption of a common customs tariff in the relations between the Community and third countries.[27] The community tariffs were gradually introduced over the same period as was needed to eliminate the internal tariffs between the Member States, namely $10\frac{1}{2}$ years: from January 1, 1958, to June 30, 1968. The common customs tariff was adopted, in its final form, as a Council regulation[28] and as such replaced the customs tariffs of the Benelux countries, Germany, France and

with an effect equivalent to customs duties to be charged by France on Italian wines.

[24] Twice the Member States decided to accelerate the establishment of the customs union: Dec. of May 12, 1960 (J.O. 1960, 1217) and Dec. of May 15, 1962 (J.O. 1962, 1284).

[25] Act of Accession, Art. 32.

[26] Case 26–62 *Van Gend en Loos* v. *Dutch Fiscal Administration* [1963] E.C.R. 1 at 12: the Court stated also that Art. 12 produces direct effects and creates individual rights which national courts must protect. The same applies to Art. 31, see Case 13/68 *Salgoil* v. *Italy* [1968] E.C.R. 453 at 460.

[27] The common customs tariff constitutes the criteria which distinguished a *custom union*, as in the case of the common market (EEC, Art. 9) from a *free trade area* as in the case, for instance, of the European Free Trade Association (EFTA).
Within EFTA, the elimination of customs tariffs only applies to goods "which are eligible for Area Tariff treatment" (EFTA, Art. 3); roughly speaking those are goods "produced within the Area of Association" (EFTA, Art. 4).

[28] Reg. 950/68 of June 28, 1968 (O.J. 1968, 172/1). The customs tariff of the European Communities is published by the Commission and regularly updated: see O.J. 1979, 342.

Italy. As to the level at which the tariffs were established, as a general rule it was equal to the arithmetical average of the duties applied in the four customs territories comprised on January 1, 1977 in the Community.[29]

Individual Member States no longer have jurisdiction over the customs tariffs they levy on goods entering their country: not only can they not modify them, either autonomously or pursuant to commercial agreements—the Community having exclusive powers in these fields—but, since the entry into force of the Council decision concerning the Communities' own resources, they have to allocate to the Community the revenue accruing from the common customs tariff.[30] The only activity left for the national authorities in this field is the actual collection of the duties for which they receive 10 per cent. of the revenue. Modifications or suspension of duties in the common customs tariff are introduced either autonomously by the Council[31] or as a measure of common commercial policy towards third countries.[32]

The customs union was completed on June 30, 1968 and given concrete form by two essential measures: the abolition of customs duties between Member States and full application of the common customs tariff. The fact that the Community as a whole is surrounded by a single common tariff barrier *vis-à-vis* third countries is conducive to increasing dependence of the various Member States upon each other, of specialisation and therefore of division of labour: in terms of trade, a customs union invariably results in shifts in the trade patterns, since, generally speaking, industrial goods become less expensive for Community consumers when imported from other Member States than when imported from

[29] The main exception to the rule of the arithmetical average provided in EEC, Art. 19 (1) are the products of the lists B, C, D and E, for which the Treaty provides a maximum and those of list F for which the duties are fixed therein. The lists constitute Annex I to the EEC Treaty.

[30] Dec. of April 21, 1970, on the replacement of financial contributions of Member States by the Communities' own resources (O.J. 1970, 94/12; O.J. 1970, 224). The Decision became effective on January 1, 1971. For further details see *infra* budgetary provisions. See also EEC, Art. 201 which provides for this transfer of resources to the Community.

[31] EEC, Art. 28.

[32] See EEC, Arts. 111 and 113 which provide for agreements with third countries. The commercial policy of the Community shall be examined *infra* under External Relations.

outside the Community; consequently internal Community trade tends to increase, while trade with third countries is reduced; in the relation with the latter the Community uses the customs union as an instrument to guarantee the effectiveness of its policy.[33]

It must be noted with regard to the common customs tariffs, that unification of tariff levels is only a very first step: a customs union calls for uniform interpretation, harmonisation of customs provisions and continuing administration.[34]

Similarly, with regard to measures having an equivalent effect to quantitative restrictions, all kinds of barriers are involved and the Commission has introduced new internal procedures so as to be able to act more rapidly and effectively against infringements. Removing technical barriers (referred to as "qualitative restrictions") to trade in industrial products is a continuing process carried out mainly by harmonisation directives: the management of the existing directives (about 120 in 1979), adapting them to technical progress and monitoring their application is becoming increasingly important.[35]

The consequences of the customs union for countries like the United Kingdom are not to be underestimated, although they cannot always be expressed in financial terms. Britain now forms part of a single market of up to 300 million people stretching from Scotland to Sicily and from Ireland to Berlin. Within this vast area, industrial products move freely, at least without tariff and quota restrictions.[36] The results, for the individual firm, are on the one hand, free access to the Community and associated markets, but

[33] Both for the voluntary restraint agreements concluded with textile exporting country (Eleventh General Report (1977), 88, 220) and for the policy to deal with the crisis in the steel industry, the Community used the technical machinery of the customs union to ensure or monitor implementation; see Twelfth General Report (1978), 100.

[34] See Thirteenth General Report (1979), 91. Uniform interpretation is guaranteed by the Court of Justice; see Case 158/78 *Biegi* v. *Hauptzollamt Bochum* (not yet published) and Case 160/78 *Intercontinentale Fleischhandelsgesellschaft* v. *Hauptzollamt München-West* (not yet published).

[35] For more details see the General Reports.

[36] As was pointed out there are still restrictions resulting from differences in internal tax levels. The Commission, however, considers that the main yardstick for measuring the extent to which the customs union has been achieved is the progress made in establishing real freedom of movement of goods between Member States: simplification of checks and other border formalities remains one of the Communities' fundamental objectives.

on the other, of course, stronger competition at home from other Community products; as will be seen *infra*, the Treaty provides for a system ensuring that competition in the common market is not distorted.

2. Free movement of persons

The Treaty distinguishes between workers and other nationals of the Member States. The freedom of movement of workers[37] is mainly based on the principle of non-discrimination on the ground of nationality, while the freedom of non-wage earners to move within the Community is, generally speaking, expressed by the right of establishment and the right to provide services.[38]

(1) *Free movement of workers*

Obstacles to free movement of workers[39] within the Community result, generally speaking, from discrimination based on nationality and from the incompatibility of the various social security system. The Treaty provides for remedies in both cases: a worker and his dependants must be treated in exactly the same way as the nationals in the host state[40] and all incompatibilities between national social provisions have to be removed.

In the first place, therefore, any discrimination based on nationality between workers of the Member States as regards employment, remuneration and other labour conditions must be abolished. Subject to limitations justified on the grounds of public policy,[41] public security and public health, it entails the right:

- to accept offers of employment actually made;
- to move freely within the territory of Member States for this purpose;
- to enter into and reside in a Member State for the purpose of employment in accordance with the provisions governing the

[37] EEC, Arts. 48–51, *i.e.* Title III, Chap. 1.

[38] EEC, Arts. 52–58 (Chap. 2) and 59 to 66 (Chap. 3).

[39] For a definition of "worker" see Art. 1 (*a*) of Reg. No. 1408/71 (O.J. 1971 (II), L 149, 416; J.O. 1971, L 149/2). See also Case 17/76 *Brack* v. *Insurance Officer* [1976] E.C.R. 1429 (preliminary ruling requested by the National Insurance Commissioner).

[40] See, *e.g.* Case 112/75 *Securité Sociale Nancy* v. *Hirardin* [1976] E.C.R. 533 at 560 (9); Case 13/76 *Dona* v. *Mantero* [1976] E.C.R. 1333.

[41] See Case 41/74 *van Duyn* v. *Home Office* [1974] E.C.R. 1337 at 1352, where the Court upheld the right of the Home Office to refuse leave to enter the U.K. to a

employment of nationals of that state laid down by law, regulation or administrative action[42];
- to remain in the territory of a Member State after having been employed in that state.

The principle of non-discrimination does not apply to employment in public service,[42] which means that public authorities may refuse to hire non-nationals; however, once a worker from another Member State is employed in public service, he must be treated in the same way as the nationals,[43] since the exception only concerns access to the post.

The basic Treaty provisions in respect to the principle of non-discrimination have been worked out in several regulations and directives drawn up by the Council[44] and by the Commission.[45]

Dutch national belonging to the Church of Scientology; the Court held that a Member State is entitled to refuse entry taking into account as a matter of personal conduct of the individual concerned, the fact that the individual is associated with some body or organisation the activities of which the Member State considers socially harmful, but which are not unlawful in that State, despite the fact that no restriction is placed upon nationals of the said Member State who wish to take similar employment with the same body or organisation. Case 36/75 *Rutili* v. *Minister of the Interior* [1975] E.C.R. 1219; Case 118/75 *Watson and Belmann* [1976] E.C.R. 1185.

See also the Dir. 64/221 (J.O. 1964, 850), extended by Dir. 75/35 (O.J. 1975, L 14/14). However, a conviction does not in itself constitute a ground for expulsion, Case 67/74 *Bonsignore* v. *Stadt Köln* [1975] E.C.R. 297 at 306 (5).

See, *e.g.* Case 48/75 *Royer* [1976], E.C.R. 497 at 513 (37), where the Court found *inter alia* that Dir. 68/360 entails an obligation for Member States to issue a residence permit; Case 118/75 *Watson and Belmann* [1976] E.C.R. at 1197 (14); Case 8/77 *Sagulo, Brenca and Bakhouche* [1977] E.C.R. 1495 at 1506 (5) and Case 30/77 *Regina* v. *Bouchereau* [1978] E.C.R. 1999 at 2014. [42] EEC, Art. 48 (4).

[43] Case 152/73 *Sotgiu* v. *Deutsch & Bundespost* [1974], E.C.R. 153 at 166. The Court added, however, that taking into consideration the fact that a worker has his residence in the territory of another Member State (for the grant of a separation allowance) does not constitute a discrimination if the scheme takes account of objective differences in the situation of workers according to whether their residence, at the time when they take up employment, is within the territory of the state concerned or abroad.

[44] EEC, Art. 49. See, *e.g.* Reg. 1612/68 on the free movement of worker within the Community (O.J. 1968, 475; J.O. 1968, 257/2) 68/360 (O.J. 1968–69, 485; J.O. 1968, L 257/13); for recent development see Thirteenth General Report (1979), 117. See also Case 48/71 *Royer* [1976] E.C.R. 497. See also the Resolution of the Council of February 9, 1976 on an action programme for migrant workers and members of their families (O.J. 1976, C 34/2).

[45] See, *e.g.* Reg. 1251/70 on the right of workers to remain in the territory of a Member State after having been employed in that state (O.J. 1970, 402; J.O. 1970, L 142/24).

The principle of non-discrimination cannot be limited of course to the sole worker himself, but must be extended to his dependants lest the practical implementation becomes meaningless. This non-discrimination as regards dependants must not be limited to the right to reside in another Member State together with the worker, it must encompass the whole treatment afforded to national dependants.[46]

Freedom of movement could nevertheless be illusory if by moving from one Member State to another the worker would lose the rights acquired under social security regulations; this applies particularly to the pension rights, both of the worker and the dependants. The Treaty has therefore provided in the adoption of a system ensuring that (a) all periods taken into account under the laws of the several countries where the beneficiary has worked will be added together for calculating the amount of his benefits and (b) that those benefits will be paid to the beneficiary in whichever Member State he resides.[47]

Freedom of movement for the worker, therefore, means applying the same treatment to the migrant worker and dependants as to the nationals of the Member State of residence.[48]

The Community provisions concerning social security have given rise to an abundant case-law of the Court of Justice mainly on

[46] The child of a deceased Italian worker who was employed in Germany must be able to take advantage of the education and training facilities available, on an equal footing with the nationals; Case 9/74 *Casagrande* v. *Landeshauptstadt München* [1974] E.C.R. 773 at 779 (8).

[47] EEC, Art. 51. The basic implementation provisions are to be found in Reg. 1408/71 (O.J. 1971, 416; J.O. 1971, L 149/2) which replaced earlier Reg. 3/58, 4/58 and 36/63 (J.O. 1958, 561 and 597; J.O. 1964, 50). The main provisions concern a broad definition of the concept "worker" (anyone who is ensured either compulsorily or voluntarily within the framework of a social security system of a Member State organised for the benefit of salaried employees), payments under health insurance to workers and pensioners, calculation of pensions, unemployment indemnities and the creation of a Consultative Committee composed of representatives of the workers, the employers and the governments.

[48] See, *e.g.* Case 15/69 *Südmilch* v. *Ugliola* [1969] E.C.R. 363 at 369 (3).

the basis of requests for preliminary rulings from national courts and tribunals.[49]

(2) *Freedom of movement of non-wage earners*[50]

The Treaty provides for the abolition of restrictions both on the right of establishment[51] and on the right to provide services.[52] The right of establishment, in so far as it concerns individuals, includes the right to take up and pursue activities as a self-employed person in another country; it implies that this person moves to another Member State. The right to provide services, on the other hand, concerns nationals of Member States who are established in a State other than that of the person for whom the services are intended. There is a great similarity between the two cases and the Treaty in fact does only provide—as in the case of the workers—that persons from Member States establishing themselves in another Member State or providing services therein are to be treated like the nationals of that other member State,[53] *i.e.* application of the principle of non-discrimination. Both rights also apply to undertakings, companies or firms although special rules are provided in the field of services to transport, banking and insurance.[54]

For both rights the Treaty makes provision for the Council, acting on a proposal of the Commission and after consulting the Economic and Social Committee and the Assembly, to draw up a general programme for the abolition of existing restrictions.[55]

Liberal professions present a particular problem because in most cases diplomas are required. Consequently, when the mere

[49] See, *e.g.* Case 1/78 *Kenny* v. *Insurance Officer*, [1978] E.C.R. 1489 and Case 10/78 *Belbouab* v. *Bundesknappschaft* [1978] E.C.R. 1915.

[50] The provisions concerning freedom of movement of non-wage earners are to be found in the Treaty under the headings "Right of establishment" (Chap. 2, Arts. 52–58) and "Services" (Chap. 3, Arts. 59–66).

[51] EEC, Art. 52.

[52] EEC, Art. 59.

[53] EEC, Art. 52, para. 2 and 60. Case 115/78 *Knoors* v. *Secretary of State for Economic Affairs* [1979] E.C.R. 399 at 410 (24) where the Court held that the beneficiaries of Community meaning in respect of activities of self-employed persons also include persons who possess the nationality of the host Member State.

[54] EEC, Art. 61. See *infra*: freedom of establishment and freedom to supply services.

[55] EEC, Arts. 54 (1) and 63 (1); the two programmes were indeed established. See General Programme for the abolition of restrictions on freedom to supply services (J.O. 32/62) and General Programme for the abolition of restrictions on freedom of establishment (J.O. 36/62).

removal of restrictions based on nationality does not insure effective freedom of establishment and supply of services, because of national regulations governing access to certain activities and their exercise, the Council must issue directives for the "mutual recognition of diplomas, certificates and other evidence of formal qualifications" and also for the "co-ordination of the provisions laid down by law, regulation or administrative action in Member States concerning the taking up and pursuit of activities as self-employed persons."[56]

The first decisions in the field of liberal professions were not taken until 1975; they concerned the free movement of doctors.[57] In 1977, the Council adopted Directive 77/249 concerning lawyers,[58] limited however to freedom to provide services; several others have been issued since.[59]

In 1979, the Commission reported that for all the professions, with the exception of lawyers, the diplomas which admit holders to the profession are or will be recognised in all Member States. Recognition of qualifications becomes an individual right of the nationals of Member States allowing genuine mobility of the members of the professions throughout the Community.[60]

Mention should be made here of the extremely important role

[56] EEC, Art. 57. See Case 136/78 *Ministère Public* v. *Auer* [1979] E.C.R. 437 at 451 (36), where the Court held that during the period prior to the implementation of the directives for the mutual recognition of diplomas and the co-ordination of national provisions the nationals of a Member State cannot rely on the provisions of a directive with a view to practice a profession on any condition other than those laid down by national legislation.

See also Case 11/77 *Patrick* v. *Ministère des Affaires Culturelles* [1977], E.C.R. 1199.

[57] Dir. 75/362 concerning the mutual recognition of diplomas, certificates and other evidence of formal qualifications in medicine (O.J. 1975, L 167/1). Another directive 75/363 concerns the co-ordination of provisions laid down by law, regulation or administrative action in respect of activities of doctors (*ibid.*, p. 17). At the same time, the Council decided to set up an Advisory Committee on Medical training and a Committee of Senior Officials on Public Health (*ibid.*, p. 19). See Twelfth General Report (1978), 90, where the Commission reports on the consequence of this liberalisation.

[58] O.J. 1977, L 78/17; this directive entered into force on March 24, 1979.

[59] Dir. 73/48 on the abolition of restrictions on movement and residence within the Community for nationals of Member States with regard to establishment and the provision of services (O.J. 1977, L 26/14), nurses responsible for general care (O.J. 1977, L 176/1), dentists (O.J. 1978, L 233/1), veterinary surgeons (O.J. 1978, L 362/1) and midwives (O.J. 1980, L 33/1 and 8).

[60] Twelfth General Report (1978), 89.

played in this field by the Court of Justice which held that the provisions concerning freedom of establishment have direct effect as from January 1, 1970 at the latest, despite the absence, in particular spheres, of the prescribed directives.[61]

Other activities present similar problems to those encountered by the liberal professions. The general programmes[62] provided for the liberalisation of 123 groups of activities, mostly situated in the industrial or craft activities; most groups have now been the object of some kind of Community measure.[63] The right for nationals of Member States to set up undertakings, agencies, branches or subsidiaries and manage them in other Member States, under the same conditions laid down for the nationals, is explicitly recognised by the Treaty.[64]

3. Freedom of establishment and freedom to supply services[65]

The freedom of establishment and the freedom to supply services were examined in the previous section insofar as they were relevant to guarantee effective application of the freedom of movement of persons. As was pointed out, both freedoms also apply to companies and firms formed in accordance with the law of a Member State and having their registered office, central administration or principal place of business within the Community.[66]

The provisions concerning freedom to offer services do not refer explicitly to undertakings, except that, services having been

[61] Case 2–74 *Reyners* v. *Belgium* [1974] E.C.R. 631 at 656: invoking the exception provided under Art. 55, Belgium refused a Dutch resident in Belgium, with a Belgian law degree, admission to the bar; this was not accepted by the Court; Case 33–74 *van Binsbergen* v. *Bedrijfsvereniging Metaalnijverheid* [1974] E.C.R. 1299, concerning a requirement of residence in order to supply services; Case 48–75, *Royer* [1976] E.C.R. 497, *inter alia* obligation to issue a residence permit; Case 118–75 *Watson and Belmann*: [1976] E.C.R. 1885, concerning the requirement to report to national authorities the presence of an alien; Case 13–76 *Dona* v. *Mantero* [1976] E.C.R., 1333, concerning the right of non-nationals to take part in football matches as professional or semi-professional players; Case 71–76 *Thieffry* v. *Conseil de l'Ordre des Avocats de Paris* [1977] E.C.R. 765, concerning the refusal to admit a Belgian lawyer with a French qualifying certificate to the profession of Advocate to the Paris Bar.

[62] J.O. 1962, 32 and 36.

[63] See Dir. 75/368, on measures to facilitate the effective exercise of freedom of establishment and freedom to provide services in respect to various activities (O.J. 1975, L 167/22).

[64] EEC, Art. 52.

[65] EEC, Arts. 52–66.

[66] EEC, Art. 58.

defined as those which are "normally provided for remuneration,"[67] the Treaty provides that they shall include: activities of an industrial character and a commercial character besides activities of craftsmen and the professions. Services in the field of transport are governed by the provisions relating to transport, and the liberalisation of banking and insurance services connected to movements of capital, shall be effected in parallel with the liberalisation of movement of capital.

The treaty provisions concerning the right of establishment entrust the Community institutions with the task, *inter alia*, of co-ordinating the safeguards which, for the protection of the interest of shareholders or others, are required by Member States of companies and firms.[68] Consequently, the Commission made proposals for various directives, several of which were adopted by the Council.[69]

The purpose of the measures is to facilitate company activities throughout the Community; the same result could also be achieved by the establishment of a uniform European company law, making it possible to set up a "European Company."[70] The proposal based on Article 235 did not meet with the approval of the Council and it is doubtful whether such legislation will ever be adopted. In this connection mention should be made of the Convention on the mutual recognition of companies and bodies

[67] EEC, Art. 60.

[68] EEC, Art. 54 (3) (*g*).

[69] A first Dir. 68/151, was adopted by the Council on March 9, 1968 (O.J. 1968 (I) 41; J.O. 1968, L 65/8); "with a view to make such safeguards equivalent throughout the Community"; they concern disclosure of particulars, validity of obligations entered into on behalf of the company and the nullity of companies with limited liability.

The second Dir. deals with the formation of public limited liability companies and the maintenance and alteration of their capital (O.J. 1977, L 26/1). The third Dir. concerns mergers (O.J. 1978, L 295/36); the fourth concerns annual accounts (O.J. 1978, L 222/11) and the proposed fifth concerns the structure of such companies; it is proposed that in companies employing more than 500 workers, the latter will have a say in the appointment of the supervisory board (J.O. 1972, C 131/49); a sixth Dir. on the prospectus to be published (J.O. 1972, C 131/61), a seventh on group accounts (O.J. 1976, C 121) and an eighth on approval of persons who carry out legal audits of company accounts (O.J. 1978, C 112/6).

[70] See J.O. 1970, C 124. The proposed Regulation provides that an European company may be formed only by way of merger or setting-up of joint holding companies or subsidiaries or by more enterprises already existing under the national law of two or more Member States. Bull. Suppl. 4/75.

corporate whose object is to enable legal persons to avail themselves fully of the Community freedoms.[71]

4. Free movement of capital

This fourth freedom, which is complementary to the freedom of movement of goods, of persons and of services, is the most difficult to specify owing to the rather general terms of the Treaty.[72] The close connexion existing between the other three freedoms and the free movement of capital is underlined by the Treaty, since restrictions on the movement of capital must be abolished by the Member States only in as far as it is "necessary to ensure the proper functioning of the common market." Since the latter is characterised by the basic freedoms, it is the movement of goods, persons and services and the right of establishment which determine the degree of freedom of movement of capital. Financial transactions across the borders of the Member States which result from movement of goods, services, etc., or which are necessary to make such movement possible are to be liberalised. The Treaty does not provide a definition of capital but since it is to be distinguished from the liberalisation of payments,[73] capital seems to refer to rather large transfers of funds for investments.

If the Treaty provisions concerning the other basic freedoms have reached a fair degree of implementation, the same cannot be said of the articles concerning capital: only two directives have been issued by the Council.[74] These directives are based on a

[71] The Convention was signed on February 29, 1968. For further details see Bull. Suppl. 2/1969.

[72] EEC, Arts. 67–73.

[73] EEC, Art. 106.

[74] Dir. implementing Art. 67 of the Treaty (O.J. 1958–1962, 49; J.O. 1960, 921). This dir. requires the Member States to grant in respect of three categories of capital movement, foreigh exchange authorisations or general permissions. The first category includes direct investments in real estate, personal capital movements and the granting and repayment of short-term and medium-term credits in respect of commercial transactions. Such transfers are essential to ensure respectively freedom of establishment, free movement of workers and free movement of goods and services.
The second category concerns operations in securities dealt with on a stock exchange, while the third category refers to operations in securities not dealt with on a stock exchange.
Dir. 72/156 on regulating international capital flows and neutralising their undesirable effects on domestic liquidity (O.J. 1972 (I) 296; J.O. 1972 L 91/13).

proposal from the Commission who, for that purpose, consulted the Monetary Committee.[75] This lack of implementation can be explained by the absence of precise treaty obligations, by the difficulties experienced by some or other Member State since the establishment of the Community and by the multiple escape clauses.[76] To date the Court has only once had occasion to rule on Articles 67 to 73.[77]

5. Approximation of laws

The proper functioning of the common market requires approximation (or harmonisation) of the laws of the Member States[78]; consequently the Treaty provides that the Council shall issue directives for the approximation of such provisions laid down by law regulation or administrative action in Member States as directly affect the establishment and functioning of the common market.[79]

It follows that the term "laws" in the title of Chapter 3 must be broadly interpreted: it covers laws, regulations and administrative action of all public authorities within the Member States. Approximation of laws must be seen as a necessary complement to the basic freedoms and, in certain cases, as a necessary condition for the effectiveness of those freedoms. As was pointed out, the freedoms are based on the principle of non-discrimination within the Member States: individuals, goods and services must be treated in a given Member State in exactly the same way as the national individuals, goods and services.

The elimination of discriminations does not, however, suffice to make free movement effective, neither does it ensure uniform national treatment throughout the whole Community of all those who operate in the common market.

Free movement of persons, goods and services can be hampered by lack of harmonised rules, and the provisions concerning the basic freedoms consequently provide for some approximation of

[75] The Monetary Committee was set up in order to promote co-ordination of policies of the Member States in the monetary field, EEC, Art. 105 (2).

[76] See EEC, Arts. 73, 108 and 109.

[77] Case 7/78 *Regina* v. *Thompson* [1978] E.C.R. 2247.

[78] EEC, Art. 3 (*h*).

[79] EEC, Art. 100.

national rules.[80] Over the years the Council has issued several directives.[81] These directives require unanimity in the Council and consultation of the European Parliament and the Economic Social Committee, when the implementation of the decision involves amendment of national legislation.

Besides impeding the proper functioning of the common market, differences between the provisions laid down by law, regulation or administrative action in Member States can distort the conditions of competition between persons and undertakings situated in one state as compared to similar legal or natural person in another.[82] If the Commission is of the opinion that such a distortion must be eliminated, it must consult the Member State concerned; if such consultation does not result in the elimination of that distortion, the Council, acting by a qualified majority, must issue the necessary directives.[83]

The Treaty thus makes a distinction between approximation of national rules which affect the common market and approximation required to eliminate distortions of competition; it is not always easy, however, to distinguish between the two cases.

By creating identical conditions under which persons and companies can operate throughout the Community, the approximation of laws constitutes an essential element of economic and social integration, in the same way as the basic freedoms do.

6. Agriculture

The common market which is characterised by a customs union, the basic freedoms and rules concerning transport, competition and social policy, extends to agriculture and trade in agricultural products[84]; consequently, the rules laid down for the establishment, operation and development of the common market apply to agricultural products. This is the principle. It seems important to

[80] See, *e.g.*: customs matters (Art. 27), mutual recognition of diplomas (Art. 57 (1)), taxation (Art. 99), export aids (Art. 112).

[81] EEC, Art. 100. Many directives were issued by the Council in pursuance of Art. 100. See, *e.g.* Dir. 77/62 co-ordinating procedures for the award of public supply contracts (O.J. 1977, L 13/1); the Council Dir. concern mainly the following fields: agriculture, customs, taxation, food commodities, pharmaceutical products and motor vehicles.

[82] EEC, Art. 101.

[83] Very few directives were issued in pursuance of these provisions.

[84] Agricultural products are those which are listed in Annex II to the Treaty.

state this from the outset since one could have imagined a common market without agriculture: some Member States produce more than they consume, others depend heavily on imports. The latter might prefer to import from third countries where food products are much cheaper; there lies a fundamental conflict of interests. Furthermore, agriculture has always been a problem which each country has attempted to solve over the years by elaborate measures. Thirdly, agriculture presents some very particular problems which clearly differentiates it from industrial production.[85] However, in the Member States, agriculture constitutes a sector closely linked with the economy as a whole[86] and the above-mentioned principle of inclusion in the common market was therefore agreed upon. But in order to take "into account the particular nature of agriculture,"[87] the inclusion took place under special terms: the operation and development of the common market for agricultural products must be accompanied by the establishment of a common agricultural policy among the Member States[88] and the necessary adjustment must be effected by degree.[89] Concretely speaking, this means that the rules laid down for the establishment of the common market apply "save as otherwise provided" in the Treaty and that the existing national organisations have to be replaced by a form of common organisation.[90]

A typical example of common market rules which are declared non-applicable to agriculture are the rules on competition: they apply to production of and trade in agricultural products "only to the extent determined by the Council."[91] In 1962, together with the

[85] Agriculture (1) is very much dependent upon climatological conditions and production therefore is somewhat problematical, (2) production cannot be reduced or increased at will to correspond to a change in demand, (3) the main factor of agricultural production, land, can only be increased at very great costs, (4) demand for agricultural products is practically inelastic.

[86] EEC, Art. 39 (2) (*c*).

[87] EEC, Art. 39 (2) (*a*) which adds that this particular nature "results from the social structure of agriculture and from structural and natural disparities between the various agricultural regions."

[88] EEC, Art. 38 (4).

[89] EEC, Art. 39 (2) (*b*).

[90] EEC, Art. 40 (2): the organisation can take one of the following forms: (a) common rules on competition, (b) compulsory co-ordination of the various national market organisations, or (*c*) a European market organisation.

[91] EEC, Art. 42.

first regulation concerning the financing of the common agricultural policy,[92] the Council issued Regulation 26 concerning the application of the rules of competition in agriculture: the application was extremely limited.[93] However, with regard to the rules concerning state aids, all the market organisation for agricultural products provide for their full implementation.

(1) *The Common Agricultural Policy (CAP)*

Proposals for a Community policy in the field of agriculture were submitted by the Commission in 1960, and based upon the work of a conference convened in pursuance of the Treaty, immediately after it entered into force.[94] The Council then adopted a certain number of basic principles which were to determine the future orientation of the common agricultural policy: free movement of agricultural products within the common market, establishment of a commercial policy jointly with the agricultural policy and a common price level for all agricultural products in the whole Community. The result should be an economic balance between supply and demand and fair earnings for those employed in agriculture. With regard to third countries, a uniform system of levies was to be established. Finally the national measures for structural reforms would be co-ordinated.

It is quite obvious that some of these objectives are contradictory, especially the balance between supply and demand on the one hand, and a fair income for farmers on the other, owing to the lack of efficiency in many sectors; after nearly 20 years of CAP, it is obvious that the Member States and the institutions have not been

[92] Reg. 25, (O.J. 1959–1962, 126; J.O. 1962, 991).

[93] Reg. 26 provides that EEC, Art. 85 (prohibition of agreements which affect trade between Member States and distort competition) and Art. 86 (abuse of dominant position which affects trade) are not applicable to agreements which form an essential part of a market-organisation or concern the production and sale of agricultural products. More important is the non-applicability of Art. 92 (incompatibility of state aids with the common market) and Art. 93 (2) (procedure against a Member State, when the Commission finds that an aid is not compatible with the common market); the only obligation left is for the Member States to help the Commission in its constant review of all existing aids (Art. 93 (1)) and to inform the Commission of any plans to grant or modify grants of aid (Art. 93 (3), first sentence). See O.J. 1959–1962, 129; J.O. 1962, 993.

[94] EEC, Art. 43 (1); the conference was held in Stresa, Italy, in July 1958; see First General Report (1958), pt. 97–101, including text of resolution of the conference.

able to solve this problem. These principles required Community action in two domains: market and price policy through the establishment of common organisations for agricultural products and structural policy.

(a) COMMON ORGANISATIONS OF AGRICULTURAL MARKETS

The common organisation of agricultural markets is based on the following principles:

(a) unity of the market: free movement of agricultural products throughout the Community;
(b) Community preference: protection of the common market against low priced imports from third countries, thereby encouraging consumers to prefer community products;
(c) financial solidarity: the common agricultural policy must be totally financed out of community funds[95]; for this purpose the European Agricultural Guidance and Guarantee Fund was set up.

If a single market for agricultural products was operative at the end of the sixties, the beginning of the present decade was marked by several monetary crises which have effectively resulted in the establishment within the EEC of five separate markets interlinked by a system of compensatory amounts[96] applied to imports and exports within the Community. In 1973, the Commission undertook steps for a gradual phasing out of these compensatory amounts; its endeavours did not meet with success until the establishment of the European Monetary System. This effectively entered into force on March 13, 1979 after agreement had been reached on a package of agri-monetary matters including the

[95] See Reg. 729/70 on the financing of the common agricultural policy (J.O. 1970, L 94/13) as amended by Reg. 1566/72 (J.O. 1972, L 167/5).

[96] Compensatory amounts are levies (or refunds) applied by Member States on agricultural products imported (exported) from (to) other Member States to offset the reduction (increase) in the price of those products due to changes in the exchange rates; *e.g.* the re-evaluation of the DM makes German agricultural products non competitive on the French market, hence refunds or export subsidies; the French products, on the other hand, become much cheaper, hence levies to protect the national production and income of German farmers. That this system is incompatible with the common market goes without saying.

See Reg. 974/71 (amended several times) on certain measures of conjunctural policy to be taken in agriculture following the temporary widening of the margins of fluctuation for the currencies of certain Member States (J.O. 1971, L 106/1).

policy to be followed with regard to the dismantling of existing monetary compensatory amounts and the creation of new ones following changes in the central rates.

The common organisations provided for in the Treaty may include all measures required to attain the objectives of the agricultural policy[97] in particular regulation of prices, aids for the production and marketing of the various products, storage and carry-over arrangements and common machinery for stabilising imports and exports.[98] The form chosen by the Council for these common organisations was the European market organisation. Such organisations have been established for practically all the agricultural products.[99]

The first proposals for what the Treaty calls European market organisations were submitted to the Council in 1961 and the first market organisation, that for cereals, was established on January 14, 1962. This first regulation[1] pertained to a transitional period—during which the existing national market organisations remained in force and were progressively replaced by the European organisation—and was replaced by a definitive one in 1967; at that time the final form of market organisation was established for most products.

Not all market organisations are identical and they can be classified into three groups according namely to the guarantee they offer the producers:

(a) for wheat, coarse grains, sugar and dairy products: a system of target and intervention prices, intervention purchases to

[97] These objectives are set out in Art. 39: (a) to increase agricultural productivity, (b) to ensure a fair standard of living for the agricultural community, (c) to stabilise markets, (d) to assure the availability of supply and (e) to ensure reasonable consumer prices.

[98] EEC, Art. 40 (3).

[99] There are to date 20 market organisations for the following products: fats (Reg. 136/66), cereals (Reg. 2727/75), pigmeat (Reg. 2759/75), eggs (Reg. 2771/75) poultry (Reg. 2777/75), rice (Reg. 1418/76), sugar (Reg. 3330/74), plants and flowers (Reg. 234/68), milk (Reg. 804/68), beef (Reg. 805/68), cider, cocoa, etc. (Reg. 827/68), processed food from vegetables (Reg. 516/77), tobacco (Reg. 727/78), wine (Reg. 317/79), flax and hemp (Reg. 1308/70), fish (Reg. 100/76), hops (Reg. 1696/71), seeds (Reg. 2358/71), fruit and vegetables (Reg. 1035/72), and dehydrated fodder (Reg. 1117/78). There is no organisation for sheepmeat, potatoes, honey and alcohol.

[1] Reg. 19, J.O. 1962, 933.

be made under certain conditions, within the Community, and external protection in the form of variable levies;

(b) for beef and veal, pigmeat, poultry and eggs: support is afforded mainly through external protection;

(c) for fruit, vegetables and wine where the determinant factor is quality control: only the standardised or graded products will be allowed on the market; in addition, measures to reduce production and a custom duty are applicable.

For a proper understanding of the functioning of those market organisations, the one applying to cereals will be examined here in some detail.

The common organisation of the market in cereals.[2] The common organisation of the market in cereals comprises a price and a trading system. The price system consists of a target price and a basic intervention price,[3] while the trading system is based on import and export licences, or threshold price and an export refund; in other words guaranteed prices within the Community and protection against third countries.

The *target price* is the price at which, it is expected, the product can be sold on the Community market during the next marketing period beginning during the following calender year; it is definitely not a fixed price: it is intended to help farmers plan their production by allowing them to calculate their minimum income. It is established once a year, before August 1, by the Council acting by a qualified majority on a proposal from the Commission and after consulting the Assembly.[4] For the 1979/1980 period the target price for, *e.g.* common wheat was fixed at 166.61 units of account per tonne.[5]

[2] This market organisation was established in its definitive form by Reg. 120/67 (O.J. 1967, 33; J.O. 1967, 2269); that reg. was superseded by Reg. 2727/75 (O.J. 1975, L 281/1)

[3] The price system in this particular market organisation also includes a guaranteed minimum price for durum wheat. This measure can be explained by the necessity to increase the production of that particular category of wheat which is in short supply within the Community. For 1979/1980 the target price was 229.43 u.a. per tonne and the single intervention price 206.06. Producers of durum wheat also receive aid of 63.95 u.a. per hectare.

[4] This is the procedure provided in Art. 43 (2); the threshold price is established without consultation of Parliament.

[5] For the 1979/1980 prices for all products, see Bull. 6–1979, 56. The target price applies for a standard quality determined by the Council for each cereal; it is fixed

The *intervention price* is the price at which the designated national authorities must buy the cereals offered to them[6]; it constitutes for the farmers the guarantee that their products, in case they cannot sell them on the market at a higher price, will at least be bought at the intervention price. For 1979/1980 the common single intervention price for common wheat was fixed at 123.39 units of account per tonne as against a target price of 166.61. In order to guarantee to producers that the market price does not fall below a minimum level, derived intervention prices for common wheat are fixed for all marketing centres except Duisburg.[7] The intervention price is fixed annually before August 1, simultaneously with the target price, by the Council on a proposal from the Commission and after consultation of Parliament. They are also fixed for a standard quality at the wholesale stage.

The *threshold price* is the price fixed for certain cereal products imported from third countries; it is fixed in such a way that, for the product imported through Rotterdam, the selling price on the Duisburg market shall be the same as the target price. Since the products have to be transported from Rotterdam to Duisburg the threshold price is equivalent to the Duisburg target price minus the transport costs from Rotterdam to Duisburg. The threshold price is fixed, for the same standard quality as the target price, by the Council acting by a qualified majority on a proposal from the Commission,[8] before March 15 for the following marketing year.[9] The threshold price of imported products is arrived at by imposing on those products a *levy* which corresponds to the difference between the threshold price and the c.i.f. price calculated for

for Duisburg (Germany) at the wholesale stage, goods delivered to warehouse, not unloaded. Duisburg was chosen since it is the area with the lowest production.

[6] Reg. 2727/75, Art. 5 (5).

[7] Reg. 2727/75, Art. 4 (1). The level of the derived intervention prices is fixed in such a way that the differences between them correspond to the disparities in prices to be expected in a normal harvest, under natural conditions of price formation on the market and allow the free movement of cereals, within the Community (*ibid.*). Since Duisburg is the area with the lowest production, prices there will be higher than in areas of high production: all the other market centres therefore have a lower intervention price (see *ibid.* para. 4). There are about 40 main market centres.

[8] Reg. 2727/75, Art. 5 (5).

[9] The marketing year for all cereals runs from August 1 to July 31 of the following year (Reg. 2727/75, Art. 3).

Rotterdam on the basis of the most favourable purchasing opportunities on the world market. The levies are fixed daily by the Commission in the form of regulations.

It should be quite clear that this system of levies on imports of agricultural products from third countries was set up to protect Community agricultural products and thereby their producers against possible unfair competition from those countries. It constitutes a practical expression of a fundamental principle underlying the European Community: Community preference.

The target prices, intervention prices and threshold prices are subject to monthly increases, phased out over all or part of the marketing year to take into account the normal increases in market prices due to additional storage and other financial costs accruing after the harvest.[10]

The export *refunds*[11] are provided to enable Community cereals to be exported on the world markets where agricultural prices are, generally speaking, lower than Community prices. Refunds are the same for the whole Community and may vary according to use or destination; they are equal to the differences between quotations or prices on the world market and Community prices; they are fixed at regular intervals by the Commission after reference to a Management Committee.

Finally, *import and export licences* are required for all imports into or exports from the Community; they are issued by the Member States to any applicant irrespective of his establishment in the Community.

It is worth noting the role of the Management Committee which was set up within each one of the market organisations to allow the Member States to follow the implementation of various rules without imposing the heavy procedure of Council decisions, but providing the possibility of bringing a matter before the Council.[12]

The implementation of the common market organisations requires an administrative machinery which the Community does not possess: it is therefore the task of the existing bodies of the Member States; as was mentioned, the import and export licences are delivered by the national authorities who also collect the levies

[10] Ref. 2727/75, Art. 6.
[11] Reg. 2727/75, Art. 16.
[12] For the Management Committee see *supra*, Chapter 3, p. 61.

and pay the refunds. Similarly, the purchases of agricultural products at the intervention prices set by the Council is the responsibility of the national intervention offices. In case of conflict concerning the application of the Community measures, responsibility lies with the Member States, not with the Community institutions,[13] even now that the agricultural levies have been attributed to the Community as own resources.[14]

(b) SOCIAL-STRUCTURAL POLICY IN AGRICULTURE

The common organisation of agricultural markets aims at a market equilibrium through prices and trade systems; at the most they are a palliative but do not contribute towards the solution of the fundamental problems of agriculture within the Community; they should be viewed as relief measures providing a temporary breathing space needed to carry out the required structural reforms. As the Commission pointed out: the question of agricultural incomes cannot be dealt with exclusively by a price policy.[15] Seeking a more durable solution, the Commission submitted to the Council in 1968 a "Memorandum of the Reform of Agriculture in the European Economic Community" (Agriculture 1980).[16] Two

[13] In several cases, the Court has, in preliminary rulings, interpreted provisions of the agricultural regulations, *e.g.* Cases 124/76 and 20/77 *Moulins-Pont-à-Mousson* v. *Office Interprofessionnel des Céréales* [1977], E.C.R. 1795 at 1811. With regard to the implementation of the agricultural measures farmers and importers/exporters of agricultural products must address themselves to the national courts and tribunals and seek redress against the national authorities: *e.g.* Case 46/75 *IBC* v. *Commission* [1976] E.C.R. 65. Similarly it is the responsibility of the national authorities to ensure collection of the levies: *e.g.* Cases 178, 179 and 180/73 *Belgium and Luxembourg* v. *Mertens* [1974] E.C.R. 383.
Many Court cases deal with the interpretation and implementation of the system of compensatory amounts in agriculture, see. *e.g.* Case 97/76 *Merkur* v. *Commission* [1977] E.C.R. 1063 concerning the accession compensatory amounts, Case 118/76 *Balkan-Import-Export* v. *Hauptzollamt Berlin-Packhof* [1977] E.C.R. 1177.

[14] See *infra*: Financing the CAP.

[15] Seventh General Report (1973), 247.

[16] An analysis of this document, also referred to as the Mansholt Plan, is given in the Second General Report (1968), 135. It can be summarised as follows: starting from (1) the social-economic situation in the Community's agriculture, the Memorandum sets out (2) the aims of an agricultural policy, (3) the concrete measures to be taken and (4) an estimate of the costs.

1. *The socio-economic situation in agriculture*: has three characteristics:
   (a) agricultural population, which dropped from 20 million in 1950 to 10 million in 1970; labour productivity rose by 7 per cent. (more rapidly than

and a half years later the Council adopted, on the basis of the proposals contained in the Memorandum, a resolution on the new guidelines for the common agricultural policy[17] closely following the measures proposed in the Memorandum. In the same resolution the Council stated that state aids in conflict with the common measures should be eliminated and considered that success in the agricultural field depended on progress made in other domains, such as economic and monetary union, regional policy and social policy. The resolution was implemented by several directives establishing the basic principles for joint action by the Community and the interested Member States in the socio-structural field.

in industry) but the annual growth rate of expenditure on foodstuffs has slackened finally, the age pyramid is quite disturbing: 50 per cent. of all farmers are over 57 years of age.

(b) the farm: the average farm within the Community is far too small only 3 per cent. of all farms have an area of 125 acres or more. The national efforts in this field have had little or no effect. This is a crucial problem because of rapid advances in mechanisation.

(c) the *marketing* problem: with outdated production structures, farmers are forced into highly intensive production methods to ensure a minimum of income: unable to adapt to the market, they go on producing to maintain that minimum. The consequence is that the price and market machinery cannot function properly and farmers' incomes are, generally speaking, lower than those of wage-earners in the Community.

2. *The aims of agricultural policy* are to modernise the structures, make more jobs available in the various regions, promote the establishment of a profit-table type farm to ensure that output is guided by demand, prevent a price policy causing the market distortion and reduce expenditure of the Guarantee Section of the Fund.
3. *Concrete measures to be taken*
   (a) For the population three types of assistance are proposed: measures for those who leave the land, measures for farmers of over 55 who are willing to give up farming and measures for those farmers who want to take up another occupation.
   (b) the size of farms should be drastically increased; modern agricultural enterprises should be set up with grants and credits. As many people will give up farming, land should become available for increasing the size of farms and land will be withdrawn from agriculture.
   (c) with regard to *marketing* it is proposed to establish European product councils to perform market intelligence, information on sales prospects, etc.
4. The *estimated costs* for a 10 year period would be 2.500 million u.a. a year to be shared by the Community and the Member States.

[17] J.O. 1971, C 52.

The *first directive*[18] on the modernisation of farms, provides for the introduction by Member States of a system of selective incentives to farms where the farmer practises farming as his main occupation. To qualify for the incentives, the farmer must draw up a plan for the development of the farm business which shows that upon implementation of the plan, the modernised farm will be capable of providing for one or two persons, an income at least comparable to that earned by persons employed in non-agricultural work in the same region. The directive also provides for special aids in certain regions where the maintenance of a minimum level of population is not assured and where a minimum amount of farming is essential in view of the need to conserve the countryside.

The *second directive*[19] concerns measures to encourage the cessation of farming and the reallocation of land for structural improvement. It provides for the grant of an annuity or a lump-sum payment to those farmers aged between 55 and 65, who practise farming as their main occupation and now leave the land. At least 85 per cent. of the land released in this manner must be made available either to farmers benefiting from the first directive or reallocated for afforestation, recreational activities, public health or other purposes.

The *third directive*[20] concerning the provision of socio-economic guidance for and acquisition of occupational skills by persons engaged in agriculture, provides for vocational retraining of persons engaged in agriculture who wish to take up an occupation outside agriculture.

Member States were given a year (until April 20, 1973, extended to December 31, 1973) to implement those directives; the draft of the implementing measures had to be submitted to the Commission for its opinion.

In 1973, the Council adopted a directive[21] on the general provisions for the regional differentiation of certain measures provided for in the three above-mentioned directives on the reform of agriculture.

[18] Dir. 72/159 (O.J. 1972, 324; J.O. 1972, L 96/1).
[19] Dir. 72/160 (O.J. 1972, 332; J.O. 1972, L 96/9).
[20] Dir. 72/161 (O.J. 1972, 339; J.O. 1972, L 96/15).
[21] Dir. 73/440 (O.J. 1973, L 356/85).

Mention should also be made of a directive on mountain and hill farming in certain less-favoured areas,[22] which together with the three other directives constitutes the basic provisions for socio-structural reform in agriculture.[23]

(c) FINANCING THE CAP

The principle of financing the expenditures resulting from the implementation of the measures referred to above, both in the market and price field and for the socio-structural policy, has always been that, since a Community price system and a Community policy were introduced, the financial consequences should be borne by the Community.[24] For this purpose the European Agricultural Guidance and Guarantee Fund which forms part of the Community budget was established.[25] In 1979, the total appropriation for commitments in agriculture amounted to 10,255,139 million units of account out of a total budget of 14,869,206,885.

7. Transport

Transport is covered in a special Title of the Treaty, but together with the free movement of goods, persons, services and capital and the common agricultural policy, it constitutes the "Foundation of the Community." With regard to the rules governing the establishment, functioning and development of the common market, transport is in a situation comparable to that of agriculture: because of particular aspects, special provisions apply. But, whilst production and commercialisation of agricultural products are subjected to the rules laid down for the establishment of the common market, in regard to transport the Treaty only provides that the "objectives of the Treaty, shall apply"[26]; in both cases, however, the Treaty calls for a common policy.

What did the drafters of the Treaty mean when they referred to the "distinctive features of transport?" Most kinds of transport require heavy investment which, due to widely varying demand, often remain idle and unproductive for long periods; there is an

[22] Dir. 75/268 (O.J. 1975, L 128/1).

[23] For other structural measures see Twelfth General Report (1978), 181. See also Thirteenth General Report (1979), 162.

[24] Reg. 25, Art. 2 (2) (O.J. 1959–1962, 126; J.O. 1962, 991).

[25] See *infra*: financing Community activities, p. 218.

[26] EEC, Arts. 74, 75.

enormous discrepancy between the infrastructure needed for various means of transport: some, like railways and inland shipping, need a specially designed infrastructure, while others, like road transport, use the road network jointly with millions of other users; another characteristic is that some means of transportation are in the hands of the State and are forced to offer services which are not economically justifiable. But whether nationalised or not, all forms of transport are subject to severe requirements with regard to public safety. Finally, air and sea transport, extending far beyond the limits of the Community, are the object of many international agreements and regulations.

On the other hand, transport is a necessary complement to the basic freedoms: free movement of goods would remain ineffective if transport conditions were discriminatory, the same applies to the freedom to offer services and, to a certain extent, to free movement of persons. Notwithstanding its particularities transport is therefore an inherent part of the common market features.

Implementation. Since the Member States are required to develop a common transport policy comprising common rules for transport between the Member States, conditions allowing non-resident carriers to operate transport services in other Member States and all other appropriate measures, the Commission at first proposed to the Council the adoption of general principles covering all aspects of a common transport policy.[27]

It soon appeared, however, that a global approach was not politically possible and that the only way to obtain at least some results, would be to proceed gradually by presenting packages of concrete proposals which would permit the Council to reach compromises gained by limited mutual concessions. During the past 10 years, the approach to working out a common transport policy

[27] Tenth EEC General Report (1967), 231.

In a memorandum concerning the orientations of a common transport policy, the Commission proposed the establishment of a system of competition in the transport field and three objectives: elimination of obstacles to the implementation of the common market resulting from transport, integration of transport at Community level and general organisation of transport within the Community. These three objectives are closely linked and would by implemented through measures based on the following principles: equality of treatment, financial autonomy of carriers, freedom of action of carriers, free choice of customers and co-ordination of investments.

became increasingly pragmatic, with the result that the Community is now making an effective contribution towards the practical solution of problems currently affecting transport; lately this tendency has been particularly marked in sea and air transport.[28]

In pursuance of this method, several regulations, directives and decisions have been carried by the Council concerning transport by rail, transport by road of both goods and passengers, and transport by inland waterways. Of course, these measures do not constitute a harmonious globally conceived transport policy; this will remain impossible as long as agreement cannot be reached on conditions of access to the markets and on publication of rates and conditions of carriage; the latter would provide the users with the necessary information to make their free choice and the Commission with an instrument to exercise an effective control.

Mention should be made here of an important development resulting from a judgment of the Court of Justice: it concerned the interpretation of Article 84 (2) and the question whether or not sea and air transport were covered by the EEC Treaty. The Court stated that, as long as the Council has not decided otherwise, sea and air transport were excluded from the rules of Title IV of Part Two of the Treaty, but that it is, on the same basis as the other modes of transport, subject to the general rules of the Treaty.[29] Since then, several Community acts have been issued in this field concerning, *e.g.* minimum rules for certain tankers entering or leaving Community ports.[30] Obviously, external events as the wreck of the *Amoco Cadiz* are going to incite a more active policy in this field.

8. Competition

Competition, according to the Commission, is the best stimulant of economic activity since it guarantees the widest possible freedom of action to all. An active competition policy, pursued in accordance with the provisions of the treaties establishing the Communities, makes it easier for the supply and demand structures to continually adjust to technological development. Through the interplay of decentralised decision-making machinery, com-

[28] See Twelfth General Report (1978), 192 and Thirteenth (1979), 172.

[29] Case 167/73 *Commission* v. *French Republic* [1974] E.C.R. 359 at 371 (31).

[30] Bull. 12–1978, 69. See Twelfth General Report (1978), 199 and Thirteenth (1979), 177.

petition enables enterprises to continuously improve their efficiency, which is the *sine qua non* for a steady improvement of living standards and employment prospects within the countries of the Community. From this point of view, competition policy is an essential mean for satisfying to a great extent the individual and collective needs of our society.[31]

It follows that competition policy is not an end in itself. It constitutes another instrument, at the disposal of the Community, to ensure that the objectives set out in the Treaty are attained. One of those objectives, it will be remembered, is economic integration through the operation and development of the common market which in turn is characterised by the basic freedoms. The ultimate test of any Community policy and any behaviour of Member States and persons in respect of Community rules is whether or not those freedoms are guaranteed to the full. All the more so, as free movement of goods is the most important of the freedoms. Trade between Member States therefore becomes the overriding criterion for compatibility with Community obligations. This rule applies especially in the field of competition.[32]

The Treaty does not define the concept "competition,"[33] but refers to certain measures which interfere with competition and are therefore prohibited, subject to exemptions granted by the Commission. Generally speaking, the rules of competition aim at preventing the introduction, within the common market, of new obstacles to trade by Member States and private parties, once the traditional protective measures such as customs duties and quotas have been abolished. The Treaty Chapter on competition contains mainly two sets of rules: those applying to enterprise—prohibiting trade restrictions through agreement and abuse of a dominant position—and rules concerning aids granted by States—the latter having effects comparable to quantitative restrictions. Other treaty provisions, concerning public enterprises[34] and state monopolies,[35] must also be considered as competition rules applying to Member States.

[31] First Report on Competition Policy (11) (annexed to the Fifth General Report).

[32] See also Cases 56 and 58/64 *Consten and Grundig* v. *Commission* [1966] E.C.R. 299 at 341.

[33] The preamble of the Treaty refers to "fair" competition, but this has no practical significance.

[34] EEC, Art. 90.

[35] EEC, Art. 37.

This does not mean, however, that Community competition policy is essentially negative. With regard to co-operation between undertakings, the Commission's declared intention is to reinforce the competitive position of enterprises, not only within the Community, but on the world market as well, by excluding, from the Treaty's prohibition agreements which have a positive effect on industrial development within the Community. This is so in the case of co-operation agreements between small and medium-sized enterprises and specialisation agreements in research and manufacture. Similarly, it will be noticed that the Treaty does not prohibit all kinds of state aids and the Commission considers that, when judiciously applied, they are an indispensable instrument for regional development. These rules will be examined, *infra*.

(1) *Competition rules applying to undertakings*[36]

(a) AGREEMENTS BETWEEN UNDERTAKINGS (ARTICLE 85)

Agreements between enterprises, which may affect trade between Member States and which have as their object or effect distortion of competition, are prohibited and automatically void, except where an exemption was granted by the Commission. Consequently, parties to an agreement must determine whether or not it impedes the free movement of goods throughout the Community and, if so, whether or not it distorts competition within the common market. If their answer to both questions is positive, it can safely be assumed that the agreement is both void and can only be implemented at their own risk, even when the agreement has been notified to the Commission as part of a request to have the prohibition declared inapplicable to said agreement. Although this rule is simple enough in its generality, it requires some explanation as regards the precise significance of various terms.

Agreements are legally enforceable contracts. This follows from the wording of the second paragraph of Article 85 according to which prohibited agreements are void, *i.e.* not binding; the term agreements therefore does not and cannot include non-binding arrangements such as "gentleman's agreements."[37] The latter may however constitute a concertation between parties, which,

[36] EEC, Arts. 85 to 89.

[37] Gentleman's agreements and other arrangements binding in honour only are not, in this writers view, prohibited, unless they are followed by prohibited practices, the latter then constituting "concerted practices" prohibited by Art. 85 (1); see

when it is followed by prohibited behaviour, constitutes a "concerted practice." Agreements, on the other hand, are prohibited whether or not they are implemented, indeed the Treaty refers to agreements "which have as their object or effect" distortion of competition. In other words, in the case of an agreement the question whether or not competition was actually distorted is irrelevant, as long as the clauses clearly show the intention of the parties to distort competition.[38] Once again, normally speaking, there must exist a contract, preferably a document, permitting the scrutiny of its clauses. Concerted practices, on the other hand, refer in the first place to the behaviour of legal or natural persons; the sole fact that this behaviour distorts competition is not sufficient for it to fall under the prohibition of the Treaty. Parallel price increases for instance, are not in themselves prohibited; they could indeed be purely coincidental or the result of a particular market situation known as oligopoly with price leadership. But parallel price increases are prohibited when they are the result of a concertation, *i.e.* some form of arrangement like a gentleman's agreement.[39] The difficulty for the Commission, in such a case, lies with the proof of the existence of such a concertation which more often than not will have to be based on circumstantial evidence.[40]

infra. If informal agreements were also included in the term "agreements" there would be no need to prohibit "concerted practices." A gentleman's agreement to carry out a forbidden practice constitutes what in U.S. law is called a "conspiracy" but there is no reason why U.S. law should determine the interpretation of Community law. In its decision of July 16, 1969 (J.O. 1969, L 192/5) in the Case *ACF Chemiefarma,* the Commission considered a gentleman's agreement as an agreement because that agreement expressly laid down written provisions binding the parties with regard to their conduct on the market; and according to the Advocate-General the binding nature of the gentleman's agreement is clearly expressed in the provision stipulating that breach of the gentleman's agreement constitutes a breach of the export agreement. Opinion of Mr. Gand, Case 41/69 *ACF Chemiefarma* v. *Commission* [1970] E.C.R. 661 at 714 (3).

[38] See Case 56/65 *Technique Minière* v. *Maschinenbau Ulm* [1966] E.C.R. 235 at 249, where the Court held that the interference with competition must result from all or some of the clauses of the agreement itself and where an analysis of the clauses does not reveal the effect on competition to be sufficiently deleterious, the consequences of an agreement should then be considered and it is then necessary to show that competition has in fact been distorted.

[39] See, *e.g. Pittsburg Corning* (J.O. 1972, L 272/35).

[40] See, *e.g.* Case 48/69 *I.C.I.* v. *Commission* [1972] E.C.R. 619 and Cases 40/73, etc., *Suiker Unie et al.* v. *Commission* [1975] E.C.R. 1663; in both cases the Court admitted the existence of concerted practices.

Decisions by associations of undertakings must be understood to include the constitutive act of a trade association and its internal rules,[41] decisions made in accordance with those rules, which are therefore binding upon the members of the association,[42] and also recommendations such as the fixing of "target prices" by an association.[43] Any such decision which affects trade between the Member States and distorts competition within the common market is automatically void.

Associations refers to any grouping of associations of undertakings with or without legal personality; a *de facto* association of associations was considered by the Commission to be an association of undertakings.[44]

Undertakings may or may not have legal personality.[45] In the latter case it must have some recognised legal status[46] otherwise they would not be able to carry out economic activities, *i.e.* conclude legally binding agreements, bring actions in the Court of Justice and be liable for the payment of fines. In other words, they must have "legal autonomy." The question whether or not an entity has the required legal status allowing it to operate on the market must be decided according to the applicable national law. The term undertaking also covers individuals, public enterprises and even Member States when they carry out commercial and economic activities.[47]

[41] *ASPA* (J.O. 1970, L 148/11).

[42] *Bomée-Stitching* (O.J. 1975, L 329/30).

[43] Case 8/72 *Cementhandelaren* v. *Commission* [1972] E.C.R. 977 at 989 (19).

[44] *Cecimo* (J.O. 1969, L 69/13).

[45] This follows *inter alia* from the wording of EEC, Art. 52 which in regard to the freedom of establishment refers to the right to set up and manage undertakings, in particular companies and firms; the latter are defined by Art. 58 as "companies and firms constituted under civil or commercial law, including co-operative societies, and other legal persons governed by public or private law, save for those which are non-profit making"; it seems therefore that where the Treaty wants to refer to entities having legal personality, it uses the terms "company" or "firm."

[46] This is the case, *e.g.* with the Dutch "Vennootshap onder Firma," the English "Partnership," and the German "Offene Gesellschaft."

[47] The economic or commercial character of these activities is what distinguishes undertakings in the sense of Art. 85 from other bodies that are engaged, *e.g.* in artistic or scientific work.

For individuals, see *Reuter/BASF* (O.J. 1976, L 254/40) and for Member States, Case 83/78 *Pigs Marketing Board* v. *Redmond* [1978] E.C.R. 2347.

Besides having legal autonomy, an entity must also have economic independence[48] in order to qualify as an undertaking within the meaning of Article 85. The Article is not concerned with agreements between undertakings belonging to the same concern and having the status of parent company and subsidiary, if the undertakings form an economic unit within which the subsidiary has no real freedom to determine its course of action on the market, and if the agreements are concerned merely with the internal allocation of tasks as between the undertaking.[49] Once these two conditions are fulfilled, the two enterprises must be, for the implementation of the competition rules, considered as one undertaking. The same applies when an agreement is concluded between two subsidiaries.[50]

If the relationship between a parent company and its subsidiary can thus result in the non applicability of Article 85, it can on the other hand bring the parent company within the jurisdiction of the Community competition rules, even when it is situated outside the Community. Indeed, since the subsidiary does not determine its own market behaviour, the latter becomes the responsibility of the parent company. Whether or not this parent company is situated within the Community becomes irrelevant since its decision has effect within the Community.[51]

Effect on trade between Member States constitutes a criterion which serves, in the first place, to determine the field of application of the Community competition rules: it is "to the extent that the agreement may affect trade between Member States that the interference with competition caused by that agreement is caught by the prohibition in Community law found in Article 85, while in the converse case it escapes those prohibitions."[52]

[48] See Case 22/71 *Béguelin Import* v. *G. L. Import Export* [1971] E.C.R. 949 at 959 (8).

[49] See Case 15/74 *Centrafarm* v. *Sterling Drug* [1974] E.C.R. 1147 at 1167 (41). The Commission had reached a similar decision in *Christiani and Nielsen* (J.O. 1969, L 165/12).

[50] *Kodak* (J.O. 1970, L 147/24). However, in this case the second condition was not fulfilled, *i.e.* it was not a simple internal allocation of tasks, since the instruction from the parent company to the subsidiary had to be incorporated in contracts concluded by the subsidiaries and third parties: the instructions, therefore, constitute an agreement between undertakings.

[51] See, *e.g.* Case 48/69 *I.C.I.* v. *Commission* [1972] E.C.R. at 662.

[52] Case 56/65 *La Technique Minière* v. *Maschinenbau Ulm* [1966] E.C.R. at 249. Since this is a question of admissibility under Community law, a formal requirement, it should logically be examined in the first place, as the Court of Justice does in all its

An agreement may affect trade when it "is capable of constituting a threat, either direct or indirect, actual or potential, to freedom of trade between Member States in a manner which might harm the attainment of the objectives of a single market between States."[53] Preventing, for instance, undertakings from importing certain products into a Member State from another one, or prohibiting them from re-exporting those products to other Member States, indisputably affects trade between Member States since they constituted a limitation of the freedom of movement of goods.[54]

With regard to agreements containing a clause granting an exclusive right of sale, the Court stated that they do not necessarily by their very nature contain elements incompatible with the common market and that, in this respect, special attention should be given to whether the agreement is capable of partitioning the market in certain products between Member States.[55] It must also be noted that the effect on trade does not have to be actual; indeed the word "may" refers to a "possible" effect on interstate commerce.

Competition is adversely affected when any kind of action by undertakings directly effects the market and is detrimental to production or sales to purchasers or consumers because it limits freedom of choice. Effective competition exists for example when a producer is forced to take into account the market behaviour of other producers within the relevant market.

This interference with competition may result from all or some of the clauses of the agreement itself. If not, then, as was mentioned

judgments; the Commission for some reason first examines the material condition: effects on competition. However, since both conditions must be fulfilled for the prohibition of Art. 85 to be applicable, it does not make a great deal of difference which condition is examined first; however, the Court's approach seems more logical.

[53] Cases 56 and 58/64 *Consten and Grundig* v. *Commission* [1966] E.C.R. at 341. The Court added that the fact that an agreement encourages an increase, even a large one, in the volume of trade between States is not sufficient to exclude the possibility that the agreement may "affect" trade in the above mentioned manner.

[54] *Ibid.* By defining the condition in this way the Court respected the Commission's interpretation according to which an agreement may affect trade when, because of the agreement, trade develops under conditions other than those which would have existed in the absence of the restrictions resulting from the agreement.

[55] See n. 48.

supra the consequences of the agreement should be considered and factors must be found which show that competition has in fact been effected.[56]

The Court of Justice has further developed and specified the meaning of distortion of competition by adding that competition must be prevented, restricted or distorted to an *appreciable* extent.[57] For instance, an "exclusive dealing agreement, even with absolute territorial protection, may, having regard to the weak position of the persons concerned in the market and the products in question, escape the prohibition of Article 85."[58] In other words, *de minimums not curat lex* also applies to the Community competition rules.

Another point emphasised by the Court is that the appreciation of the effects on competition may not be purely theoretical but the "competition in question must be understood within the actual context in which it would occur in the absence of the agreement in dispute." One must take into account, therefore, the nature and quantity, limited or otherwise, of the product covered by the agreement, the position and importance of the parties on the market for the products concerned, the isolated nature of the disputed agreement or, alternatively, its position in a series of agreements, the severity of the clauses limiting trade or, alternatively, the opportunities allowed for other commercial competition in the same product by way of parallel re-exportation and importation.[59]

According to the Treaty, distortion of competition must take place *within the common market*. It follows that an agreement between two undertakings situated within the Community which limits competition within a third country is not prohibited by Community law,[60] unless of course the behaviour of the parties to the agreement outside the Community indirectly affects interstate

[56] See n. 52, *ibid.*

[57] *Ibid.* For more details as to the meaning of the term "appreciable" see the Commission's Notice concerning agreements of Minor Importance of December 19, 1977; (O.J. 1977, C 313/3). See also the following Commission decisions: *SOCEMARS* (J.O. 1968, L 201/4) and *Intergroup Trading* (*Spar*) (O.J. 1975, L 212/23) where the effects were considered to be minor; but in *Reuter/BASF* (O.J. 1976, L 28/19) this was not the case.

[58] Case 5/69 *Völk* v. *Vervaecke* [1969] E.C.R. 295 at 303.

[59] See n. 52, *ibid.* at 250.

[60] *e.g. Rieckermann* (J.O. 1968, L 276/25).

trade and competition within the Community.[61] Another consequence is that an agreement concluded between undertakings situated outside the Community, but having effect on interstate trade and competition within the Community, is prohibited by the Treaty. The same applies of course when one of the parties is situated within the Community.[62] And finally, it should be noted that the expression "within the Community" does not necessarily refer to competition in several Member States or even all nine; adverse effect on competition in one single Member State is also to be considered as taking place within the Community, and forbidden when interstate trade is also affected; this will practically always be the case when the agreement covers the whole territory of one Member State.[63]

Nullity (Article 85 (2)). Any agreements or decisions prohibited by the Treaty are automatically void.[64] This statement requires some clarification: a distinction must be made between "new" agreements and "old" ones. What distinguished the two groups is the question whether they were concluded before or after March 13, 1962. The latter date refers to the moment when Regulation 17, the first regulation implementing Articles 85 and 86, became effective.[65] Nullity applies without reservation to all *new agreements* (*i.e.* those concluded after March 13, 1962[66]) prohibited by the Treaty, whether or not they were notified[67] to the Commission in a procedure to obtain an exemption from the prohibition under Article 85 (3), or whether they were exempted from notification.[68]

The situation is different with *old agreements* (*i.e.* those which were in existence at the time Regulation 17 entered into force). The Court held[68a] that in those cases the general principle of contractual certainty, particularly when the agreement has been notified in

[61] *e.g.* Cases 6 and 7/73 *Commercial Solvents Corporation* v. *Commission* [1974] E.C.R. 223 at 252 (33).

[62] *e.g. Franco-Japanese Ballbearings* (O.J. 1974, L 343/19).

[63] *e.g.* Case 8/72 *VCH* v. *Commissin* [1972] E.C.R. 977 at 999 (29).

[64] EEC, Art. 85 (2).

[65] O.J. 1959–1962, 87; J.O. 204/62.

[66] For the new Member States: Denmark, Ireland and U.K., this date became June 30, 1979.

[67] Reg. 17, Art. 4; thus notification has no suspensive effect.

[68] Case 48/72 *Brasserie de Haecht* v. *Wilkin* (No. 2) [1973] E.C.R. 77 at 86 (9, 10).

[68a] Case 59/77 *De Bloos* v. *Bouyer* [1977] E.C.R. 2359 at 2369 (8).

accordance with Regulation 17, requires that the agreement may only be declared to be automatically void after the Commission has taken a decision by virtue of that regulation. Since certain old agreements are exempted from notification, another distinction must be made between the latter—these are simply valid—and the old agreements which must be notified in order to be exempted—these are "provisionally valid" since they may still become void if the exemption is refused by the Commission.[69]

The declaration of inapplicability of the prohibition (Article 85 (3)). A declaration of inapplicability, or exemption, may be given by the Commission[70] under certain limited conditions, either for individual agreements or for categories of agreements.[71] Exemption in individual cases may only be granted once the Commission has been notified of the agreement concerned and the four conditions provided in Article 85 (3) are fulfilled:

(1) the agreement must contribute to improving the production or distribution of goods or to promoting technical and economic progress;
(2) consumers must get a fair share of the resulting benefit;
(3) the agreement may not impose restrictions which are not indispensable for the objectives under (1) and (2);
(4) the agreement may not afford the parties the possibility of eliminating competition in respect of a substantial part of the products in question.

The exemptions may not enter into force on a date earlier than the date of notification[72]; they must be issued for a specified period and conditions and obligations may be attached thereto; they may be renewed but also revoked even with retroactive effect.[73]

Exemptions for categories of agreements can only be provided by the Council in the form of regulations or directives.[74] This

[69] Case 13/61 *Bosch* v. *Van Rijn* [1962] E.C.R. at 52.
[70] Before Reg. 17 became effective, only the national authorities in the Member States could grant such an exemption (EEC, Art. 88); with the entry into force of the said Reg., this exclusive right passed to the Commission (Reg. 17, Art. 9 (1)).
[71] EEC, Art. 85 (3).
[72] Reg. 17, Art. 6 (1). Agreements should therefore be notified on the day they become effective, otherwise parties run the risk of having to consider this agreement void between the date of entry into force of the agreement and the date on which the exemption becomes effective, *i.e.* at the earliest the date of notification.
[73] Reg. 17, Art. 8.
[74] EEC, Art. 87 (2) (*b*).

technique was only used in two instances: certain categories of exclusive dealing agreements and categories of specialisation agreements.[75]

(b) ABUSE OF DOMINANT POSITION

Interstate trade and competition can be adversely affected not only by several undertakings acting or behaving jointly, but also by an individual enterprise or a group of undertakings enjoying a dominant position within the common market or in a substantial part of it. Article 86 therefore must be understood in conjunction with Article 85 which it complements; together they constitute the common rules of the Community competition policy based on the basic principle set out in Article 3 (*f*) which provides for the institution of a system ensuring that competition in the common market is not distorted, thereby requiring *a fortiori* that competition must not be eliminated. This requirement is so essential that without it numerous provisions of the Treaty would be pointless. Thus the restraints on competition which the Treaty allows under certain conditions because of the need to harmonise the various objectives of the Treaty are limited by that fundamental requirement.

The methods used to eliminate competition are irrelevant: both practices which may directly affect the market and are detrimental to production or sales, to purchasers or consumers, and changes to the structure of an undertaking which lead to competition being seriously disturbed in a substantial part of the common market, are prohibited by Article 86.[76]

[75] Reg. 19/65 was the first to be adopted pursuant to this provision; it empowered the Commission to exclude by regulation from the prohibition, certain agreements concluded between only two undertakings (J.O. 1965, 533). This was done by Reg. 67/67 on the application of Art. 85 (3) of the Treaty to certain categories of exclusive dealing agreements (O.J. 1967, 10; J.O. 1967, 849).

See also Reg. 2821/71 (O.J. 1971, 1032; J.O. 1971, L 285/46) followed by Reg. 2779/72 on the application of Art. 85 (3) to categories of specialisation agreements (O.J. 1972 (28–30 Dec.) 80; J.O. 1972, L 292/23, amended by Reg. 2903/77.

[76] *Continental Can* (J.O. 1972, L 7/25) and Case 6/72 *Europemballage and Continental Can* v. *Commission* [1973] E.C.R. 215. This case constitutes the first major breakthrough in the implementation and interpretation of Art. 86. The Court states that the latter must be based upon the spirit, general scheme and wording, as well as on the system and objectives of the Treaty. Most of the remarks made above about Art. 86 are taken from this judgment; see *ibid.* at 243.

The Treaty refers to abuse "of" a dominant position, but this does not mean that a link of causality must exist between the dominant position and its abuse. Indeed, the strengthening of the position of an undertaking may constitute an abuse and be prohibited regardless of the means and procedure by which it is achieved. It also follows from the case law of the Commission[77] and the Court of Justice[78] that to be considered as "dominant," the position of an undertaking must be viewed in relation to a relevant product market, and in this context substitution with regard to both demand and production constitutes an essential element of appreciation.

As for the concept of "dominant position," it relates to a position of economic strength enjoyed by an undertaking which enables it to prevent effective competition being maintained on the relevant market, by giving it the power to behave to an appreciable extent independently of its competitors, customers and ultimately of its consumers. It follows that dominance is not only a question of sheer size, but that it can also derive from a combination of several factors which, taken separately, would not necessarily be determinative.[79]

More difficult is the definition of "abuse," except that it has to be specified with regard to competition: any behaviour of an undertaking enjoying a dominant position which interferes with one of the basic freedoms or the free choice of purchasers or consumers or freedom of access to business, must be viewed as limiting competition and therefore as an "abuse."

[77] The most important Commission decisions concerning Art. 86 were taken in the following cases: *GEMA* (J.O. 1971, L 134/15), *Continental Can* (*supra*), *ZOJA* (J.O. 1972, L 229/51), *General Motors* (O.J. 1975, L 23/14), *United Brands* (O.J. 1976, L 95/1), *Hoffman-La Roche* (O.J. 1976, L 223/27), *ABG/Oil companies* (O.J. 1977, L 117/1).

[78] The most important Court rulings were given in the following cases: Case 6/72 *supra*, n. 76; Case 26/75 *General Motors* v. *Commission* [1975] E.C.R. 1367; Cases 6 and 7/73, *ICI-CSC* v. *Commission* [1974] E.C.R. at 223; Case 13/77, *GB-INNO-BM* v. *ATAB* [1977] E.C.R. 2115; Case 27/76 *United Brands* v. *Commission* [1978] E.C.R. 207; Case 77/77 *BP* v. *Commission* [1978] E.C.R. 1513.

[79] Eighth Competition Report (1978), 29. A trader can be in a dominant position on the market for a product only if he has succeeded in acquiring a substantial part of this market. Although it is far from negligible, a market share of between 40 and 45 per cent. does not permit the conclusion that the undertaking in question automatically controls the market. The percentage must be assessed having regard to the strength and number of the competitors.

In connection with the provisions of Article 86, mention should be made of the Commission proposals for a regulation on the control of concentrations between undertakings.[80] As the Commission pointed out, the process of industrial concentration is on the increase and although mergers can increase competition within the common market, it is essential to preserve the unity of this market, to ensure that it remains open and to maintain effective competition. Obviously excessive concentration is likely to obstruct these aims[81] and since Article 86 only allows the Commission to intervene once abuse has taken place, some kind of preventive control seems required. To date no decision has been taken by the Council on this proposal.

Regulation 17.[82] Regulation 17 is the first regulation "to give effect to the principles set out in Article 85 and 86" and generally speaking, it sets out the procedure to be followed when the Commission decides:

(1) to give a *negative clearance*[83] (Article 2): this is issued at the request[84] of undertakings which want to make certain that their agreement is not prohibited by Article 85 or 86. Before granting a negative clearance, the Commission must publish the essential content of the application and invite interested parties to submit observations;

(2) to oblige undertakings to put an *end to infringements*, when it finds that the latter exist, either upon application of Member States or natural or legal persons or upon its own initiative (Article 3). In this connection attention should be drawn to the limitation period in proceedings under competition.

[80] See O.J. 1973, C 92/1.

[81] Third Competition Report, 29.

[82] O.J. 1959–1962, 87; J.O. 1962, 204.

[83] Complete lists of decisions taken by the Commission are to be found in the annual Reports on Competition Policy published in conjunction with the General Reports. The first decision taken under Reg. 17 concerned a request for negative clearance: *Grosfillex-Fillistorf*, March 11, 1964 (J.O. 915/64); the last decision to date was issued on July 14, 1975, *Intergroup Trading Spar* (O.J. 1975, L 212/3). About 14 decisions were taken in all and the disuse of this procedure can be explained by the greater security which has existed since the Commission and the Court defined the various concepts of the Treaty provisions.

[84] See Reg. 27 fixing form, content and other details concerning application and notifications (O.J. 1959–1962, 132; J.O. 1962, 1118); it was amended by Reg. 1133/68 (O.J. 1968, 400; J.O. 1968, L 189/1) and Reg. 1699/75 (O.J. 1975, L 172/11).

(3) to issue a declaration *granting an exemption* from the prohibition of Article 81 (1) (Article 6)[85];

(4) to impose *fines* or *penalties* (Articles 15 and 16).[86]

In the last three cases, the Commission, before deciding, must make known to the undertakings concerned the points to which it objects and which it has taken into consideration, and give the undertakings an opportunity to express their views thereon (Article 19),[87] and invite interested third parties to submit their observations. In those cases, the Commission must also consult the Consultative Committee on Cartels and Monopolies.

Commission announcements. To clarify its competition policy the Commission has issued announcements, notices or communications concerning the following subjects:

(1) *Exclusive agency contracts made with commercial agents*[88]: the Commission declared that contracts concluded with commercial agents in which such agents, with respect to a particular part of the common market, undertake to negotiate business transactions for the account of an undertaking, or to do so in the name and for the account of the latter, or to do so in their own name and for the account of the latter, are not prohibited by Article 85 (1).

(2) *Patent licences agreements*[89]: some clauses specifically mentioned in this communication are not covered by the prohibition of Article 85 (1);

(3) *Co-operation agreements*[90]: in this notice the Commission first indicates that it encourages co-operation between small and medium-sized enterprises, where such co-operation enables

[85] See *supra*: declaration of inapplicability of the prohibition of Art. 85 (1).

[86] In several cases fines have been imposed by the Commission for infringement of Art. 85 (1): *e.g. Hoffman-La Roche* (O.J. 1976, L 223/27); in one case for submitting incomplete information: see Bull. 11–1971, p. 55 (5) and in another case the Commission imposed a periodic payment for each day the undertaking failed to fulfil an obligation imposed by the Commission (J.O. 1972, L 299/51).

[87] See Reg. 99/63 (O.J. 1963–64, 47; J.O. 1963, 2268) laying down implementing provisions for those hearings.

[88] J.O. 1962, 2921.

[89] J.O. 1962, 2922. See also Case 24/67 *Parke, Davis* v. *Probel* [1968] E.C.R. 55 and several other judgments *inter alia*, Case 16/74 *Centrafarm* v. *Winthrop* [1974] E.C.R. at 1183.

[90] J.O. 1968, C 75/3.

them to work more rationally and increases their productivity and competitiveness on a larger market; the Commission then lists a number of agreements which do not restrict competition;

(4) *Agreements of minor importance*[91]: this announcement also follows from the desire of the Commission to promote co-operation between small and medium-sized enterprises. The notice lists a number of criteria which allow undertakings to acquire the certainty that their agreement does not fall under the prohibition of Article 85 (1);

(5) *Subcontracting agreements*[92]: the notice offers a general guide as to clauses often contained in subcontracting agreements and which are not caught by Article 85 (1);

(6) *Imports of Japanese products*[93]: the Commission reminds undertakings concluding agreements with Japanese firms and which are intended to restrict imports of Japanese products into the Community that such agreements do not fall outside Community competition rules because one of the parties is situated outside the Community. It urges those undertakings concerned to notify those agreements.

Relationship between Community and national competition rules. In one of its judgments,[94] the Court of Justice had to answer the question whether or not Community and national competition law could be applied simultaneously to the same agreement. The Court considered that Community and national law consider cartels from different points of view; the former regards them in the light of the obstacles which may result for interstate trade, while the latter proceeds on the basis of considerations which are particular to it. This implies that one and the same agreement in principle, may be the object of two sets of parallel proceedings. However, if the ultimate general aim of the Treaty is to be respected, the parallel application of the national system can only be allowed in so far as it does not prejudice the uniform application throughout the common market of the Community rules on cartels and the full effect of the measures adopted in implementation of those rules.

[91] J.O. 1977, C 313/3. This Notice replaces the Notice published in J.O. 1970, C 64/1.
[92] O.J. 1979, C 1/2.
[93] J.O. 1972, C 111/13.
[94] Case 14/68 *Wilhelm* v. *Bundeskartellamt* [1969] E.C.R. 1.

The Court based this rule on the fact that "the EEC Treaty has established its own system of law, integrated into the legal systems of the Member States, and which must be applied by their courts. It would be contrary to the nature of such a system to allow Member States to introduce or to retain measures capable of prejudicing the practical effectiveness of the Treaty. The binding force of the Treaty and of measures taken in application of it must not differ from one state to another as a result of internal measures, lest the functioning of the Community system should be impeded and the achievement of the aims of the Treaty placed in peril. Consequently, conflicts between the rules of the Community and national rules in the matter of the law on cartels, must be resolved by applying the principle that Community law takes precedence."[95]

As long as this rule is applied, national authorities may take action against an agreement in accordance with their national law, even when an examination of the same agreement, from the point of view of its compatability with Community law, is pending before the Commission.[96]

However, to avoid conflict, the best solution is that as soon as the Commission starts proceedings, the national authorities, and this includes tribunals, should suspend their procedure.[97] But it is

[95] *Ibid.* at 14 (6).

[96] This means that when, *e.g.* the Commission has made it known that it intends to grant an exemption from the prohibition of Art. 85 or has granted such an exemption, national authorities may no longer prohibt or declare void the agreement concerned on the basis of their national law, othewise the agreement would be void in one Member State and valid in all the others. Similarly, national authorities may not consider an agreement which was found by the Commission to be prohibited under Art. 85 to be valid. However, when applying national law, national authorities are under no obligation to take into account possible infringements of Community law, as long as the Commission has not opened proceedings, and nothing prevents those authorities from prohibiting agreements under national law which are void under Community law or from imposing fines upon the undertakings concerned, even if fines were already imposed by the Commission, just as, *vice versa*, the Commission is not prevented from imposing fines after an undertaking has been fined under national law. See Case 7/72 *Boehringer* v. *Commission* [1972] E.C.R. 1281 at 1289, when the two cases are identical, the fines should be offset against one another.

[97] In Case 48/72 *Brasserie de Haecht* v. *Wilkin-Janssen*, the Court considered that "whilst the principle of legal certainty requires that in applying the prohibition of Article 85, the sometimes considerable delays by the Commission in exercising its powers should be taken into account, this cannot however absolve the (national)

for the national judge to decide whether there is cause to suspend proceedings in order to allow the parties to obtain the Commission's standpoint, unless of course it is established that the agreement does not have any perceptible effect on competition or trade between Member States or that there is no doubt that the agreement is incompatible with Article 85.[98]

Application of competition rules to certain agreements. After this brief analysis of the Community competition rules it might be useful to indicate how they have been applied by the Commission and the Court of Justice to the main types of agreements.[99]

The following are very likely to fall under the prohibition of Article 85 (1): (a) agreements relating to prices and conditions of sale[1]; (b) limitations on markets and productions[2]; (c) agreements whereby a vendor agrees not to compete within the market of the purchaser[3]; (d) exclusive dealing agreements such as supply agreements[4]; collective exclusive dealings[5]; and (e) joint purchasing[6] and joint selling agreements.[7]

Special mention should be made of exclusive dealing agreements, *i.e.* agreements between suppliers and intermediaries providing for limitation of the commercial activities of one or both parties. These agreements are prohibited as soon as they provide geographical restrictions since this risks the re-introduction of partitions within the common market.[8] Of particular interest are

court from the obligation of deciding on the claims of interested parties who invoke the automatic nullity" [1973] E.C.R. 77 at 87 (11).

[98] *Ibid.* The national judge is in the same position here as when parties ask for a preliminary ruling (EEC, Art. 177, see *supra*).

[99] This section is based on Bellamy and Child, *Common Market Law of Competition* (Sweet and Maxwell, 1978) with the kind permission of the authors.

[1] See, *e.g. International Quinine Agreement* (J.O. 1969, L 192/5) and Case 41/69 *ACF Chemiefarma* v. *Commission* [1970] E.C.R. 661.

[2] See, *e.g. Julien Van Katwijk* (J.O. 1970, L 242/18).

[3] See, *e.g. Reuter BASF* (O.J. 1976, L 254/40).

[4] See, *e.g. Bayer Gist* (O.J. 1976, L 30/13).

[5] See First Competition Report 35 *et seq.* and Case 71/74 *Frubo* v. *Commission* [1975] E.C.R. 563. See also Reg. 67/67 on the application of Art. 85 (3) of the Treaty to certain categories of exclusive dealing agreements (O.J. 1967, 10; J.O. 1967, 349).

[6] See, *e.g. Belgian Industrial Timber*, Bull. 10–1975, 23.

[7] See, *e.g. SEIFA* (J.O. 1969, L 173/8).

[8] See, *e.g.* Cases 48, etc., *Suiker Unie et al.* v. *Commission* [1975] E.C.R. 73 at 2006 (535).

the selective distribution agreements, *i.e.* limitation of the sales points of a given product[9] and distribution systems in general.[10]

Reference should also be made to industrial property rights with respect to the Community competition rules although these rights are generally used by their owners to prevent import into a given country and therefore enter into conflict with the principle of free movement of goods under Article 30 of the Treaty; it is in regard to this principle that most cases concerning property rights brought before the Court have been decided upon.[11] The position of the Court can be summarised as follows: the Treaty provisions do not affect the existence of exclusive rights attached to patents and licences, trade-marks and copyright, but may limit their use in so far as it restricts trade between the Member States.

(2) *Competition rules applying to Member States*

As was mentioned at the beginning of the section on competition, obstacles to the free movement of goods can result not only from illegal behaviour of undertakings but also from interferences of national authorities: both are prohibited by the Treaty. Member States do affect trade and competition by establishing or maintaining state monopolies, by acting through public enterprises or by granting subsidies to undertakings. The Treaty provides rules for the abolition and prevention of those interferences recurring.

(a) STATE MONOPOLIES OF A COMMERCIAL CHARACTER[12]

Member States were required by the Treaty to adjust their monopolies of a commercial character[13] so as to ensure that, by the end of the transitional period,[14] no discrimination regarding the conditions under which goods are procured and marketed exists

[9] See *Omega* (J.O. 1970, L 242/22), *SABA* (O.J. 1976, L 28/219), *BMW* (O.J. 1975, L 29/1) and *Junghans* (O.J. 1977, L 30/10).

[10] See, *e.g. Fedetab* (O.J. 1978, L 224/29).

[11] See, *e.g.* Cases 78/70 *Deutsche Grammophon* v. *Metro* [1971] E.C.R. 487.

[12] EEC, Art. 37. A state monopoly is a body through which a State, in law or in fact, directly or indirectly, supervises, determines or appreciably influences imports or exports between Member States.

[13] Commercial means that production monopolies are not affected by the Treaty because in a real common market these monopolies do not constitute an obstacle to free trade.

[14] December 31, 1969.

force of the Treaty about a dozen such monopolies existed in the six original Member States[15]; the timetable of the Treaty was not respected by the Member States and in 1978 the Commission reported that it hoped "that by the end of the year its work on state monopolies of a commercial character will have reached a point where none of the remaining monopolies are at variance with Article 37 of the EEC Treaty."[16] Therefore, if no new monopolies are introduced, Article 37 would be one of the few Treaty provisions having received a full and satisfactory implementation.

(b) PUBLIC ENTERPRISES[17]

A public enterprise, in the sense of Article 37, is any undertaking[18] whatever its public or private status, on whose economic behaviour the state may exert influence by virtue of its direct or indirect financial participation or by legal provisions governing its establishment. It follows that what is essential is the "control" a national authority exercises over an enterprise.[19] The logical consequence of this subordinate position of the public enterprise in respect to a public authority, places upon the latter the entire responsibility for the behaviour of the enterprise. Therefore, whether the undertaking, which is by definition under state control, acts illegally on instructions of the national authority[20] or whether the latter has not taken the necessary measures to prevent its public enterprise from acting in such a way, it is the Member State—to be understood here as any public authority—which is considered as having acted.

This explains why Article 90 imposes obligations exclusively upon the Member State—not on the public enterprises—and why

[15] See First Competition Report, 160 *et seq*.

[16] Eighth Competition Report, 181.

[17] EEC, Art. 90.

[18] Undertaking to be understood as defined for Art. 85 (1); see *supra* p. 156.

[19] A parallel can be drawn here with the above-mentioned relationship between a parent company and its subsidiary; see *supra* p. 157.

[20] Member States might indeed be tempted to implement through the undertakings certain measures which are prohibited when taken directly by the State. Art. 30 constitutes a good example: it prohibits any restriction on imports or exports; if a Member State in a notice of public contracts indicates that it will only consider tenders proposing national products, it would violate Art. 30. If an undertaking were to do the same, no action could be taken. The Member State might, therefore, order an undertaking under its control to issue the notice in its stead.

Article 90 (3) provides that the Commission shall, in order to ensure the application of the provisions of Article 90, address directives and decisions only to the Member States.[21]

An interesting provision of Article 90 is that concerning undertakings "entrusted with the operation of services of general economic interest"[22] since they shall be subject to the Treaty rules, in particular those on competition, only "in so far as the application of such rules does not obstruct the performance in law or in fact, of the particular task assigned to it."

Owing to the very important role played by "public enterprises" as producers and traders within the common market, it is to be expected that the provisions of Article 90 will be applied much more vigorously in the future.

(c) AIDS GRANTED BY STATES

The common market, as described in the preceding sections, implies that all those who operate therein do so only with their own resources and at their own risk. These resources can be artificially increased and the risks reduced by agreements between enterprises, as well as by State aids. Aids, whatever their form or size, invariably modify market conditions and, therefore, affect competition and interstate trade. Article 92 states that aids are incompatible with the common market when they distort competition and affect trade between the Member States; it seems difficult to imagine state aids favouring certain[23] enterprises which would not distort competition and affect trade between the Member States.

[21] Such a decision is now in preparation, see Eighth Competition Report, 31.

[22] See Case 10/71 *Ministère Public Luxembourg* v. *Muller* [1971] E.C.R. 723. A typical example of such enterprises is in the transport sector; it appears, however, that the provisions of Art. 90 are relevant only for these undertakings which are in competition with other enterprises which are not controlled by the State; it is no surprise that the competition rules concerning the abuse of dominant positions do not apply to railways, postal service, telecommunications, gas and electricity. See also Cases 155/73 *Sacchi* [1974] E.C.R. 409 and 127/73 *Belgische Radio en Televisie* v. *Sabam* [1974] E.C.R. 313.

[23] The reference to "certain" enterprises establishes a distinction between what is commonly considered as "aids," *i.e.* measures favouring a limited number of undertakings, and general economic measures which favour all the undertakings operating within a given country; the latter measures are not caught by Art. 92. Distortion resulting from those general measures must be eliminated through approximation of legislation; see *supra* p. 138.

However, state aids also constitute an instrument of structural development policy when certain legitimate objectives of economic growth cannot be attained solely by the interplay of market forces, or not within an acceptable time-limit, or without unacceptable social frictions. The Treaty therefore, having stated the principle of incompatibility of state aids with the common market, provides for certain categories of aids which either are or may be considered by the Commission to be compatible with the common market.[24]

To allow the Commission to declare certain aids compatible with the common market, Member States must notify the Commission of any plans to grant or alter aids. Until the Commission has decided on the compatibility of the plans,[25] the Member State concerned may not put its proposed measures into effect. If the Commission comes to the conclusion that the aid cannot be considered compatible with the common market, it opens up a procedure which allows all interested parties to express their opinion; once this is done, the Commission takes a final decision. During the procedure, the measures may not be applied, unless the Council decides that they are compatible.

If a Member State were to apply an aid either without waiting for the procedure to be closed or without informing the Commission, the following would happen: any interested party can ask the national judge to declare the aid illegal,[26] the Commission can ask the Court to adopt interim measures requiring the Member State to cease the infringement,[27] and finally having declared the aid to be

[24] Any aid therefore which does not fall within one of those categories is automatically prohibited (see, *e.g.* J.O. 1972, L 10/22: Belgian aids to undertakings in difficulty which the Commission ordered to be abolished). The possibility exists of extending the categories of aids which can be declared admissible by the Commission: Art. 92 (*d*). *e.g.* Dir. 77/338 on aid to shipbuilding (O.J. 1978, L 98/19) which created the category of production aids to shipbuilders. See Case 74/76 *Iannelli* v. *Meroni* [1977] E.C.R. 557 at 574 (11): the incompatibility is "neither absolute nor unconditional."

[25] According to Art. 93 (3), the Commission must be notified "in sufficient time to enable it to submit its comments"; as for the Commission, once it has been informed, it has, according to the Court, two months to make up its mind; see Case 122/73 *Nordsee* v. *Germany* [1973] E.C.R. at 1522 (4).

[26] Indeed, the last sentence of Art. 93 (3) has direct effect: Case 120/73 *Lorenz* v. *Germany* [1973] E.C.R. at 1481 (4).

[27] Cases 31/77 R. and 53/77 R. *Commission* v. *U.K.* and *U.K.* v. *Commission* [1977] E.C.R. 921.

incompatible, the Commission can "require from the recipients [of the aid] the repayment, within certain time limits, of the grants awarded."[28]

Apart from a category of aids, which are compatible *de jure*,[29] the Treaty provides for aids which can be declared compatible by the Commission; these are regional development aids and aids to certain industries.

(i) *Regional development aids.*[30] The implementation of the Treaty provisions in regard to regional aids has presented the Commission with considerable problems: the granting of aids has remained a national responsibility and the fact that the Community's regional policy is in its initial stage has made the co-ordination of national policies in this field very difficult. It constitutes furthermore a very sensitive matter, since in certain Member States the choice of the development areas is often influenced by internal political considerations; the powers of the Community in this field are therefore sometimes resented as an interference with national "policies."

The absence of co-ordination did result in the implementation by Member States of policies seeking to attract new industries to their depressed areas by offering more and better incentives than their neighbours, thereby initiating stiff competition between the Member States or even their own regions. The Commission, therefore, in close liaison with the Member States, developed "principles of co-ordination of national regional aid schemes"[31] which

[28] Case 70/72 *Commission* v. *Germany* [1973] E.C.R. 813 at 828 (10).

[29] *e.g.* aids having a social character, aids which make good the damage caused by natural disasters and aids granted in Germany to areas affected by the division of the country. Although, these aids are compatible, they must be notified to the Commission which must make sure that they fall within these categories.

[30] The Treaty distinguishes between under-developed regions and other regions where aids for development are needed; where the latter are concerned the aids may not "adversely affect trading conditions, to an extent contrary to the common interest," while no such condition is provided for the depressed areas.

[31] The first principles which applied only to the "central regions" of the six original Member States are embodied in a Commission communication to the Council (J.O. 1971, C 1111/7) and adopted in the form of a resolution by the representatives of the governments of the Member States in Council (O.J. 1974 (2nd) IX, 57; J.O. 1971, C 1111/1). See also Act of Accession, Art. 154; in pursuance of this provision, the Commission sent to the Council an adapted version of the Principles of co-ordination in 1973 (Bull. 6–1973, 23). The latest version of the

have since 1971 constituted the main feature of the Community's policy in this field. Plans to alter existing aids or to introduce new ones are examined as to their compatibility with the common market by the Commission, on the basis of these principles[32]; they are valid for an initial period of three years.

(ii) *Aids to certain industries.* The application of the Community rules to industrial aids, as opposed to regional aids, is easier generally speaking since their scope is much more limited and the measures more clearly defined. In this field also, the Commission undertook to clarify and publicise its policy by a communication to the Council describing the general principles in industry aids and outlining

Principles was sent to the Council on December 21, 1978 (O.J. 1979, L 311/9); as in the past, the principles have five main aspects (see Eighth Competition Report 116 *et seq.*):
are divided into four categories: (a) the least developed regions: Ireland, the Mezzogiorno, Northern Ireland, Berlin and the French Overseas Departments; the ceiling is 75 per cent. of investment or 13,000 EUA per job created. No ceiling was set for Greenland because of its special situation; (b) development regions in France, Italy and Northern Ireland, where the ceiling is 30 per cent. of initial investment or 5,500 EUA per job created subject to an overall ceiling of 40 per cent. of initial investment; (c) the Zonenrandgebiet in Germany and North Jutland and certain islands of Denmark: ceiling 25 per cent. or 4,500 EUA per job with an overall ceiling of 30 per cent.; (d) all the other development areas, *i.e.* the more central and industrialised regions of the Community: ceiling 20 per cent. or 3,500 EUA, subject to an absolute ceiling of 25 per cent.;

(2) *transparency*: some progress was made here, since all forms of aid can, at least, be calculated now; the common method of evaluating regional aids was first based entirely on fixed investment; an alternative denominator, expressed in EUA per job created by the investment, was introduced, subject, however, to an overall ceiling expressed as a percentage of the initial investment;

(3) *regional specificity*: refers mainly to the necessity of a clear definition of the assisted areas based upon the respective nature, acuteness and urgency of the socio-economic problems prevailing in the region;

(4) *sectoral repercussions*: methods are being worked out to assess and control the incidence of regional aids on various industrial sectors; in case of overcapacity, for instance, limitation or exclusion of all aids including regional aids must be possible (see, *e.g.* synthetic fibres, Seventh Competition Report, 164);

(5) *system of supervision*: supervision is carried out by the Commission by means of *a posteriori* communications submitted to it concerning the most significant cases of application, *i.e.* investments above 4 million EUA when they consist of creation or extension entailing the creation of new jobs or 3 million EUA in other cases.

[32] See, *e.g.* Dec. concerning the Belgian Law on Economic Expansion (J.O. 1972, L 105/13).

the specific criteria used in the scrutiny of national schemes.[33] Guidelines have also been developed in particular where an industry is in a crisis or where the Community industry is insufficiently competitive to take advantage of rapid growth in world demand; this is the case for shipbuilding,[34] textiles,[35] man-made fibres[36] and steel.[37]

(iii) *General aid schemes.* A general aid is a measure granting assistance to undertakings but which is not justified by the need to develop the region where the undertaking invests or to restructure the industry to which the undertaking belongs. These schemes do not fall within one of the categories provided for by the Treaty as being suitable to be considered compatible with the common market. The Commission, therefore, is unable to take a definitive

[33] O.J. 1979, L 31/9 and Eighth Competition Report 132.
The Commission policy on industry aids is based on the rules of the Treaty which aim to ensure that competition is not distorted; unilateral granting of aid by Member States endangers the functioning of the common market; however, in many cases, aid is justified because it contributes to the achievement of the Community's economic and social aims. Aid should be authorised when it is needed to correct serious regional imbalances, to encourage or speed up certain essential changes or developments in certain industries, to permit smooth cutbacks in certain activities when this is desirable for social reasons or to neutralise certain distortions of competition due to action outside the Community. On the basis of these principles the Commission has developed the following criteria against which it examines the sectoral aid proposals notified to it:
(i) aid should be limited to cases when it is justified by circumstances within the industry concerned;
(ii) aid should lead to restoration of long-term viability rather than preserving the *status-quo*;
(iii) since adjustments take time, a limited use of resources to reduce the social and economic costs of change is admissible;
(iv) unless granted for a short period, aid should be progressively reduced and clearly linked to restructuring;
(v) the intensity of the aid should be proportionate to the problem it is designated to resolve;
(vi) industrial problems and unemployment should not be transferred from one Member State to another as a consequence of aid.

[34] Four successive Directives were issued by the Council, see Eighth Competition Report 135.

[35] General principles for the textile industry were elaborated in 1971 and refined and extended to 1976 (First Competition Report 144 and Sixth Competition Report 134).

[36] Request to the Member States for appropriate measures (Seventh Competition Report 164).

[37] General principles adopted in 1977 (Seventh Competition Report 204).

position on such aid schemes and requires the Member States, when applying these schemes, to notify in advance either the regional or sectoral programmes adopted to implement them, or failing this, the significent cases of aid grants.[38]

It is clear that in the field of state aids the Commission has been given wide powers to ensure that the measures, which the Member States intend to implement to achieve national, regional and industrial objectives, do not jeopardise the Community's endeavours to ensure that the aims set out in the Treaty are attained.

Conclusion with regard to the competition policy. The Community competition policy must be seen, not as an end in itself, but as an effective instrument in the hands of the Commission to ensure that the objectives set out in the Treaty are attained. The prohibitions provided by the Articles 85 and 86 are of course of great importance, and logical interpretation as much as systematic application is an essential requirement for the indispensable legal certainty. Furthermore, without the knowledge that the rules are strictly and objectively implemented, it will not be possible to convince the undertakings operating within the common market that fulfilling the Treaty obligations is in their own interest as much as in the interest of the purchasers and consumers.

The same considerations apply of course to the incompatibility of state aids with the common market, the adjustment of state monopolies and the abolition of illegal measures in the case of public enterprises. The Member States have a right to know how the Commission intends to interpret and apply the relevant provisions and must have the assurance that the Commission will prosecute any failure of other Member States to comply with the Treaty obligations in this particularly sensitive field.

More important, however, are the discretionary powers vested in the Commission, especially by Articles 85 (3) and 92 (3). It is with its power to declare the prohibition of Article 85 (1) inapplicable in certain cases, that the Commission is in a position to pursue a real policy. Agreements, mergers, dominant positions, etc., tend to reinforce the competitive position of Community undertakings on the common market and on the world markets. Economic strength and technological progress require co-operation between

[38] Eighth Competition Report 151, which also describes a certain number of schemes approved by the Commission.

undertakings and between the latter and the public authorities. Similarly, by considering aids compatible with the common market under certain conditions, the Commission is able to develop, in close co-operation with the Member States, a Community structural policy which will contribute to the development of economic activities throughout the Community.

As will be seen *infra*, the policies developed through the implementation of the competition rules are further strengthened by the contributions from the financial instruments which the Community administers; mention should be made here of the orientation section of the agricultural fund, the regional fund, the social fund, the ECSC funds, the Community borrowing and loan facilities and the Euratom funds. The ultimate goal of all these policies and instruments is the same: *i.e.* to strengthen the structure of the regions and Community industry. It is essential to keep all this in mind in order to see the competition rules in their true relation to Community objectives.

9. Regional policy

Regional policy is not explicitly provided for under the Treaty[39] since, at the time the Treaty was drafted, it was assumed that the differences existing between the various regions, if not eliminated would at least be strongly reduced by the functioning of the common market. At the time the Treaty was signed[40] there were only two areas within the Community of the Six which presented serious underdevelopment or other economic problems: The Mezzogiorno in Italy and the Zonenrandgebiet in Germany. Some provisions had furthermore been made for the development of these areas: the European Investment Bank was to provide the necessary resources for "developing less developed regions,"[41]

[39] There are, however, some indications in the Treaty referring to the problems of certain regions: the fifth para. of the Recitals: "anxious to strengthen the unity of their economies and to ensure their harmonious development by reducing the differences existing between the various regions and the backwardness of the less favoured regions"; Art. 2 refers to the promotion of a harmonious development of economic activities "throughout the Community" and also Art. 92 (3) provides that aids granted by States may, as an exception to the general rule, be considered to be compatible with the common market when they are intended "to promote the economic development of areas where the standard of living is abnormally low or where there is serious underemployment."

[40] March 25, 1957.

[41] EEC, Art. 130 (*a*): those regions were understood to be in the South of Italy.

while the Treaty provided the possibility to grant State aids to the above-mentioned German regions.[42] More important, however, was the fact that the functioning of the common market, with the resulting development of economic activities, continuous and balanced expansion and accelerated raising of the standard of living, would more or less automatically eliminate the problems caused by the regional disparities.

After all, although they were less developed, less favoured or even backward, these areas had two great advantages: large reserves of manpower much in demand for an expanding industry, and vast expanses of land at a time when the central, industrialised areas were already suffering from excessive concentration.

The establishment, functioning and development of the common market achieved spectacular results in most of these areas as evidenced by a doubling and even trebling of the per capita income. This, however, was not sufficient within a Community where similar developments were taking place in the well developed areas. The result was that although the gap may not have widened between richer and poorer regions, it was kept relatively stable, depending on the method of calibration, *e.g.* GNP per inhabitant.[43] It goes without saying that such discrepancies are no longer politically or socially acceptable and create a major problem for the Community as a whole. On the one hand, it becomes increasingly difficult to achieve the required convergence of Member States' economic policies[44] as long as some of them—and their number has increased with enlargement—have to devote a large fraction of their GNP to the development of their less favoured regions, with all the economic consequences such as

[42] Art. 92 (2) provides that—as an exception to the principle of incompatibility of state aids with the common market—are nonetheless compatible "aid granted to the economy of certain areas of the Federal Republic of Germany affected by the division of Germany, in so far as such aid is required in order to compensate for the economic disadvantages caused by that division."

[43] It is generally admitted that the ratio in 1960 between the average income in Hamburg and Sicily was in the order of 3 to 1, the difference being 2; after the figure doubled for Hamburg to 6 and trebled in Sicily to 3, the difference increased by 50 per cent.

[44] See EEC, Art. 2: "progressively approximating the economic policies of the Member States"; Art. 6: "Member States shall . . . co-ordinate their respective economic policies" and Art. 145: "the Council shall . . . ensure co-ordination of the general economic policies of the Member States."

inflation, balance of payment problems and exchange rate fluctuations. A recent example is the European Monetary System (EMS), introduced in March 1979: the disciplines it implies in economic and monetary matters could not be accepted by the Member States with weak economies, *i.e.* those with regional problems, without "measures designed to strengthen the economies of the less prosperous Member States of the EMS," which consisted mainly in transfers of resources from the richer countries.[45]

On the other hand, regional imbalances within the common market may have a disruptive effect: Member States have shown dangerous tendencies to have recourse to protective measures where, for instance, low productivity and inflation have resulted in increased prices and diminished competitiveness for their industries.

It has even been argued that far from strengthening the unity of the economies and reducing the differences between the various regions, the functioning of the common market has increased the relative backwardness of the less favoured areas of the Community. It took the governments of the Member States many years to see the problem or at least to formally recognise it as such; and once it was recognised as a major problem it still took them several years before measures were taken to attempt to solve the problem. It was at the conference of Heads of State or of Government held in Paris in October 1972, that it was agreed that a high priority should be given to the aim of correcting the structural and regional imbalances which might affect the realisation of economic and monetary union.[46] They invited the Commission to present a report analysing the regional problems which arise in the enlarged Community and to put forward appropriate proposals. They undertook to co-ordinate their regional policies and invited the Community institutions to create a Regional Development Fund.[47]

A "Report on Regional Problems in the enlarged Community"[48] was presented to the Council in 1973, containing an analysis of the

[45] See *infra*, Economic and Monetary Policy and Bull. 12–1978, 12.

[46] Bull. 10–1972, 9.

[47] It was further stated that this fund would be set up before December 31, 1973, and would be financed from the Community's own resources from the beginning of the second phase of Economic and Monetary Union; it was also provided that interventions by the Fund should take place in conjunction with national aids.

[48] Bull. Suppl. 8/73. The report concluded that the main imbalances are to be found in (a) predominantly agricultural areas; (b) regions affected by industrial change,

regional problems and policy instruments; the same year the Commission sent a proposal for a regulation establishing a European Regional Development Fund[49] together with other proposals[50] and a draft decision establishing a Committee for Regional Policy which would facilitate the co-ordination of the regional policies of the Member States.

It is not unimportant to record the various facts and dates because it shows that the Commission responded immediately to the request of the 1972 Summit Conference and produced all the required proposals within an extremely short period of time, but it shows also that, despite official declarations and commitments at the highest level, there was no way of speeding up the decision-making process of the Council[51]; the time limit of December 31, 1973, decided upon in Paris was not met. Once again, a meeting of the Heads of Governments at Paris, in December 1974, decided that the European Regional Development Fund would be put into operation on January 1, 1975,[52] although at the Copenhagen Summit Conference in December 1973, the same Heads of Governments had decided that the Fund would be established on January 1, 1974.[53]

Notwithstanding all these commitments, it was not until March 1975 that the regulation establishing the Regional Fund was formally adopted by the Council[54] together with a decision setting up a Regional Policy Committee.[55]

i.e. marked by dependency on old industries; and (c) regions of structural unemployment.

[49] O.J. 1973, C 86.

[50] For more details see Bull. 10–1973, 13.

[51] One must, however, bear in mind that the developing economic crisis due partly to the increase in oil prices and the U.K. request for "renegotiation" of the terms of accession did nothing to simplify matters, although it could also be argued that as the general economic situation deteriorated the more urgent it became to provide for the less prosperous regions.

[52] Bull. 12–1974, 10. This Summit decided on the first endowment of this fund and the way the fund would be divided among the Member States.

[53] Seventh General Report (1973), 488 (7).

[54] Reg. 724/75 (O.J. 1975, L 73/1). This Reg. is based upon EEC, Art. 235. The creation of the Regional Fund required a modification of the Financial Regulation concerning the Community budget (O.J. 1975, L 73/45) and the financing of the first endowment of the Fund necessitated a regulation on the transfer of funds out of the appropriations held in reserve by the Agricultural Fund (O.J. 1975, L 73/8).

[55] O.J. 1975, L 73/47.

It is interesting to note that, although a Regional Fund was finally set up, no provisions were made to develop a Community Regional Policy. It appears, therefore, that in the first place the Regional Fund was seen as an instrument to transfer supplementary resources to the poorest regions of the Community, although the system of reimbursement to the Member States of their own regional aids which was laid down for the Fund contributions, totally defeated this purpose. Nothing proves that the principal recipients of the Fund resources used those grants to increase the financial aid allotted to the deprived areas. In the absence of a real Community policy, the Fund became, in most cases, merely a transfer of resources from the richer to the poorer Member States[56] although it is explicitly stated in the preamble to the Fund Regulation, that the Fund's assistance should not lead Member States to reduce their own regional development efforts, but should complement these efforts.

However, since the regulation was to be re-examined after three years, the Commission was asked to make at that time the "appropriate proposals for the Community's regional policy."[57] The importance of this provision should be emphasised, because it implies that the Community itself has a responsbility for the elimination of unacceptable regional differences and, consequently that the Member States not only have lost their exclusive sovereign rights in this field, but must in the future co-ordinate their national policies.

Proposals for a Community regional policy,[58] together with amendments to the existing Fund regulation, were forwarded by the Commission to the Council in July 1977.[59] Due to difficulties encountered with the introduction in the Fund of the proposed quota free section, *i.e.* which would not be submitted to repartition of resources in national quotas, and because of a conflict which arose between the European Parliament and the Council with

[56] An exception are Fund grants for infrastructure which, as in the U.K., go directly to the local authorities which finance them, although these amounts are deducted from the borrowing ceiling of those authorities.

[57] Reg. 724/75, Art. 2 (2).

[58] Bull. Supp. 2/77: "Community Regional Policy: New Guidelines."

[59] O.J. 1977, C 161/11.

regard to the Fund's endowment for the period 1978–1980[60] and the modification of the existing regulation,[61] it was not until February 1979, that the amendments were formally accepted by the Council, together with a resolution concerning the guidelines for a Community regional policy.

COMMUNITY REGIONAL POLICY

The Commission felt that a few simple, positive actions were required as a first step towards a Community Regional policy, rather than lengthy and general statements of intention; consequently, it proposed to initiate measures along the following lines and asked the Council to endorse these policies in the form of a resolution; this summarises the actions proposed by the Commission.

(1) *Comprehensive analysis* of the evolution of the socio-economic situation in all the Community regions: regional policy is an integral part of economic policy and the comprehensive system of analysis will make it possible to establish a common basis of assessment of the problems at Community level.[62]

[60] At its meeting of December 1977, the European Council agreed on the endowment of the Regional Fund for the period 1978–1980 for a total of 1.850 million EUA, notwithstanding the fact that the Council had previously agreed with Parliament that the Fund resources would be considered as non-obligatory Community expenditure and, consequently, fall within the exclusive competence of Parliament. At the end of 1977, when the Community budget comprising the Fund expenditure of the first of the three years period had to be approved, Parliament increased slightly the amount fixed by the European Council, but a year later a real conflict emerged when Parliament decided on a Fund endowment of a billion EUA as against the 620 decided upon by the European Council; the final endowment was 945. A new conflict threatens with the 1980 budget, although the Council itself has proposed the sum of 850, thereby accepting that the ceiling set by the European Council does not hold.

[61] The delay with the adoption of the regulation amending Reg. 724/75 was partly caused by the protracted discussions between the Council and the Parliament during the conciliation procedure (see *supra* under European Parliament); Parliament wanted the Council to accept many more of the Commission's proposals, *inter alia*, a large quota free section, simpler procedures and advances.

[62] The finding of this analysis will be the object of a report to be sent to the Council every two and a half years, so as to coincide alternate years with the presentation of the Community's medium-term economic policy programme. The first report should be presented in 1980.

(2) *Assessment of the regional impact* of all Community policies: it is obvious that all Community policies have regional implications, particularly as regards employment; consequently, the Commission decided to take a more systematic account of these implications when formulating and implementing those policies. This approach must not, however be understood in a negative way, *i.e.* the avoidance of measures and action which have a detrimental effect on some regions. In the first place such actions might be required, despite negative regional consequences, but in those cases the Community should endeavour to counteract the unfavourable results by positive intervention: this is the purpose of the quota-free section of the Regional Fund. In the second place, however, it is even more essential that all Community policies and measures do contribute actively to the solution of regional problems and thereby to the reduction of the regional imbalances within the Community. To this end the Commission now applies the Regional Impact Assessment (R.I.A.), whenever possible.

(3) *Co-ordination of national regional policies* is essential to achieve a progressive, balanced distribution of economic activities throughout the Community. For the practical implementation of this, the Commission can not only rely upon the Regional Policy Committee, whose main task it is to ensure such co-ordination, but now it also has at its disposal regional development programmes established by the Member States according to a joint plan.[63] It should be noted that an investment may only benefit from the Fund Assistance if it falls within the framework of a regional development programme. There is, therefore, a formal link between

[63] O.J. 1976, C 69/2. In accordance with Reg. 724/75, Art. 6 these programmes were transmitted to the Commission by the end of 1977 for all regions eligible for assistance from the Fund. The programmes were examined by the Commission's staff, supplemented and then submitted to the Regional Policy Committee, which gave its opinion in June and October (Bull. 6–1978, 9 and 40 and 10–1978, 38). The Commission then expressed its opinion concerning the programmes and made recommendations to the Member States, both as to the contents of the programmes and future actions in the field of regional policy (O.J. 1979, L 143/7 and 9). A summary and a comparative analysis was published by the Commission (Studies-Series Regional Policy, No. 15).

these programmes and the working of the Regional Development Fund which will be examined briefly.

(2) EUROPEAN REGIONAL DEVELOPMENT FUND (ERDF)[64]

To execute its regional policy, the Community has two instruments at its disposal: the Regional Fund and the Regional Policy Committee. Although the European Parliament and the Commission consider the Fund's endowment to be insufficient, it plays a major role in carrying out the regional policy both of the Community and the Member States. Except for five per cent. the resources are distributed among the Member States according to quotas fixed in the regulation.[65]

The Fund was set up to help correct the regional imbalances within the Community which have resulted in particular from the predominance of agriculture, industrial change and structural unemployment. The main part of the Fund's resources is used to support regional policy measures taken by the Member States. Fund contributions are therefore limited to investments in industry and infrastructure located in regions and areas designated by Member States in applying their own systems of regional aids.

The Fund's assistance is decided upon by the Commission, generally speaking after seeking the opinion of the Fund Committee,[66] and in certain cases the Regional Policy Committee. Member States submit requests for assistance in the form of individual projects. The contribution from the Fund may either supplement aid granted to the relevant investment by national authorities or be credited to those authorities and considered as a partial repayment of such aid.[67]

[64] An updated version of Reg. 724/65 establishing a European Regional Development Fund was published in O.J. 1979, C 36/1. The amendments were introduced by Reg. 214/79 (O.J. 1979, L 35/1).

[65] Art. 2 (3) (*a*); the main beneficiaries are Italy (39.39 per cent.), the U.K. (27.03), France (16.86) and Ireland (6.46); calculated per inhabitant Ireland gets by far the most out of the ERDF. The receipts of the other Member States are purely symbolic: Belgium 1.39 per cent., Denmark 1.20, Germany 6, Luxembourg 0.09 and Netherlands 1.58.

[66] The Fund Committee can be compared to an agricultural management committee, see *supra* p. 61.

[67] All Member States have to date chosen the second alternative with the result that the money paid out by the Fund is practically always kept by the national exchequers thus making it virtually impossible to check whether the Fund resources do indeed increase the financial assistance to the regions.

Of great importance is the introduction of the "quota free" section: the resources thus available may be used to finance specific Community regional development measures as opposed to national development measures; these measures must be linked with Community policies and with measures adopted by the Community in order to take better account of their regional dimension or to reduce their regional consequences.[68] An interesting aspect of the quota free section is that the resources will be allocated on the basis of special programmes rather than individual projects.

THE REGIONAL POLICY COMMITTEE

As mentioned above, this Committee was set up with a view to contributing to the co-ordination of the regional policies of the Member States; its mandate, however, is much larger since its task is to examine problems relating to the regional development progress that has been made or will be made towards solving the problems and the regional policy measures needed to further the achievement of the Community's regional objectives.[69] In practice, the Committee fulfills a role comparable in certain ways to that of the Committee of Permanent Representatives: it expresses the views of the governments of the Member States on various questions related to regional development. On the other hand, it endeavours to have the opinion of the committee accepted by the national administrations. In other words, it constitutes a vital link between the national and the Community view.

CONCLUSION

Community regional policy is still in the developing stage: the very first steps have just been taken to arrive at a comprehensive approach to the problems created by the regional discrepancies within the Community. The means to implement such a policy are still extremely modest but the foundations have been laid which

[68] In October 1979, the Commission made its first proposals for the utilisation of the non-quota resources; the first is linked with the future enlargement of the Community and aims at preparing the most exposed regions to make the necessary structural adaptations, three take into account the decline in the steel industry and in shipbuilding and the energy problem and the last provides for cross-border development in Ireland and Northern Ireland.

[69] Dec. 75/185 Art. 2 (O.J. 1975, L 73/47).

will allow the Community to remedy one of its most dramatic shortcomings.

10. Industrial policy

If undertakings are the object of explicit Treaty provisions such as those concerning the right of establishment, the freedom to provide services and the free movement of capital on the one hand, and those concerning competition on the other, there is no reference to industry in the Treaty.[70] It is true, of course, that two objectives of the Treaty are the development of economic activities and balanced expansion, both of which are normally the result of industrial growth, but the drafters of the Treaty obviously did not see the need for Community intervention in the growth and adaptation process of industry at large. However there are two exceptions: (i) the coal and steel industry which falls within the ambit of the European Coal and Steel Community which has its own objectives and policies for achieving them[71]; and (ii) atomic energy and its uses in industry, the development of which is promoted by the Euratom Treaty.[72]

This corresponded to the more or less liberal conceptions prevailing with regard to economic policies at that time and which find their expression in the fundamental freedoms, which constitute the characteristics of the common market reinforced by the rules of competition. This was feasible as long as the economies of the Member States continued to develop, but as soon as the recession of the seventies set in, certain industries supported by a number of Member States requested Community intervention. Although the Heads of State or Government in 1972 considered it necessary to seek to establish a single industrial base for the community as a whole,[73] and agreed that objectives will need to be defined and the

[70] The only exception being a reference to "economic activities" in Art. 92 (3) which provides that aid to facilitate the development of certain economic activities may be considered by the Commission as compatible with the common market, notwithstanding the general principle of incompatibility of state aids with the common market.

[71] See *supra*, Chap. 4, the Coal and Steel Community.

[72] See *supra*, Chap. 4, Euratom.

[73] Communiqué issued at the Paris Summit of 1972 (Bull. 10–1972, 19) which referred to the removal of technical barriers to trade and elimination, particularly in the fiscal and legal fields, of barriers which hinder closer relations and merger between firms, the rapid adoption of a European company statute, the progress-

development of a common policy in the field of science and technology ensured and that "appropriate means should be drawn up by the Community's institutions before January 1, 1974,"[74] no comprehensive industrial policy was decided upon.

Instead various limited measures were adopted which were applicable either to industry as a whole, *e.g.* public contracts,[75] or more specifically to certain sectors. The latter approach became the only possible one. Over the years the Community adopted measures mainly to regulate and sometimes to help the reconversion of specific industries in crisis, such as steel, shipbuilding, textiles, footwear[76] or to encourage the development of new technology such as data processing and electronics, aerospace and telecommunications.[77]

It is doubtful whether the Member States will ever agree to transferring wider powers with regard to industry as a whole to the Community institutions.

11. Tax provisions and VAT

INDIRECT TAXES

The objective of the Treaty provisions concerning taxation[78] is to prevent any discrimination in taxation between imported products and products originating within a Member State. As was explained, the basic freedom of movement of goods throughout the Community, obtained by the elimination of customs duties and quotas, would be meaningless without the other freedoms and furthermore, could be jeopardised by government intervention in other fields such as state monopolies, public enterprises and state aids and by actions of undertakings. The same applies to

ive and effective liberalisation of public contracts, the promotion on a European scale of competitive firms in the field of high technology, the transformation and conversion of declining industries, under acceptable social conditions.

[74] Thirteenth General Report (1979), 85–90.

[75] See Dir. 70/32 (J.O. 1970, L 13/1), Dir. 71/304 (J.O. 1971, L 185/1), Dir 71/305 (J.O. 1971, L 185/5) and Dir. 77/62 (O.J. 1977, L 13/1).

[76] Eleventh General Report (1977) 89 and 98, which also mentions the building industry, wood, paper and petrochemicals.

[77] See Thirteenth General Report (1979), 88.

[78] EEC, Arts. 95–99.

internal taxation[79]: it can be used as a powerful weapon to protect domestic products from competition by imported goods.

If to date, the common market is not yet a single market within which all products circulate freely as in a national market, this is mainly due to the existence of differences in taxation from one Member State to the other; if turnover taxes, excise duties and other forms of indirect taxation, including countervailing measures applicable to trade between Member States, had been harmonised as provided for by Article 99, there would no longer be any need for customs controls at the internal borders of the Community.[80]

On the basis of the mandate granted by this provision, the Commission submitted to the Council, *inter alia* proposals for directives concerning the introduction of a common value added tax system in all the Member States. Two directives were adopted in 1967.[81] The principle of VAT as defined in the first Directive, involves the application to goods and services of a general tax on consumption which is exactly proportional to the price of the goods and services, regardless of the number of transactions which take place during the production and distribution process before the stage at which tax is charged. This implies that on each transaction VAT will be calculated on the price of the goods or services chargeable at that stage, but that the VAT already paid on the various costs components must be deduced.

The second directive specifies the method of implementing the principle which is now uniformly applied in all the Member States; unfortunately, the Member States were allowed to determine the rate of the tax. The system was introduced on July 1, 1972.[82] Since a small part of the VAT revenues were to accrue to the Community

[79] The Court found that Art. 95 constitutes, in the field of taxation the indispensable foundation of the common market; after January 1, 1962 (beginning of the second stage) citizens within the Community can ask the national courts to enforce Art. 95 (1); in other words Art. 95 (1) has direct effect (Case 57/65 *Lütticke* v. *Hauptzollamt Sarrelouis* [1966] E.C.R. 205).

[80] This is, of course, a slightly exaggerated statement since the elimination of all border controls on goods implies harmonisation of all other legislative and administrative provisions which impose various requirements in the field of packaging, quality control, technical control, etc.

[81] O.J. 1967, 14 and 16; O.J. 1967, 1301 and 3.

[82] See however the Fourth Dir. on the introduction of VAT in Italy (J.O. 1971, L 283/41).

as own resources,[83] the Council issued a Sixth Directive establishing a common basis of assessment.[84]

DIRECT TAXES

The Treaty does not contain specific provisions regarding harmonisation of direct taxes, but Article 100 provides the necessary powers.[85] Several proposals for directives were submitted to the Council; very few were adopted,[86] notwithstanding the fact the Council and the representatives of the Member States recognised that harmonisation was necessary to achieve the effective liberalisation of movement of persons, goods, services and capital to accelerate economic integration.[87]

12. Economic and monetary policy

The economy is one of the main responsibilities of the European Economic Community; the Treaty itself calls for "the application of procedures by which the economic policies of Member States can be co-ordinated and disequilibria in their balances of payments remedied"[88] and provides for measures to be taken by the institutions and the Member States with regard to conjunctural policy,[89] balance of payments[90] and commercial policy.[91] Mention should be

[83] See *infra*: Financing Community Activities, p. 218.
[84] O.J. 1977, L 145/1; see also Thirteenth General Report (1979), 107.
[85] See Programme for the harmonisation of direct taxes, Bull. 1967, Supp. 8.
[86] See, *e.g.* Twelfth General Report (1978) 121.
[87] Resolution of March 22, 1971 (J.O. 1971 (28/1)).
[88] EEC, Art. 3 (*g*).
[89] EEC, Art. 103. Several Regs. Dirs. and Decs. were issued in pursuance of this provision; see, *e.g.* Dec. 74/120 (O.J. 1974, L 63/16) on the attainment of a high degree of convergence of the economic policies of the Member States; the guidelines provided therein were adjusted several times; see Dec. 80/67 adopting the annual report on the economic situation in the Community and lying down the economic policy guidelines for 1980 (O.J. 1980, L 17/20).
[90] EEC, Arts. 104–109. The most used provisions are those of Arts. 105 (co-ordination of economic policy), see, *e.g.* Dec. 64/300 on co-operation between the Central Banks (J.O. 1964, 1206) and the programmes for medium term economic policy (O.J. 1977, L 101/1) and 108 (Community action in case a Member State is in difficulties as regard its balance of payments), see, *e.g.* Dec. 71/143 setting up a machinery for medium-term financial assistance (J.O. 1971, L 73/15) and Dec. 78/154 authorising the U.K. to take certain protective measures (O.J. 1978, L 45/30).
[91] Commercial policy will be examined *infra* under External Relations, p. 203.

made here of the programmes of the Council and the governments of the Member States on medium-term economic policy,[92] of the Monetary Committee which was set up to keep the monetary and financial situation of the Member States and the Community under review[93] and of the Annual Report on the Economic Situation in the Community adopted by the Council in pursuance of the decision of 1974 on the attainment of a high degree of convergence of the economic policies of the Member States.[94]

The measures provided in the Treaty do not of course constitute an overall Community policy in the economic and monetary field, nor is it certain that the Member States at this point are prepared to accept a Community policy replacing their own. However, the deterioration of the general economic situation has persuaded the member States that a greater convergence of the national economic and monetary policies was essential for their own survival and that of the Community.

CO-ORDINATION OF ECONOMIC POLICIES

Short-time economic and monetary policies have been co-ordinated over the years by the Commission and the Council working together, but here again a more comprehensive approach was required. At the European Council meeting in Copenhagen in April 1978, the Community agreed on a common economic policy strategy[95] in order to contribute to overall international action to promote world economic recovery and facilitate progress towards economic and monetary union. In the light of this agreement, it was felt by the Community institutions that "concerted action" would boost the multiplier effect of national measures and alleviate the balance-of-payments and public finance constraints which limit the scope of economic policy measures. This concerted action was in turn defined by the European Council in Bremen[96] and

[92] So far four programmes covering a five year period have been adopted; see J.O. 1967, 1513; 1969, L 129/1; 1971, L 49/1 and O.J. 1977, L 101/1.

[93] EEC, Art. 105 (2) and the rules governing the Monetary Committee (J.O. 1958, 390).

[94] See n. 89.

[95] Bull. 4–1978, 11. It was agreed that this common strategy would cover economic and monetary affairs, employment, energy, trade, industrial affairs and relations with the developing world.

[96] Bull. 6–1978, 17; the President of the European Council referred to "common approach" and "co-ordinated approach."

implemented by the institutions.[97] The aims were to achieve an appreciable increase in economic growth and to reduce unemployment by fighting inflation, ensuring greater monetary stability, stepping up international trade, making progress in the energy field, reducing regional disequilibria and activating demand in the Community.[98]

EUROPEAN MONETARY SYSTEM(S)[99]

At its Bremen meeting in July 1978, the European Council outlined a scheme for establishing closer monetary co-operation. This was the creation of a European Monetary System, leading to a zone of monetary stability in Europe. The Council asked that the detailed rules necessary for the functioning of such a system be worked out.[1] The discussion leading to the final adoption of the EMS centres on two key questions: the system itself and the actions needed to strengthen, under the system, the economies of the less prosperous Member States.

The final system had four main characteristics: a European monetary unit,[2] an exchange rate and intervention mechanism,[3]

[97] Dec. 78/658 O.J. 1978 L 220/27 and Bull. 7/8–1978, 22.

[98] Twelfth General Report (1978) 70. Under this concerted action guidelines were defined for the Thirteenth General Report (1979), 65.

[99] The analysis of the EMS and the Resolution of the European Council of December 5, 1978 concerning the establishment of a European Monetary System is extracted from the Twelfth General Report (1978) 76 *et seq*.

[1] Bull. 6–1978, 17.

[2] The European monetary unit, called ECU, is at the centre of the system; at present its value and composition are identical with those of the EUA. The ECU serves as a *numéraire* (each currency has a central rate expressed in this unit), as the basis for a "divergence indicator," as denominator for claims and liabilities, arising under the intervention mechanism and credit mechanism; finally it serves also as a means of settlement between the monetary authorities of the Community.

[3] The exchange rate and intervention mechanism borrows some of its features from the "snake" which it has replaced, but it involves major innovations. The central rates of the national currencies expressed in ECU are used to establish a grid of bilateral exchange rates around which 2.25 per cent. fluctuation margins are established, except for Italy and Ireland which were given a 6 per cent. margin during the initial phase. The intervention mechanism is supported by unlimited very short-term credit facilities. Settlements are made through the European Monetary Co-operation Fund (EMCF). To serve as a means of settlement, an initial supply of ECUs was provided by this Fund against the deposit of 20 per cent. of the gold reserves and 20 per cent. of the dollar reserves currently held by the Central Banks of the Member States.

a credit mechanism,[4] and a transfer mechanism.[5] The EMS came into operation on March 13, 1979.[6]

ECONOMIC AND MONETARY UNION

On the basis of a report drawn up by a committee under the chairmanship of Prime Minister and Minister of Finances of Luxembourg, Mr. Pierre Werner, the Council and the representatives of the governments of the Member States expressed their political will to establish an Economic and Monetary Union according to a plan starting in phases on January 1, 1971.[7] The final objective was the establishment of an area within which persons, goods, services and capital would move freely forming an individualised entity within the international system and having in the economic and monetary fields powers and responsibilities allowing its institutions to administer the union. Community instruments would be created whenever necessary. They also decided on the measures which were to be taken during the first stage ending on December 31, 1973.[8]

In 1972 the Council and the representatives of the governments of the Member States decided to establish the "snake." This restricted the maximum divergence between the currencies of any two Member States to 2.25 per cent. while the whole system would float against the dollar. They also decided on the establishment of the European Monetary Co-operation Fund.[9]

[4] The existing credit mechanisms: short-term monetary support and short-term and medium-term credit are maintained and strengthened. They will be consolidated into a single fund under the definitive arrangements.

[5] Under the transfer mechanism the new borrowing and lending instrument and the European Investment Bank make up to 1 million EUA per year available to Italy and Ireland on special conditions for the financing of selected infrastructure projects and programmes.

[6] See, Regs. 3180/78 and 3181/78, O.J. 1978, L 379/1 and 2.

[7] Resolution of March 22, 1971, J.O. 1971, C 28/1.

[8] These measures included: co-ordination of short-term economic policies, measures in the regional and structural field, co-ordination of monetary and credit policies, narrowing the fluctuations of exchange rates, etc.

[9] Reg. 907/73 (O.J. 1973, L 89/2). The Fund has legal personality and should promote the proper functioning of the "snake," interventions in Community currencies on the exchange markets and settlements between Central Banks leading to a concerted policy on reserves. The Fund is provisionally installed in Luxembourg.

If the first stage of the economic and monetary union was successfully implemented the deteriorating general economic situation prevailing at the end of 1973 made the transition to the second stage impossible. Notwithstanding this setback, achievement of the union remains a fundamental objective of the future.[10] Discussion of the objectives of economic and monetary union was revived in 1977 when the Commission presented a paper to the European Council entitled "The prospect of economic and monetary union"[11] on the basis of which the Commission also sent an action programme for 1978.[12] In preparing and implementing the measures of economic policy the Council and Commission are assisted by an Economic Policy Committee[13] and the European Institute for Economic and Social Policy Research.[14]

13. Social policy[15]

Apart from the extremely important measures provided by the Treaty concerning free movement of workers and related social security advantages, the Commission's task in the social field is wide and varied since it must promote co-operation between the Member States in matters relating to employment, labour law and working conditions, basic and advanced vocational training, social security, prevention of occupational accidents and diseases, occupational hygiene and the right of association, and collective bargaining between employers and workers.

The Treaty preamble indicates that the essential objective of the efforts of the Member States is the constant improvement of the living and working conditions of their peoples and in the enumeration of the activities of the Community, reference is made to the "creation of a European Social Fund in order to improve employ-

[10] However the expression was somehow dropped from the official vocabulary (see the General Reports 1974–1977) to be replaced by economic and monetary policies action; it reappeared again in 1977, see Eleventh General Report (1978), 74.

[11] Bull. 10–1977, 15.

[12] Bull. 2–1978, 16. The Commission proposes to act on three main points: (i) increased convergence of economies and economic policies; (ii) progress in the creation of a single competitive market and (iii) development of Community structural and social policies.

[13] Dec. 74/122 (O.J. 1974, L 63/21).

[14] See Twelfth General Report (1978), 78.

[15] EEC, Arts. 117–128.

ment opportunities for workers and to contribute to the raising of their standard of living."[16] The same objectives are repeated under the specific social provisions but this time not as a goal in itself but as a means to achieve their harmonisation. This constitutes an essential requirement for achieving economic integration within the European Community; in the previous sections much emphasis was placed on the uniformity of the common market, the convergence of the economic policies of the Member States, even economic and monetary union.[17] However, these objectives can only be achieved if the main differences which still exist within the Community are eliminated or reduced to acceptable proportions. In this respect regional discrepancies constitute a major obstacle to further integration and a threat to the internal cohesion of the EEC[18]; these regional differences are in turn best illustrated by the uneven distribution of income per head; it is therefore by closing the gap between the average income in the richer and in the poorer regions that real progress will be made towards European unification.

The draftsmen of the Treaty expressed the conviction that this would be achieved, *inter alia* through the functioning of the common market which would result in the harmonisation of social systems and approximation of other relevant legal and administrative provisions.[19] Their expectations were only partly fulfilled in that standards of living did rise considerably in the poorer regions, but they also did in the richer ones with the result that no harmonisation took place. As was pointed out in the section devoted to regional policy, market forces alone do not bring about, at least not under acceptable conditions, the necessary convergence. Public authorities must therefore intervene actively and, when necessary, with considerable financial means.

Of the various fields in which the Commission has the task to promote close co-operation between Member States, employment inevitably constitutes the most urgent one. The guiding principle for Community action in this domain is that social measures, *e.g.* national aids, intervention by the various Community funds, vocational readaptation, etc., should form an integral part of the indus-

[16] EEC, Art. 3 (*i*).
[17] See *supra*: Economic and Monetary Policy, p. 189.
[18] See *supra*: Regional Policy, p. 177.
[19] EEC, Art. 117, para. 2.

trial restructuring policy.[20] Here again[21] it may be said that social policy cannot be seen in isolation, but constitutes one aspect of the overall economic policy of the Community. Employment problems cannot be solved as such; job-creation is the result of investments which in turn are dictated by economic growth unless they are artificially induced through incentives. In times of economic recession most Member States rely very heavily on this method of direct intervention. The Commission paper examined at the fourth tripartite conference logically put forward an overall strategy involving in particular the stimulation of growth, intensified structural readaptation measures, besides certain work-sharing measures and, for the future, a greater role for the service sector.[22]

Nevertheless direct measures to support the categories worst hit by the recession were required and the Commission's action gave priority in particular to young people, women, migrants and workers affected by restructuring operations.[23]

With regard to *employment of women*, special reference should be made to several decisions of the Court interpreting the principle of equal treatment for men and women as regards pay, access to employment, vocational training and promotion, and working conditions.[24] In this field the other institutions of the Community also took several measures[25] including directives on equal treatment.[26]

Mention should also be made here of the impressive efforts of the Community in the field of *vocational training* together with the European Centre for the Development of Vocational Training.[27]

EUROPEAN SOCIAL FUND

The Treaty provides for the establishment of a European Social Fund in order to improve employment opportunities for workers

[20] Twelfth General Report (1978), 123.
[21] The same is true, *e.g.* for competition and regional policy; see *supra*.
[22] Twelfth General Report (1978), 124.
[23] For more details see the annual Reports on the development of the Social Situation in the Community published by the Commission together with the General Report, in pursuance of Art. 122.
[24] Case 80/70 *Defrenne* v. *Belgium* [1971] E.C.R. 445 and Case 43/75 *Defrenne* v. *Sabena* [1976] E.C.R. 455.
[25] See Commission publication: "Women and the European Community"; see also Eleventh General Report (1977), 127.
[26] Dir. 75/117 (O.J. 1975, L 45/19); Dir. 76/207 (O.J. 1976, L 39/40).
[27] See Eleventh General Report (1977), 123. See also the General Guidelines for a Community level programme on vocational training, J.O. 1971, C 81/5.

and thereby contribute to raising the standard of living. The objectives are the same as those mentioned earlier and the Fund constitutes the Community's financial instrument to achieve them. The Fund is administered by the Commission which is assisted by a Social Fund Committee composed of representatives of governments, trade unions and employers organisations. The Fund's resources are provided by the Community budget from the Community's own resources. The main function of the Fund is to reimburse Member States or public bodies for expenditure incurred for (a) vocational retraining and resettlement allowances and (b) unemployment benefits.

A new regulation came into operation in 1972[28] as the Council had decided to reform the Fund.[29] It was decided that the assistance provided for in Article 125 would no longer be granted and the Fund would take action in two instances: (1) when employment is affected by Community policies (Article 4); in those cases, the Council will decide on an *ad hoc* basis and (2) when unemployment is not brought about by Community measures, but results indirectly from the working of the common market or impedes the harmonious development of the Community (Article 5); in this case assistance is granted on the basis of implementing provisions by the Commission.[30]

Finally, *social protection* measures issued by the Community and measures regarding *living and working conditions* and *health and safety*[31] should be mentioned.

14. The European Investment Bank[32] (EIB)

The Treaty provides for the establishment of a European Investment Bank to facilitate the economic expansion of the Community by opening fresh resources.[33] In fact the Bank was mainly

[28] Reg. 858/72 on certain administrative and financial procedure for the operation of the European Social Fund (O.J. 1972, 353; J.O. 1972, L 101/3).

[29] Dec. 71/66 (O.J. 1971 52; J.O. 1979, L 28/15), amended by Dec. 77/801 (O.J. 1977, L 337/8).

[30] In 1979, the total budget of the Fund available for granting assistance came to 767.5 million EUA of which 306 million EUA were for Art. 4 operations and 461.5 million EUA for Art. 5. Thirteenth General Report (1979), 115.

[31] For all those measures see details in the annual Social Reports.

[32] EEC, Arts. 129–130 and Protocol on the Statute of the European Investment Bank annexed to the EEC Treaty.

[33] EEC, Art. 3 (*j*).

intended to provide financial resources for the economic development of Southern Italy, the Mezzogiorno. This is still the case, but other regions have been added, first by the enlargement of the Community in 1973 and secondly by the economic crisis of the 1970's. More than two thirds of the Bank's loans go to the development regions of the Community.[34]

The EIB has legal personality and its Members are the Member States.[35] Its statute is laid down in a Protocol annexed to the EEC Treaty. The EIB operates on a non-profit making basis; it grants loans and gives guarantees to facilitate the financing of all sectors of the economy. Decisions regarding these loans are taken by the Board of Directors on proposals from the Management Committee. However, before deciding on the financing of a project, the Bank must secure the opinion of the Commission; when the Commission delivers an unfavourable opinion, the Board of Directors may not grant the loan (or guarantee) unless its decision is unanimous (the director nominated by the Commission abstaining).

The Bank is directed and managed by a Board of Governors, a Board of Directors and a Management Committee.

The *Board of Governors* consists of the ministers of finance of the Member States; it lays down general directives for the credit policy of the Bank; it also decides on possible increases in the subscribed capital, on grants of special interest bearing loans to the Bank to finance specific projects by Member States and on the granting of loans for investment projects to be carried out entirely or partially outside the European territory of Member States.

The *Board of Directors* consists of 18 directors and 10 alternates nominated by each Member State and the Commission and appointed by the Board of Governors for five years.[36]

The *Management Committee* consists of a president and four

[34] EEC, Art. 130 provides that the Bank shall grant loans and give guarantees which facilitate the financing of "projects for less developed regions." In 1978, the Mezzogiorno alone attracted 1,958.9 million EUA or nearly 30 per cent. of the total finances for the Member States: EIB Annual Report 1978, 45.

[35] EEC, Art. 129.

[36] Protocol, Art. 11. Those figures will become 19 and 11 after Greek accession (Protocol No. 1, Art. 4 to the Greek Accession Treaty).

vice-presidents appointed by the Board of Governors on a proposal from the Board of Directors.[37]

Besides the loans to finance projects in less developed regions of the Community *the Bank provides loans from its own resources for*: large industrial projects, or projects of common interest to several Member States when those projects cannot be entirely financed by the means available in the individual Member States. The same kind of projects can also be financed from resources provided by the new borrowing and loan facilities of the Community[38] which are administered by the Bank. The Bank also provides loans for projects situated outside the territory of Member States either from its own resources[39] or under mandate, for the account and at the risk of individual Member States, the EEC or Euratom; they consist mainly in financial aid provided for under various agreements, financial protocols and decisions concerning Greece, Turkey, the African, Caribbean and Pacific States, the Overseas Countries and Territories (French) and Portugal, Yugoslavia and Lebanon.[40] The Bank also finances operations on special conditions and risk capital operations from the resources of Member States directly (Turkey) or through the intermediary of the European Development Fund[41] and accounted for under the Bank's special section.[42]

By the decision of the Board of Governors of June 19, 1978, the subscribed capital of the Bank was increased to 7,087,500 million units of account. The four larger Member States subscribe about one billion and a half each, Belgium and The Netherlands a little more than 400 million, Denmark 200, Ireland 50 and Luxembourg 10.

[37] The number of vice-presidents will be increased to five after Greek Accession (Protocol No. 1, Art. 6).

[38] This new instrument was set up in October 1978. Dec. 78/870 (O.J. 1978, L 298/9; see also Bull. 10–1978, 21) empowers the Commission to contract loans of up to 1,000 million EUA and to on-lend the proceeds for the purpose of financing investment projects that contribute to priority Community objectives with regard to energy, industry and infrastructure. The Commission decides which projects are eligible for assistance and the EIB acting in accordance with a general mandate, vets applications and grants the loans (Twelfth General Report 1978, 78). See also Thirteenth General Report (1979), 59.

[39] Between 1958 and 1979, the Bank loaned 1,165.8 million EUA outside the Community and 11,654.5 inside from its own resources.

[40] Between 1963 and 1978, loans granted in those regions amounted to 744.9 million EUA from the Bank's own resources.

[41] See *infra*, p. 212.

[42] Between 1963 and 1978: 575.7 million EUA. See EIB Annual Report 1978, 89.

Through its sound financial operations both inside and outside the Community the EIB has acquired a world-wide reputation as one of the major financial institutions for economic development.

15. External relations

The ECSC Treaty explicitly provides that in international relations the Community enjoys "the legal capacity it requires to perform its functions and attain its objectives."[43] No similar provision is to be found in the EEC Treaty which only states that "the Community shall have legal personality,"[44] but one can repeat here the words of the International Court of Justice concerning the United Nations Organisation: it is destined to exercise activities and enjoy rights which can only be explained if it possesses a large measure of international personality and the capacity to act on the international level.[45] This, together with the fact that the Community is a body created by international Treaty concluded between sovereign states, automatically confers upon it, albeit in a limited way, international legal personality. It should be noted that this has never been challenged by any State[46] and was explicitly recognised by the Court of Justice which stated that the fact that the Community has legal personality means that "in its external relations the Community enjoys the capacity to establish contractual links with third countries over the whole field of objectives defined in Part One[47] of the Treaty."[48] Thereby the Court defined

[43] ECSC treaty, Art. 6. This international legal personality is not therefore a full one, comparable to that of an independent State; it should be compared rather to the recognition of the United Nations Organisation by the International Court of Justice, see Annuaire 1948–49, 61.

[44] EEC treaty Art. 210. See also Euratom Treaty, Art. 184.

[45] Annuaire 1948, 49, 61.

[46] Even the U.S.S.R. have agreed after years of abstention to open negotiations with the Community as such. See Twelfth General Report 1978, 301.

[47] Part One of the EEC Treaty refers to the "Principles" and contains basic provisions such as Art. 2 which lays down the objectives of the Community and the means to attain them and Art. 3 which specifies some of the Community's activities.

[48] Case 22/70 *Commission* v. *Council* (AETR) [1971] E.C.R. at 274 (14). See, *e.g.* International Rubber Agreement, Court of Justice, Opinion 1/79 (October 4, 1979), Draft Convention of the International Atomic Energy Agency on the physical protection of nuclear materials, facilities and transports, Ruling 1/78 of the Court pursuant to Euratom Art. 103 (3) [1978] E.C.R. 2151 and Cases 3, 4 and 6/76 *Kramer* [1976] E.C.R. 1279 concerning the North-East Atlantic Fisheries Convention.

the extent, *ratione materiae*, of the competence of the Community in the treaty-making field: it mainly concerns commercial relations[49]; this logically follows from the economic nature of Community activities.[50] The Court also determined that the authority to conclude international agreements arises not only from an express conferment by the Treaty[51] but may equally flow, even implicitly, from other provisions of the Treaty[52] and from measures adopted within the framework of those provisions by the Community institutions.[53] To establish in a particular case whether the Community has the authority to enter into international commitments, the whole scheme of Community law must be considered as well as its substantive provisions.[54]

Having defined the scope of the Community's powers in this field, there remains the question of the relationship with the Treaty-making competence of the Member States. According to the Court, any problem in this domain must be resolved on the basis of the subject-matter of the agreement to be concluded. If it is a common commercial policy measure as prescribed by the Treaty, this policy having been conceived in the context of the operation of the common market, it cannot be accepted that the Member States should exercise a power concurrent to that of the Community, either in the Community sphere or in the international sphere. In such cases, therefore, the Community has exclusive power to participate in the relevant international agreement.[55]

Each time the Community, with a view to implementing a common policy envisaged by the Treaty, adopts provisions laying

[49] See EEC, Art. 3 (*b*) which refers to a "common commercial policy towards third countries."

[50] See Case 36/74 *Walrave* v. *Union Cycliste Internationale* [1974] E.C.R. at 1417 (4) where the Court determined that Community law only applies to economic activities within the meaning of Art. 2 of the Treaty.

[51] As is the case with Arts. 113 and 114 for tariffs and trade agreements and with Art. 238 for association agreements.

[52] See Opinion 1/76, *Fund for inland waterway vessels* [1977] E.C.R. 741 at 755 (4): the competence exists even when the internal power has not yet been used to adopt a common policy, but flows by implication from the provisions of the Treaty creating the internal power and in so far as the participation of the Community is necessary for the attainment of one of the objectives of the Treaty.

[53] Cases 3, 4 and 6/76, *Kramer* [1976] E.C.R. 1279 at 1308 (17/18).

[54] *Ibid.* at 19/20.

[55] Opinion 1/75 *OECD Local Cost Standard* [1975] E.C.R. 1355 at 1363. See also Opinion 1/78 *Nuclear Materials Convention* [1978] E.C.R. 2151.

down common rules, whatever form these may take, Member States, acting individually or even collectively, no longer have the right to undertake obligations with third countries affecting those rules. As and when such common rules come into being, the Community alone is in a position to assume and carry out contractual obligations towards third countries affecting the whole sphere of application of the Community legal system.[56]

In other fields where the Community enjoys the right to conclude agreements with third countries or international organisations, this right becomes exclusive from the moment it is exercised.[57] As long as this has not been done Member States have the power to assume commitments; however, this authority is only of a transitional nature and Member States are bound by Community obligations[58] in their negotiations: they are under a duty not to enter into any commitment which could hinder the Community in the carrying out of the tasks entrusted to it by the Treaty.[59]

No mention was made yet of other aspects of external relations such as the exchange of ambassadors, international representation or what is generally known as "foreign policies."

With regard to the first item: diplomatic relations with third countries, the only relevant Treaty provision is to be found in the Merger Treaty, in the Protocol on the privileges and immunities of the European Communities, where it is provided that the Member State in whose territory the Communities have their seat shall accord the customary diplomatic immunities and privileges to

[56] Case 22/70 *supra*, n. 48, at 274 (17–18). See also Opinion 1/76 *supra*, n. 52.

[57] See answer to Parliamentary question No. 173/77 (O.J. 1978, C 72/1).

[58] The Court referred in particular to EEC, Art. 5.

[59] Cases 3, 4 & 6/76 *supra*, n. 53, at 1310–1311. See *infra*: commercial policy through agreements. See also EEC, Art. 111 (4) obliging Member States to bring about adjustments of tariff agreements in force with third countries. See also EEC, Art. 234 which provides that the entry into force of the Treaty does not affect existing agreements concluded between one or more Member States and one or more third countries. If, however, such agreements are not compatible with the Treaty, the Member States concerned must take the appropriate steps to eliminate the incompatibilities. It would indeed be unacceptable if third countries, through previous agreements, were to enjoy the same advantages accorded by Member States to each other as part of the establishment of the Community without accepting at the same time the obligations and constraints resulting from such establishment.

missions of third countries accredited to the Communities.[60] Reference could also be made to the statements issued after the extraordinary Council session of January 28 and 29, 1966, held in Luxembourg where it is provided that credentials of Heads of Missions of non-Member States accredited to the Community will be submitted jointly to the President of the Council and to the President of the Commission, meeting together for this purpose.[61]

The representatives of the Commission in various third countries enjoy the same diplomatic immunities and privileges also; this is the case for the delegations to certain international organisations, *e.g.* the Commission delegations to the ACP countries, to the Southern Mediterranean countries, to the United Nations, and the OECD.[62] Without it being more explicitly provided in the Treaty, the Community thus exercises the right of active and passive legation.

With regard to foreign policy in general, mention was made in the section on the Council of what is referred to as "political co-operation"[63]; it was explained that it concerns co-operation between Member States in the field of foreign affairs.[64] Although within the general framework of the Community, it takes place at intergovernmental level, it does not, strictly speaking, constitute a Community foreign policy. Nevertheless, through its economic weight, the Community plays an ever-increasing role in world trade and on the international scene in general which is not adequately expressed by the Treaty provisions.

The complex network of relations which have been established over the years around the world by the Community can be grouped under the following headings: commercial policy, international organisations, industrialised countries, Mediterranean countries, developing countries, state trading countries and diplomatic relations.

[60] Protocol, Art. 17. For a list of the missions accredited to the Community see "corps diplomatique accrédité auprès des Communautés Europeénnes," D. G. External Relations.

[61] For text, see Sweet and Maxwell, *European Community Treaties* (4th ed.), p. 249.

[62] For a list of Commission delegations see Directory of the Commission.

[63] See *supra*, p. 50.

[64] See, *e.g.* Thirteenth General Report (1979), p. 271.

(1) *Commercial policy*

The Treaty provides for "the establishment of a common customs tariff and for a common commercial policy towards third countries,"[65] and the two are complementary. The common customs tariff was examined earlier in relation to the free movement of goods. A common commercial policy towards third countries implies the elimination of all tariffs within the Community, but this, in turn, requires a common customs tariff as a *conditio sine qua non* for a customs union.[66]

However, external tariffs also constitute one of the main instruments of commercial policy and indeed the duties of the common customs tariff can be lowered or raised according to the needs of commercial policy. There are two procedures for such modifications, the autonomous modification[67] and modifications through agreements with non-Member State countries.[68] For such agreements the Commission makes recommendations to the Council, which authorises the Commission to open the necessary negotiations.[69] In case the implementation of the common commercial policy were to lead to economic difficulties in a Member State, the Commission may authorise that state to take the necessary protective measures,[70] which can deviate from the provisions regarding free movement of goods.[71]

Mention must be made here of a Council decision of 1961 on the progressive standardisation of agreements concerning commercial relations between Member States and third countries in order to eliminate disparities existing between the arrangements of the

[65] EEC, Art. 3 (*b*).

[66] EEC, Art. 9 (1).

[67] EEC, Art. 28. See also Art. 25.

[68] EEC, Arts. 111 and 113, first para.; the latter provides that after the transitional period has ended, the common commercial policy shall be based on uniform principles, particularly in regard to changes in tariff rates, the conclusion of tariff and trade agreements, the achievement of uniformity in measures of liberalisation, export policy and measures with regard to trade to be taken in case of dumping or subsidies. See Cases 21, 24/72 *International Fruit Company* v. *Produktschap voor groenten en fruit* [1972] E.C.R. at 1227, where the Court found that the Community is bound by the provisions of the General Agreement for Tariffs and Trade.

[69] EEC, Art. 113 (3); these negotiations are conducted in close consultation with a special Committee appointed by the Council.

[70] EEC, Art. 115.

[71] Case 62/70 *Bock* v. *Commission* [1971] E.C.R. 897 at 909 (14).

various Member States with third countries.[72] On the basis of this decision the Commission examines the Member States' trade arrangements with non-Member countries to check them for compatibility with the Community's developing commercial policy.[73] The Council, acting on a proposal from the Commission, authorises Member States to renew or extend existing agreements. Another Council decision[74] established a consultation procedure for co-operation agreements to be concluded between Member States and third countries. Member States must inform the Commission and the other Member States of any agreement relating to economic and industrial co-operation, which they propose to negotiate or renew with third countries and of any commitments and measures proposed by the authorities of the Member States concerned as part of the co-operation agreements. The Commission and a Member State may request prior consultation to ensure that the agreements are consistent with common policies, to encourage co-ordination and to examine the advisability of unilateral action which should be taken by the Commission.

With regard to *imports* in general, various rules exist within the Community applicable to trade with State-trading countries[75] and to other non-Member countries.[76] All the measures taken by the Community institutions in this field concern further liberalisation, thereby confirming the basically liberal common commercial policy of the Community. The various regulations and decisions concerning imports establish freedom of import for a wide range of products.[77] They also allow, however, for supervision,[78] in order to guarantee that the imports of particular products will not prejudice the interests of the Community producers, and for the introduction of safeguard measures in the event of serious danger. The most important of those measures are those which can be imposed

[72] J.O. 1961, 1274 and O.J. 1959–1962, 84.
[73] See, *e.g.* O.J. 1978, L 44, L 123 and L 225.
[74] Dec. 74/393 O.J. 1974, L 208/23.
[75] See *infra*, p. 212 and Reg. 925/79 (O.J. 1979, L 131/1).
[76] For more details see the annual General Report and the Bulletin. For textile products, *e.g.* see Thirteenth General Report 1979, 27 and O.J. 1979, L 131/15.
[77] See Twelfth General Report 1978, 250 and Thirteenth (1979) 224.
[78] See, *e.g.* system of surveillance introduced on imports of footwear (O.J. 1978, L 188/28). See *ibid.* for voluntary restraint agreements concluded between the Community and third countries for iron and steel products, textile products and footwear.

by the Commission when applying the Community anti-dumping rules.[79] Several such procedures are initiated each year,[80] either at the request of Member States, any natural or legal person, or any association, not having legal personality, acting on behalf of a Community industry, which considers itself injured or threatened by dumping. The Commission may then apply an anti-dumping duty on the dumped products. Other specific measures of commercial policy have been taken by the Community institutions for various products, namely to ensure that the internal arrangements operate properly[81] or to counteract protectionist measures adopted by certain industrialised countries.[82]

Where *exports* are concerned, the principle of freedom of export for almost all the headings of the common external tariff was established by the Council in 1969.[83] Community quantitative exports quotas for certain products are fixed by the Council, sometimes on a yearly basis.[84] Another important item of commercial policy is to be found in the export credit system, with or without insurances or guarantees, applied by the various Member States. In October 1970, the Council adopted two directives concerning the introduction by Member States of common insurance policies for medium and long-term transactions based on suppliers credit and intended for public and private buyers.[85] Various other directives and decisions were adopted by the Council in an effort to harmonise the policies of the Member States in this field.[85a]

[79] See Reg. 459/68 on protection against dumping or the granting of bounties or subsidies, by non-Member countries (O.J. 1968, 80; J.O. 1968, L 93/1) based upon EEC, Arts. 111, 113 and 227. This Reg. was recently codified by Reg. 3017/79 (O.J. 1979, L 339/1). See Case 113/77 R *NTN TOYO* v. *Council* [1977] E.C.R. 1721; Case 119/77 R *Nippon Seiko* v. *Council and Commission* [1977] E.C.R. 1867 and Case 121/77 R *Nachi Fuyikoshi* v. *Council* [1977] E.C.R. 2107.

[80] See, *e.g.* Thirteenth General Report 1979, 26.

[81] See, *e.g.* for iron and steel products, Thirteenth General Report 1979, 26.

[82] See, *e.g.* for footwear, Twelfth General Report 1978, 255.

[83] Reg. 2603/69 establishing common rules for exports (O.J. 1969, 590; J.O. 1969, L 324/25); for an updated version of the Annex, see O.J. 1975, C 287/50.

[84] See Reg. 915/78 (O.J. 1978, L 119/9).

[85] Dirs. 70/509 and 70/510 (O.J. 1970, 762 and 782; J.O. 1970 L 254/1 and 26).

[85a] See, *e.g.* Dir. 71/86 on harmonisation of basic provisions in respect of guarantees for short-term transactions (political risk) (O.J. 1971, 71; J.O. 1971, L 36/14) and Dec. 73/391 on consultation and information procedure in matters of credit, insurance, credit guarantees and financial credits (O.J. 1973, L 346/1).

(2) *International organisations*

The Commission is instructed by the Treaty to maintain such relations as are appropriate with all international organisations[86] and especially with the organs of the General Agreement for Tariffs and Trade,[87] the organs of the United Nations and its specialised agencies,[88] the Council of Europe[89] and the Organisation for Economic Co-operation and Development.[90]

(a) GENERAL AGREEMENT FOR TARIFFS AND TRADE

After the Kennedy Round of trade negotiations of 1967, in which the EEC played a major role,[91] the Community participated actively in the Tokyo Round of multi-lateral trade negotiations which started in 1973.[92] The final package of negotiated agreements provides for cuts in industrial and agricultural tariffs and the strengthening of the GATT rules by drawing-up a series of "codes" in non-tariff fields such as public contracts and subsidies. Implementation of such agreements comes within the sphere of the common commercial policy.[93]

(b) UNITED NATIONS

The Community, represented by the Commission, participates as observer in the meetings of the General Assembly, while the position of the Member States on the main issues debated at the U.N. is generally set out by the President of the Council of the European Communities. The Community also participates actively in the work of all the specialised agencies of the U.N.[94]

[86] EEC, Art. 229, second para.
[87] EEC, Art. 229, first para.
[88] *Ibid.*
[89] EEC, Art. 230. [90] EEC, Art. 231.
[91] See Tenth EEC General Report (1966), para. 310 and First General Report (1967), 381.
[92] See Bull. 4–1979, 8 *et seq.*
[93] *Supra*, p. 203; see also Dec. 80/271 (O.J. 1980, L 71/1).
[94] The Economic and Social Council, the Economic Commission for Europe, the Economic and Social Commission for Asia and the Pacific, the United Nations Conference on Trade and Development, the United Nations Industrial Development Organisation, the World Food Council, the Food and Agricultural Organisation (FAO), the International Labour Organisation, UNESCO, the IMF and International Bank for Reconstruction and Development, the World Intellectual Property Organisation, the International Atomic Energy Agency, the GATT and the United Nations Conference on Technical Co-operation among Developing

(c) ORGANISATIONS FOR ECONOMIC CO-OPERATION AND DEVELOPMENT

As the Commission points out "the OECD continued to be the forum *par excellence* where the industrialised Western countries could exchange views on the major economic problems of the world and together work out solutions to some of them.[95] The annual ministerial meetings are attended by the Commission, which furthermore participates regularly in the work of the various OECD committees.

(d) OTHER ORGANISATIONS

Agreements of co-operation were also concluded by the Commission with the Committee of Ministers of the Council of Europe,[96] the Central Commission for the Navigation of the Rhine[97] and the International Bureau of Weights and Measures.[98]

(3) *Industrialised Countries*

On January 1, 1973, after the first enlargement of the Community, free trade agreements with Austria, Switzerland, Portugal and Sweden came into force. Similar agreements were concluded with Iceland, Norway and Finland, this completing the series of Agreements between the Community and EFTA countries.[99] Trade regulations with the United States, Japan, Canada, Australia and New Zealand are not regulated by special agreements,[1] but intensive contacts between the parties concerned are aimed at eliminating problems resulting from low-priced imports from those countries into the Community, especially, agricultural products. The imbalance of trade with most of those countries also creates problems.[2]

Countries. For details see the annual General Report and the Bulletin, *e.g.* Thirteenth General Report (1979), 242 *et seq*.

See also Convention between the EEC and the U.N. Relief and Works Agency for Palestine Refugees (UNWRA) (O.J. 1976, L 203/40).

[95] Twelfth General Report 1978, 272.

[96] Not yet published.

[97] J.O. 1961, 1027.

[98] J.O. 1966, 614.

[99] For a summary of those agreements, see Sixth General Report 1972, 22 and Seventh General Report 1973, 400.

[1] With Canada the Community concluded a framework Agreement for commercial and economic co-operation in 1976 (O.J. 1976, L 260/1). See also Tenth General Report (1976) 276.

[2] For further details, see, *e.g*. Thirteenth General Report (1979), 248 *et seq*. and Bull.

(4) *Mediterranean countries*

Because of their geographical proximity to the Community, the countries of the Mediterranean basin are of extreme importance to the development of trade. From the outset, systems were set up to deal pragmatically with trade, to help improve the organisation of markets and production, and the commercial and tariff machinery. However, the disparity of these systems created difficulties. At the Paris Summit of October 19 and 20, 1972, it was stated therefore by the Heads of State or Government that the Community attaches essential importance to honouring its commitments towards the Meditterranean countries with whom agreements have been or are to be made, agreements which require an overall and balanced handling."[3] The Council decided to examine a global approach to the problems arising in the region and, on the basis of a Commission proposal, worked out the substance of a general Community policy towards the Mediterranean countries, covering trade, economic, technical and financial co-operation and also co-operation on labour. This "global approach" did not meet with great enthusiasm from the three Maghreb countries (Algeria, Morocco and Tunisia), Spain and Israel which were the first to be approached by the Commission on this subject. However, the Community pursued its efforts and over the years concluded agreements with all the countries of that region.

Mention must be made here in the first place of the association agreements which are explicitly provided for in the Treaty[4] and which may involve reciprocal rights and obligations, common action and special procedures. Several of such association agreements were concluded with various Mediterranean countries, but, a distinction must be made between those associations which constitute a prelude to membership of the Community (Greece and Turkey) and the others (Cyprus, Malta, Morocco and Tunisia). The association agreement with Greece[5] will end on Greek accession, which leaves the association with Turkey[6]. In 1978, it was

[3] Bull. EC 10–1972, p. 9.

[4] EEC, Art. 238.

[5] The association agreement with Greece was signed in 1961 (J.O. 1963, 294/63; O.J. 1974 (2nd) I, 1).

[6] The association agreement with Turkey was signed in 1963 (J.O. 1964, 3687). The relations with the EEC are essential for Turkey: 40 per cent. of its exports were at that time destined for the Community from which 30 per cent. of all its imports came. Before a customs union could be created with this country the latter had to

decided to do everything possible to reactivate and consolidate the association, particularly in view of the enlargement of the Community.[7] Besides the association agreements with Greece and Turkey, agreements were concluded with Cyprus,[8] Malta,[9] the Maghreb countries,[10] Yugoslavia,[11] Israel,[12] the Mashreq countries[13] (Egypt, Jordan Lebanon, Syria), Spain[14] and Portugal,[15] which leaves Libya and Albania as the only Mediterranean countries not connected in one way or another with the Community.

(5) *Developing countries*

The main feature of the Community policy towards developing countries is the ACP-EEC agreement,[16] which establishes commercial, industrial and financial relations with 57 African, Caribbean and Pacific countries on the one hand and the Community and the nine Member States on the other. This relationship grew out of a quite different set of links, which existed at the time of signature of the EEC Treaty, between most of those ACP countries and several Member States. The Treaty provides for "the association of the overseas countries and territories in order to increase

accelerate its industrialisation, modernise its agriculture and improve its infrastructure. Therefore, various phases were provided for in the agreement to progressively achieve the objectives of the association with the financial help of the Community. An Association Council has limited powers of decision and possible conflicts should be solved through arbitration; finally contacts are instituted with Parliament and the Economic and Social Committee.

[7] Twelfth General Report (1978), 281. See also Bull. EC 5–1979, 87; the third EEC–Turkey Financial Protocol, signed on May 12, 1977, came into force on May 1, 1979. O.J. 1979, L 67/14. It provides for 310 million EUA to be committed by October 31, 1981.

[8] O.J. 1973, L 133/1; the agreement was completed by various protocols, see Twelfth General Report 1978, 281 and Thirteenth (1979), 255.

[9] J.O. 1971, L 61/1; see also Bull. 3–1976 and Bull. 9–1978.

[10] Algeria, O.J. 1978, L 263/1; Morocco, O.J. 1978, L 264/1; Tunisia, O.J. 1978, L 265/1.

[11] An agreement was concluded in 1973 and expired in 1978; see Twelfth General Report 1978, 283.

[12] Agreement of May 11, 1975, O.J. 1975, L 136/1. See also O.J. 1978, L 270/1.

[13] Egypt, Syria, Jordan and Lebanon (O.J. 1978, L 266, 269, 268 and 267).

[14] An agreement was concluded in 1970 (J.O. 1970, L 182/1); see also Twelfth General Report 1978, 242.

[15] O.J. 1978, L 274/1 and J.O. 1972, L 301/164. See Protocol O.J. 1978, L 274/1.

[16] In its latest form, *i.e.* Lomé II, the agreement was signed on October 31, 1979.

trade and to promote jointly economic and social development.[17] Consequently the Member States decided to associate with the Community the non-European countries and territories which have special relations with Belgium, France, Italy and the Netherlands.[18] This was of course extended to the United Kingdom after enlargement.[19] These countries and territories are listed in Annex IV of the Treaty.[20] Drafted at a time when most of these countries and territories were dependent, the principle of a special association was maintained after they gained independence.

For a first period of five years, the details and the procedure for the association were determined by an implementing convention[21] annexed to the Treaty.[22] This convention was replaced by an agreement negotiated between the Community and the emerging African and Malagasy states. This first agreement, known as the Yaoundé I Convention[23] still bears the marks of the paternalistic approach of most European countries towards their former colonies. A second Yaoundé Convention, similar to the former entered into force on January 1, 1971,[24] it did not apply to the United Kingdom, Ireland and Denmark until January 31, 1975.[25]

An entirely new agreement was signed at Lomé (Togo) on February 28, 1975, between the European Community and 46 countries situated in Africa, the Caribbean and the Pacific.[26] It entered into force on April 1, 1976,[27] and expired on March 1, 1980.

[17] EEC, Art. 3 (*k*). See also Preamble to the Treaty (seventh indent) "intending to confirm the solidarity which binds Europe and the overseas countries and desiring to ensure the development of their prosperity, in accordance with the principles of the Charter of the United Nations."

[18] EEC, Art. 131.

[19] Act of Accession, Art. 23 (1).

[20] This list was modified by Act of Accession, Art. 24 (2).

[21] This was of course a Convention concluded between the Member States, not with the overseas countries and territories.

[22] EEC, Art. 136.

[23] Convention of Association between the European Economic Community and the African and Malagasy states associated with the Community; it entered into force on June 1, 1964 (J.O. 1964, 1431).

At the same time an agreement was concluded by the representatives of the Governments laying down measures and procedures for the application of the Yaoundé Convention (J.O. 1964, 1490).

[24] J.O. 1970, L 282/1 and O.J. 1974 (2nd), I, 5.

[25] Act of Accession, Arts. 109 and 115 (1).

[26] O.J. 1976, L 25/1. This number was progressively increased to 57.

[27] O.J. 1976, L 85/1.

As mentioned, the Lomé II Convention was signed on October 31, 1979. These Conventions differ from the Yaoundé Conventions in that they aim to establish a kind of partnership between the developing countries and the Community. It will be noted that although there are 66 signatories, the Lomé Convention is legally speaking a bilateral agreement between the ACP States[28] on the one hand and the Community on the other. The Convention provides for three institutions, a Council of Ministers, a Committee of Ambassadors and a Consultative Assembly.

In respect to the trade co-operation the ACP countries enjoy, without reciprocity for the Member States, free entry into the Community for all products originating in those countries, including processed products originating in other ACP countries and for most of their agricultural products. The Member States only have the guarantee that they will not be treated worse than any other industrialised country and that all of them will be treated equally.

An entirely new feature of the Lomé Convention is the stabilisation of export earnings (STABEX). This is the setting up of machinery assuring those ACP countries whose revenues derive mainly from a simple product, a certain level of export earnings by protecting them from income fluctuations due to the play of the markets or production hazards. The agreement also provides for an undertaking by the Community to purchase from certain ACP countries at guaranteed prices cane sugar for an indefinite period, and an undertaking from these countries to supply specific quantities annually.

Another important element is the place assumed by industrial co-operation, with its industrial co-operation committee and industrial development centre. The purpose is to integrate firms and entrepreneurs into the ACP-EEC co-operation.

[28] The ACP countries, signatories of the Lomé II Convention are: Bahamas, Barbados, Benin, Botswana, Burundi, Cameroon, Cape Verde, Central African Empire, Chad, Comoros, Congo, Djibouti, Dominica, Equatorial Guinea, Ethiopia, Fiji, Gabon, Gambia, Ghana, Grenada, Guinea, Guinea-Bissau, Guyana, Ivory Coast, Jamaica, Kenya, Lesotho, Liberia, Madagascar, Malawi, Mali, Mauritania, Mauritius, Niger, Nigeria, Papua New Guinea, Rwanda, St. Lucia, Solomon Islands, Sao Tome Principe, Senegal, Seychelles, Sierra Leone, Somalia, Sudan, Surinam, Swaziland, Tanzania, Togo, Tonga, Trinidad and Tobago, Tuvalu, Uganda, Upper Volta, Western Samoa, Zaire, Zambia.

Finally the Lomé Convention provides for financial co-operation to the sum of 5,227[29] million units of account for five years, *i.e.* 4542 million for the European Development Fund (grants 2,989, special loans 504, risk capital 280, Stabex 550, Minerals 280) and 685 from the European Investment Bank as commercial loans.[30] Notwithstanding the relative modesty of the financial support, the Community through its special relationship with the ACP countries, plays an important role in the development of the Third World. It should be noted that besides their contribution to the Development Fund, most Member States of the Community provide an important aid bilaterally to a large number of the ACP countries.

Besides the ACP countries, the Community co-operates with other African countries with the member countries of the Association of South East Asian Nations, with South Asia and with Latin America.[31]

(6) *State-trading countries*

In 1974, the expiry of the bilateral trade agreements with the Member States led the Council to lay down autonomous trade arrangements for 1975 and to send to relevant countries a model for a possible agreement which the Community might conclude with each one of them. The model envisaged a long-term non-preferential agreement, based on reciprocity, ensuring that both sides have equal rights and obligations. No reactions were received. However, contacts were maintained or established with Romania, the Council for Mutual Economic Assistance (COMECON) and China.[32]

(7) *Other aspects of external relations*

Mention must be made here of the food aid operations and emergency aid granted by the Community. The latter are implemented via international organisations and are generally prompted by situations resulting from political events[33] or from

[29] In the Lomé I Convention the amount was 3,466 million EUA.

[30] See Bull, 9–1979, 11.

[31] For all these aspects, details can be found in the annual Gen. Rep. and the Bull.

[32] See Twelfth General Report (1978), 300. With China a trade agreement was concluded in 1978 and a textile agreement was signed in April 1979. See Thirteenth General Report (1979), 228.

[33] Lebanon, Bangladesh, Nicaragua.

natural disasters.[34] The Community, on the other hand, also participates in various international commodity agreements for example tin,[35] cocoa,[36] textiles,[37] and wheat.[38]

16. Environment and consumers

(a) ENVIRONMENT

At the Summit Conference at Paris in 1972, the Heads of State or Government of the enlarged Community emphasised the importance of a Community environmental policy. They invited the Community institutions to establish, before July 31, 1973, a programme of action accompanied by a precise timetable.[39] The programme proposed by the Commission was adopted by the Council and the Representatives of the Governments of the Member States on November 22, 1973.[40] It defines the terms of a Community policy for environment. It sets the objectives, states the principles, selects the priorities and describes the measures to be taken in the next two years. The aim of a Community environment policy is to improve the quality of life, and the surrounding and living conditions of the Community population. The Council adopted eleven principles of which three deserve particular mention: the necessity of preventive action; the responsibility of the polluter[41] and the need for action to be taken at the most appropriate level. From the

[34] *e.g.* Malaria epidemics in Turkey, floods in India, etc.

[35] J.O. 1972, L 90/1 and O.J. 1976, L 222/1.

[36] O.J. 1973, L 324/20.

[37] O.J. 1974, L 118/1.

[38] O.J. 1974, L 219/24.

[39] Sixth General Report 1972, 12. See also Bull. 10–1972, 20.

[40] Seventh General Report (1973), 235 and O.J. 1973, C 112/1. A resolution on the continuation and implementation of a European Community policy and action programme on the environment was adopted on May 17, 1977 (O.J. 1977, C 139/1); this programme covers the period until 1982.

[41] The "polluter-pays" principle means that the expenses of preventing and eliminating pollution should, in principle, be paid by the polluter. It requires, however, careful assessment. The indiscriminate application of this principle to certain sensitive sectors of the economy, suddenly subjecting them to stricter rules, could have undesirable social and regional consequences. Special arrangements and transitional periods can avoid these consequences: implementing procedures and exceptions must be defined. This was done in a resolution of the Council (Bull. 11–1974, 11) and in a notice sent to the Member States by the Commission concerning the application of the treaty provisions on state aids to anti-pollution investments (Bull. 11–1974, 39). (Also: O.J. 1975, L 194/1.)

end of 1973 the Commission submitted to the Council several drafts for regulations, directives, recommendations and resolutions under the programme of action.[42]

On March 5, 1973, the representative of the governments of the Member States meeting in Council concluded an agreement concerning the information[43] of the Commission and the Member States with a view to harmonisation throughout the Community of priority measures to protect the environment.

At the international level, the Community participates actively in the work of organisations concerned with topics closely linked to the projects being carried out in the Community.[44]

The Council set up a European Foundation for the Improvement of Living and Working Conditions.[45]

After the pollution caused by the *Amoco Cadiz* disaster, the Commission put forward a number of proposals for measures regarding the protection of the marine environment; the Council approved some measures on the control and reduction of pollution caused by hydrocarbons discharged at sea.[46]

Although the Treaty does not provide for any measures in the field of environment protection, it has been possible to develop a comprehensive policy to cope with one of the major problems of modern times: measures enacted by the institutions in respect to the environment are mainly based on EEC, Article 235.

(b) CONSUMERS[47]

Guidelines for Community action in this field were laid down in a Preliminary Programme contained in a Council Resolution of 1975.[48] The programme refers, *inter alia* to protection of consumer health and safety, protection of the economic interests of the consumer (misleading advertising, unfair commercial practices,

[42] For details see "State of the Environment," Second Report by the Commission (1979).
[43] O.J. 1973, C 9/1.
[44] United Nations Environment Programme, Paris Convention for the Prevention of Marine Pollution, Strasbourg Convention on the protection of International Water (Eighth General Report 1974, 136 and Thirteenth (1979), 139).
[45] O.J. 1978, L 139/1.
[46] O.J. 1978, C 37/3 and O.J. 1977, L 240/1.
[47] Full details can be found in the annual Reports published by the Commission since 1977 on Consumer Protection and Information Policy.
[48] O.J. 1975, C 92/1.

etc), advice, help and redress, consumer information and consumer consultation and representation. A great number of measures have already been adopted by the Community institutions to implement this programme.[49]

17. Energy policy

The necessity for the Community to develop an energy policy has been generally accepted for only a few years. Although the Treaty does not mention it explicitely, it follows directly from its contents. A common market could not function properly if national measures were maintained, which directly or indirectly, impede trade in certain forms of energy. Furthermore, it is clear that the problems particular to certain sectors cannot be solved on a national basis. Although two forms of energy, coal and nuclear energy are regulated in the Coal and Steel and in the Euratom Treaties respectively, many aspects remain to be considered, and furthermore an overall approach seems required. As the Commission expressed it "much effort is still needed, primarily at national level, but the prescribed objectives will not be achieved without Community-level co-ordination of Member States' policies and Community action wherever appropriate and necessary.[50]

In 1968, the Commission submitted a memorandum containing the "First Guidelines for a Community Energy Policy" to the Council.[51] The principles of this memorandum were approved in 1969. On this basis, the Commission made proposals relating to the amendment of Chapter VI of the Euratom Treaty, the Community's supply of enriched uranium, the regulations governing notification to the Commission of import programmes for hydrocarbons and investment projects of Community interest in the petroleum, natural gas and electricity sectors.[52] This memorandum was brought up to date and amplified in 1972 by a memorandum on "The problems and resources of the energy policy for 1975–1985" and another one on "Necessary progress in Community energy policy."[53] These documents were supplemented in

[49] See Thirteenth General Report 1979, 140.
[50] Twelfth General Report 1978, 201.
[51] See Second General Report 1968, 251.
[52] See Fourth General Report 1970, 207 *et seq*. The main accent was on security of supply, stable and low prices.
[53] See Sixth General Report 1972, 230.

1973 by a communication from the Commission to the Council concerning the guidelines and priority actions for a Community energy policy.[54]

At the Paris Summit Conference in 1972, the Heads of Government gave the Community institutions the task of formulating, as soon as possible, an energy policy guaranteeing reliable and lasting supplies on satisfactory terms. Much of the Copenhagen Conference in 1973 was devoted to the situation arising from the energy crisis. The results of the discussions were recorded in a document annexed to the final communiqué of the Conference. Some of the intentions expressed at those conferences—and reaffirmed at the Paris Summit Conference in 1974—were given substance in the course of 1974.[55]

The Council took a decision setting up an Energy Committee composed of representatives of the Member States and chaired by the Commission. It has the task of ensuring the co-ordinated application by Member States of measures taken by the Community, facilitating information and consultation between Member States and the Commission regarding supply and foreseeable trends in supply and helping the Commission to prepare the proposals which it intends to put forward.[56] In accordance with the wishes expressed at the Copenhagen Conference, the Commission transmitted to the Council a communication entitled "Towards a new energy policy strategy for the Community."[57]

At the 1975 Rome meeting of the European Council it was decided to ask the Commission to submit proposals for appropriate mechanisms to protect existing sources and to ensure the development of alternative sources of Community energy, on reasonable economic conditions and also to encourage conservation in the use of energy.[58] These proposals were to serve as guidelines for the meeting of the Commission on energy of the Conference on International Economic Co-operation (North-South dialogue).

[54] Bull. Suppl. 6/73.
[55] Eighth General Report 1974, 189. See, *e.g.* Reg. 1729/76 (O.J. 1976, L 198/1).
[56] Eighth General Report 1974, 190–191.
[57] Bull. Suppl. 4/74. For an analysis, see Eighth General Report 1974, 191. Several resolutions were adopted by the Council on the basis of this Communication (see *ibid.*).
[58] Bull. 12–1975, 63.

Finally, in 1978, the European Council at its Bremen meeting, endorsed Community energy objectives which basically are to reduce the Community's dependence on imported energy to 50 per cent. to limit net oil imports by the Community, to achieve energy savings and to make optimum use of the Community's resources. Unfortunately, the proposals of the Bremen Council[59] and those of the Bonn Economic Summit[60] have only partly and then with great difficulty been embodied in Council decisions.[61] Very little was achieved, therefore, in the way of an overall energy policy for the Community although several measures were adopted in various fields.

In the *coal* sector the Commission publishes annually a short-term outlook for coal in the Community[62] and various aid systems have been authorised. Although the Council reaffirmed the important role of coal in the Community's energy policy, no agreement could be reached on proposed Community aids for financing cyclic stocks of coal[63] or to promote the use of coal for electricity generation.[64]

With regard to *nuclear energy*, the Community grants subsidies to undertakings carrying out prospecting programmes for uranium on the territories of the Member States and in 1977 the Council authorised the Commission to borrow up to one billion European units of account on the financial markets in order to grant loans for the construction of nuclear power plants.[65] The Supply Agency continues to play its role in the conclusion of supply contracts mainly with the United States and Canada while various research

[59] Bull. 6–1978, 17.

[60] Bull. 7/8–1978, 7.

[61] This lack of follow-up constitutes a typical example of the unsatisfactory decision-making process at the level of the Council composed of representatives of the governments of the Member States. It is relatively easy for the heads of the same governments to take important non-binding decisions when meeting in the European Council and leave the implementation to other ministers in the Council of the European Communities, obviously without the necessary instructions to carry through commitments undertaken elsewhere.

[62] *e.g.* "The Community coal market in 1978 and forecasts for 1979" (O.J. 1979, C 120, 1).

[63] O.J. 1977, C 87/6.

[64] O.J. 1977, C 22/4.

[65] O.J. 1977, L 88/9.

projects are carried out in the Communities Joint Research Centre.[66]

The main preoccupation of the past years concerns the *oil* supply, for which the Community is practically entirely dependent on imports from third countries. Member States are now required to maintain a minimum level of stocks of crude oil or oil products.[67] Measures were taken to equip the Community to take effective Community-wide action in the event of oil supply difficulties[68] and Member States now have to inform the Commission concerning imports[69] and investments projects of Community interest in the oil, natural gas and electricity sectors.[70] No solution has yet been found to the problem of overcapacity in refining.

Notwithstanding those first measures the Member States were ill-prepared for the 1973 energy crisis which caused serious internal problems for the Community. It does not seem that much was learned from that troubled period and the Member States do not seem ready to address the energy problems from a Community point of view.

18. Financing Community activities[71]

1. *Financial contributions of the Member States and Community's own resources*

Under the first European Treaty, the Coal and Steel Community could meet its expenditure out of its own resources which it obtained by imposing a levy on the production of coal and steel.[72]

[66] See, *e.g.* Thirteenth General Report (1970), 180.

[67] See Dec. 68/414 (J.O. 1968, L 308/14) and modified by Dec. 72/425 (J.O. 1972, L 291/154).

[68] See Dec. 77/186 on the exporting of crude oil and petroleum products from one Member State to another in the event of supply difficulties (O.J. 1977, L 61/23) and Dec. 77/706 on a Community system for reducing energy consumption (O.J. 1977, L 292/9). See for the implementation of the several Community decisions in this field: answer to Parliamentary Question 449/79 (O.J. 1979, C 288/21).

[69] Reg. 1055/72 (J.O. 1972, L 120/3).

[70] Reg. 1056/72 (*ibid.* at 7).

[71] With regard to the budgetary procedure and the respective powers of Commission, Council and Parliament, see *supra*, p. 29: participation in budgetary procedure.

[72] ECSC Treaty, Art. 49. The ECSC was also empowered to procure funds by contracting loans; this facility was used extensively see, *e.g.* ECSC borrowing and lending operations in Thirteenth General Report 1979, 56. The same Art. 49 added, somewhat optimistically, that the ECSC "may receive gifts."

The situation was different under the EEC and Euratom Treaties which provide that the budget revenue, irrespective of any other revenue, shall include contributions from Member States,[73] but the Commission was to submit proposals to the Council to replace the financial contributions by the Community's own resources, in particular by revenue accruing from the common customs tariff.[74] The Community's own resources were introduced by the Council Decision of April 21, 1970[75] while at the same time the Treaty of April 22, 1970 amended certain budgetary provisions of the basic treaties and the Merger Treaty to confer certain budgetary powers upon the European Parliament.[76]

THE DECISION OF APRIL 21, 1970

The main features of this decision on the Replacement of Financial Contributions from Member States by the Community's own resources can be summarised as follows:

(1) Although the Treaty only refers to revenue accruing from the Common Customs Tariff, the Decision provides that both the agricultural levies[77] and the Common Customs Tariff

[73] EEC, Art. 200. Under this provision the budget revenue consisted mainly of financial contributions of Member States on the following scale: Belgium 7.9 per cent., Germany 28, France 28, Italy 28, Luxembourg 0.2 and The Netherlands 7.9 per cent; this applied to all expenditures except those of the Social Fund which were on a slightly different scale.

[74] EEC, Art. 201. A memorandum to this effect was submitted to the Council on July 16, 1969, see Third General Report 1969, 320.

[75] O.J. 1970 (1), 224; J.O. 1970, L 94/19. This decision (70/243) became effective on January 1, 1971.

[76] The new budgetary powers of the European Parliament were analysed, *supra*, p. 79: participation in budgetary procedure. This treaty became effective on January 1, 1971.

[77] Dec. 70/243, Art. 2 (*a*) refers to: "levies, premiums, additional or compensatory amounts, additional amounts or factors and other duties established or to be established by the institutions of the Communities in respect of trade with non-Member countries within the framework of the common agricultural policy, and also contributions and other duties provided for within the framework of the organisation of the markets in sugar (hereinafter called 'agricultural levies')." The inclusion of these levies in the own resources was also provided for by Reg. 25 (O.J. 1959–1962, 126; J.O. 1962, 991) on financing the common agricultural policy (Art. 2 (1); also in pursuance of the same Reg. the European Agricultural Guidance and Guarantee Fund forms part of the Community budget; on the other hand Reg. 139 (J.O. 1966, 965) provided that 90 per cent. of all the levies collected by the Member States must accrue to the Guarantee section of the Agricultural Fund.

duties[78] constitute own resources to be entered in the budget of the Communities.

(2) The decision provides for a system which made it possible to achieve the transfer of revenue from customs duties progressively over a period of four years. From January 1, 1971 onwards, the total budget of the Community was financed, irrespective of other revenue,[79] from the Community's own resources.

(3) Since revenue accruing from the levies and duties is not sufficient to ensure that the budget of the Communities is in balance, additional tax revenue was allocated to the Communites, *i.e.* that accruing from the application of a rate not exceeding one per cent. of the basis used for assessing the value added tax, determined in a uniform manner for the Member States. The uniform basis of assessment was provided for in the Sixth Council Directive on the harmonisation of the law of the Member States relating to turnover taxes—common systems of value added tax.[80]

As from 1980, the Community's expenditures are entirely financed by the revenue accruing from agricultural levies, customs duties and a percentage of the VAT collected by the Member States.

In connection with the decision of April 21, 1970, three resolutions recorded in the minutes of the Council meeting of that date should be mentioned. First, the Council undertakes to make no amendments to the estimate of Parliament's expenditure, as long as there is no conflict with any Community rules. Parliament thus gained sole responsibility for its own budget. The second resolution concerns Community acts which have financial implications

[78] *Ibid.* Art. 2 (*b*): Common Customs Tariff duties and other duties established or to be established by the institutions of the Communities in respect of trade with non-member countries (hereinafter called "customs duties").

[79] Other revenues are, *e.g.* the fines imposed on undertakings for violation of the Community competition rules; see *supra* under competition policy.

[80] Dir. 77/388 (O.J. 1977, L 145/1). As for the degree of implementation of the Dir. see O.J. 1979, C 172/8. Since not all the Member States had taken the necessary internal measures Dec. 70/243 could not be implemented to the full until 1979. Before that date the Community's budget was financed from revenue accruing from agricultural levies, customs duties, value added tax and the financial contributions of those Member States which had not yet applied the Sixth Dir. See Regs. 2891/71 and 2892/77 implementing Dec. 70/243 of April 21, 1970 (O.J. 1977, L 336/1 and 8).

and provides for collaboration between the Council and the Assembly in this field. This resolution gave rise to the Joint Declaration of the European Parliament, the Council and the Commission of March 4, 1975[81] providing for a conciliation procedure to be followed for Community acts of general application which have appreciable financial implications and for which adoption is not required by virtue of acts in existence.[82] The third Resolution concerns co-operation between the Council and the European Parliament in matters of budgetary procedure. Everything possible must be done to ensure close co-operation at all levels between the two institutions, with regard to the budgetary procedure. In particular it provides that the President in office or another member of the Council should be present at the deliberations of the European Parliament on the draft budget.

That this budgetary concertation procedure has had little effect is proved by the fact that on December 13, 1979 the European Parliament in a historic decision, rejected the 1980 draft budget after the Council failed to take into account most of the modifications proposed earlier by the European MP's.[83]

COMMUNITY'S OWN RESOURCES COLLECT IN THE UNITED KINGDOM

The agricultural levies, customs duties and VAT revenue which constitute the Community's own resources are collected by the Member States and transferred to the Community. The latter refunds to each government 10 per cent. of the amounts paid in order to cover expenses incurred in collection.[84]

The United Kingdom's share of customs duties and agricultural levies was, at the end of 1979, particularly high, due, *inter alia*, to the fact that a large share of the United Kingdom imports still come from non-Member countries. As the United Kingdom trade, as a consequence of its membership of the Community, shifts increasingly from third countries to other Member States, the United Kingdom share of duties and levies transferred to the Community

[81] O.J. 1975, C 89.

[82] See *supra*, p. 29 participation of Parliament in the legislative procedure.

[83] It was the first time this happened in the history of the Community. The decision was taken by 288 votes to 64, thereby easily exceeding the two-thirds majority of the votes cast required by EEC, Art. 203 (8). See also *supra* under European Parliament, participation in the budgetary procedure, Chap. 3 I (3).

[84] Dec. 70/243, Art. 3 (1).

will decrease. It should be remembered, however, that the introduction of the system of own resources implies that the transfer of revenues accruing from levies and duties cannot be considered as national financial contributions.[85] The claim for "broad balance" between these transfers and the Community expenditures in a given country is, therefore, legally, unfounded.[86] This does not mean, however, that a better balance within the Community budget should not exist, *i.e.* that at present the expenditure under the Common Agricultural Policy—from which the United Kingdom is only a minor beneficiary—is much too high and should be proportionally reduced in favour of structural policies and their instruments, such as the Social and Regional Funds.[87]

In pursuance of the Act of Accession[88] the Community's own resources and, where appropriate, the financial contributions referred to in the Decision of April 21, 1970, are due by the new Member States in full from January 1, 1978, subject, however, to certain conditions[89] the consequences of which are that the United Kingdom for instance will contribute to the full from January 1, 1980, onwards.

In 1976, a budget correcting mechanism was introduced to enable payments to be made to Member States which, due to special economic conditions, are considered to bear a disproportionate burden in financing the budget.[90]

[85] It should be noted for instance that often duties and levies are collected by the authorities of the country where the products first enter the Community although the destinees of those products, *i.e.* those who bear the costs of these duties and levies, are situated in other Member States; since the duties and levies are the same in all the Member States the point of entry for a given product is determined solely on the basis of transport considerations.

[86] See Commission's answer to Parliamentary questions 1020/77, 604/78 and 607/78, O.J. 1979, C 28/1–3 and question 50/79, O.J. 1979, C 164/9–11.

[87] With regard to the budgetary imbalances and the problems of economic convergence see EUROPE Documents, Agence Europe of November 9, 1979, No. 2785, suppl. 1073 and of November 28, 1979, No. 2798, suppl. 1077. The effect of the shift in trade and the reduction of the budgetary imbalances will only be felt in the medium-term; this is the reason why the Commission has proposed the introduction of correcting measures of a temporary nature.

[88] Act of Accession, Arts. 127–132. For Greece, see Act of Accession of May 28, 1979, Arts. 124–127 (O.J. 1979, L 291).

[89] *Ibid.* Art. 131.

[90] Reg. 1172/76, O.J. 1976, L 131/7. This was one of the results of what is sometimes referred to as the "British renegotiation"; see Bull. 3–1975, 6, on the decision of the European Council at Dublin (March 10 to 11, 1975).

2. *The Community budget, revenue and expenditure*

All items of revenue and expenditure of the three Communities must be included in estimates to be drawn up for each financial year and be shown in the budget.[91] The revenue and expenditure shown in the budget must balance.[92] The financial year runs from January 1 to December 31.[93] The structure of the general budget and the form in which it is to be presented are determined by Financial Regulations.[94] The budget consists of separate sections dealing with the revenue and expenditure of each institution. The section dealing with the Commission provides for expenditure in the following fields: agriculture, social, regional, research-energy-industry-transport and development co-operation besides administrative expenditures. The total appropriations for commitments in the 1979 budget stood at over 14 billion European units of account.[95]

COMMITMENT AND PAYMENT APPROPRIATIONS

The Community budget contains "non differentiated" and "differentiated" appropriations. Under the former, commitments can be made during the financial year and the corresponding payments during two years. The latter, the differentiated appropriations, provides for both commitments, *i.e.* the maximum which may be committed during the financial year, and payments which may be disbursed and which correspond to commitments made during the same financial year or previously. The system of commitment and payment appropriations is particularly suited for longer term operations such as research projects and infrastructure

[91] One important item not covered by the Community budget is the European Development Fund: the resources destined to finance aid to developing countries are used to fund Community programmes in the associated states, but these funds do not pass through the budget. It will be noted that the activities of the European Investment Bank do not appear on the budget either.

[92] EEC, Art. 199; Art. 20 of the Merger Treaty provides that this applies to the revenue and expenditure of the EEC and Euratom with the exception of that of the Supply Agency and the Joint Undertakings and, for the administrative expenditure of the ECSC, all in accordance with the appropriate provisions of the treaties establishing the three Communities.

[93] EEC, Art. 203 (1).

[94] See O.J. 1977, L 356/1, Arts. 15 and 16; for the latest amendment see O.J. 1979, L 160/1.

[95] For the 1979 budget see O.J. 1979, L 124 and Twelfth General Report (1978), 42.

investments. The total amount for the Community's financial participation in such a project can be committed at the start of the project but the payments only have to be made as the work progresses over the year.[96]

COMPULSORY AND NON-COMPULSORY EXPENDITURE

The Treaty of July 22, 1975, amending certain financial provisions of the existing Treaties introduced the concept of "expenditure necessarily resulting from this Treaty or from acts adopted in accordance therewith,[97] otherwise referred to as "compulsory" expenditures. A budgetary item is considered compulsory when the principle and the amount of the expenditure (either a figure or a precise mechanism for arriving at it) are statutorily prescribed in the Treaties, secondary legislation, international conventions or private-law contracts.[98] In practice, however, expenditures are classified in one or the other category in a rather pragmatic way, by agreement between Parliament and the Council.[99] As was pointed out before,[1] the distinction is important with regard to the budgetary powers of the European Parliament. The increase of non-compulsory expenditures is limited to a maximum annual rate established by the Commission[2] and the last word on this category of expenditure belongs to the Parliament.[3]

(3) *The European Unit of Account (EUA) and the European Currency Unit (ECU)*

The establishment of a unit of account is provided for by the Treaty,[4] and the Community first used a parity unit of account defined by reference to a given weight of fine gold. On account of the severe disturbances in international monetary relations and the

[96] The commitment and payment appropriations are used mainly for Euratom research and investment appropriations and for regional fund expenditures.

[97] EEC, Art. 203 (4).

[98] D. Strasser, *The Finances of Europe* (New York 1977), 33. Another definition given by the Council reads: "expenditure in respect of which, by virtue of existing enactments, no budgetary authority, be it the Council or the European Parliament, has the right freely to determine the appropriations."

[99] It was agreed for instance that the expenditures for the Regional Fund were to be considered as "compulsory" in 1975–6 and 7 and as non compulsory afterwards.

[1] See *supra*, p. 29, participation in budgetary procedure.

[2] EEC, Art. 203 (9).

[3] Non compulsory expenditures amount to roughly 25 per cent. of the budget.

[4] EEC, Art. 207.

replacement of the systems of fixed parities of the various currencies with regard to the United States dollar by floating exchange rates, the Community decided to introduce a new unit of account, referred to as a "basket" unit of account or European unit of account, which reflects the day-to-day fluctuations between the various currencies on the foreign exchange markets.[5] A "basket" unit of account is made up of different national currencies; the European unit of account is thus defined by reference to a sum of fixed amounts of Member States' currencies. The value of the EUA in any national currency moves in line with changes in the weighted average of exchange rates in all the currencies in the basket; in other words, it reflects the aggregate movement in those currencies.[6] The value of the EUA in the Member States' currencies is determined each day by the Commission on the basis of the official exchange rates notified by the Member States' central banks. The rates are published daily in the *Official Journal*.[7] The EUA was introduced in the general budget of the Community in 1978. The establishment of the European Monetary System in 1979 made it possible to introduce the ECU—a monetary unit having the same definition as the EUA[8]—for the operations of the European Monetary Co-operation Fund on March 13, and for the common agricultural policy on April 9, 1979. The ECU/EUA is now used in all areas of Community activity without exception. The Community has thus returned to using a single unit of account after a period of several years during which units of account of very different nature had existed side by side.[9]

[5] The old unit of account was until 1979 used in connection with the common agricultural policy.

[6] Bull. 1–1979, 96.

[7] *Ibid.* at 97.

[8] "The ECU is identical with the EUA, though, unlike the EUA, it provides for a revision clause enabling changes to be made to its composition. It is a 'basket' unit made up of specific amounts of Member States' currencies, determined mainly by reference to the size of each Member State's economy." Bull. 3–1979, 133. On September 28, 1979 the ECU/EUA was worth £0.649544.

[9] Bull. 3–1979, 132. See also Bull. 9–1979, 102.

Chapter 7

COMMUNITY LEGAL ORDER

As was pointed out at the beginning of this book, the Treaties establishing the European Communities are more than agreements which merely create mutual obligations between the Member States. Generally speaking, this conclusion was reached on the basis of the following facts. The Treaties have created quasi governmental bodies—the institutions—independent from the national public authorities and endowed with legislative, administrative and judicial sovereign rights. These rights were transferred to them by the Member States and they affect both the national governments and the citizens. The Treaties thus present many analogies with national constitutions: it can be said therefore that, although they started as international treaties, they have become the "constitution" of the European Communities.

As has been shown, the law embodied in the Treaties—primary European law—is constantly being expanded, made specific, implemented and applied by the various acts and measures of the Community institutions—secondary law. The Treaties have, therefore, as the Court of Justice found, established a legal order of their own and indeed, "by creating a Community of unlimited duration, having its own institutions, its own personality, its own legal capacity and capacity of representation on the international plane and, more particularly, real powers stemming from a limitation of sovereignty or a transfer of powers from the states to the Community, the Member States have limited their sovereign rights, albeit within limited fields, and have thus created a body of law which binds both their nationals and themselves.[1]

This view is shared as will be seen by many national courts such as the German Supreme Administrative Court which stated that

[1] Case 6/64 *Costa* v. *ENEL* [1964] E.C.R. at 593.

Community law constitutes "a separate legal order, where provisions belong neither to international law nor to the municipal law of the Member States."[2]

DIRECT APPLICABILITY

Community law is not only separate from national law, it is also independent, which means that rights can be conferred and obligations imposed directly by Community provisions upon the national authorities and upon the citizens of the Member States. There is indeed no necessity for Member States to intervene in order that those provisions have a binding effect[3] or, as Article 189 expresses it, are "applicable"; furthermore, Member States are committed not to interfere with the application of Community law. This latter obligation follows from Article 5 of the Treaty which provides, *inter alia*, that Member States "shall abstain from any measure which could jeopardise the attainment of the objectives of this treaty."

More important than the acceptance of this "legal autonomy" of the Community legal system is the understanding of its *raison d'être*. The European Treaties, it will be remembered, aim at establishing within the territories of the Member States a single market characterised by the basic freedoms and constituting a geographical area wherein Community rules apply with the same force and with exactly the same meaning and effect to all who operate thereon.[4] Therefore, the very nature of the law created by

[2] C.M.L. Rev. 1967, 483. See *infra*.

[3] This is what is meant by s. 2 (1) of the European Community Act 1972: these provisions "are without further enactment to be given legal effect or use in the United Kingdom." In other words "reception" of Community law into the national sphere is and cannot be required. Anyway reception is only required by those who adhere to the dualist theory and furthermore "if one accepts, as is logical and in one view inevitable, that Community law is *sui generis* then in strictness monist/dualist argument is excluded, since it is an argument properly limited to international law strictly so called," which is not the case with Community law. See Mitchell, "British law and British Membership," *Europarecht*, 1971, April–June, 109.

[4] As the Court pointed out in Case 6/64 see n. 1, at 594, "the executive force of Community law cannot carry from one State to another in deference to subsequent domestic law, without jeopardising the attainment of the objectives of the Treaty set out in Article 5 (2) and giving rise to the discrimination prohibited by Art. 7."

the European Treaties implies uniform interpretation and application; without those characteristics there can be no Community. Community law is either uniform in all the Member States or it is not.

DIRECT EFFECT

If the consequence of direct applicability for the Member States is non-interference, for the citizens it means the possibility to invoke the Community rules in their national courts in order to protect the rights which those rules confer upon them.[5] Applicability of Community law must indeed be understood both in the negative way—obligations imposed upon national authorities, institutions and persons—and in the positive way—rights for those, in favour of whom, these obligations have been provided. In law, every obligation has a right as its corollary. It is of course the same in Community law, *e.g.* the obligations imposed upon the Member States may have as their corollary rights for their citizens. It is those rights which the national courts and tribunals must uphold, in pursuance of Article 5 of the Treaty.[6] It is thus not only regulations which, because they are "directly applicable,"[7] are as such suited "to grant to the citizens rights which the national tribunals are under obligation to protect,"[8] but all binding Community acts whatever their nature or form.[9] Consequently, the question arises

[5] This was clearly stated by the Court in Case 43/75 *Defrenne* v. *Sabena* [1976] E.C.R. at 474 (24): "in such a situation, at least, Article 119 is directly applicable and may thus give rise to individual rights which the courts must protect." In other words direct applicability implied direct effect.

The same position of the Court became already apparent in Case 2/74 *Reyners* v. *Belgium* [1974] E.C.R. 631 at 651 (25) although less clearly stated; referring to Art. 52 the Court held that "the rule on equal treatment with nationals is one of the fundamental legal provisions of the Community. As a reference to a set of legislative provisions effectively applied by the country of establishment to its own nationals, this rule is, by its essence, capable of being directly invoked by nationals of all the other Member States" and the Court concluded by answering that "Article 52 of the Treaty is a directly applicable provision."

[6] EEC, Art. 5 refers to the "Member States" and this expression covers all the national authorities whether legislative, administrative or judicial. See, *e.g.* Case 33/76 *Rewe* v. *Landwirtschaftskammer Saarland* [1976] E.C.R. 1989 at 1997 (5): "applying the principle of co-operation laid down in Article 5 of the Treaty, it is the national courts which are entrusted with ensuring the legal protection which citizens derive from the direct effect of the provisions of Community law."

[7] EEC, Art. 189. [8] Case 93/71 [1972] E.C.R. 287 at 293 (5).

[9] *e.g.* provisions of directives, decisions and agreements concluded by the Com-

as to which provisions of Community law, which impose a clear and unconditional obligation upon a Member State, an institution or a person, do not have "direct effect."[10] The answer is only those which leave, to the addressee of the obligation, a discretionary latitude. For instance, with regard to Article 90 (2), the Court stated that "Its application involves an appraisal of the requirements, on the one hand, of the particular task entrusted to the undertaking concerned and, on the other hand, the protection of the interests of the Community. This appraisal depends on the objectives of general economic policy pursued by the states under the supervision of the Commission. Consequently, . . . Article 90 (2) cannot at the present stage create individual rights which the

munity can have direct effect; for directives, see Case 21/78 *Delkvist* v. *Anklagemijndigheden* [1978] E.C.R. 2327 at 2340 (21); and Case 51/76 *Nederlandse Ondernemingen* v. *Inspecteur der Invoerrechten en accijnzen* [1977] E.C.R. at 126, where the Court reiterated that if regulations, because they are directly applicable, may by their very nature have direct effects, "it does not follow from this that other categories of acts mentioned in [Article 189] can never have similar effects" and that "it would be incompatible with the binding effect attributed to a directive by Article 189 to exclude, in principle, the possibility that the obligation which it imposes may be invoked by those concerned." The Court goes on to state that "in particular, where the Community authorities have, by directive, imposed on Member States the obligation to pursue a particular course of conduct, the useful effect of such an act would be weakened if individuals were prevented from relying on it before their national courts and if the latter were prevented from taking it into consideration as an element of Community law" (*ibid.* at 127 (23)).

Author's comment: obviously, by establishing a causal link between direct applicability and direct effect the Court is at pain to justify direct effect of acts which are not directly applicable. The theory developed in the text above which sees direct effect as a corollary of any obligation imposed on a third person by Community law provides a simpler approach.

This idea was developed by the Court itself in one of its earlier judgments: Case 26/62 [1963] E.C.R. at 12: "these rights [of individuals] arise . . . also by reason of obligations which the Treaty imposes in a clearly defined way upon individuals as well as upon the Member States and upon the institutions of the Community." Case 33/70 *Sace* v. *Italian Ministry for Finance* [1970] E.C.R. 1213 at 1224 and Case 91/78 *Hansen* v. *Hauptzollant Flensburg*. For decisions see Case 33/70, *supra* and for agreements Case 91/78, *supra*.

[10] Originally, the question was put the other way round: which Community provisions have direct effect; the answer given by the Court was that "it is necessary but also sufficient that the provision which is being invoked lends itself by its very nature to produce direct effects in the legal relations existing between the Member States and their citizens; that EEC Art. 95 (1) prohibiting discrimination, provides for a clear and unconditional obligation, that this obligation was not made dependent upon any condition nor its implementation or effectiveness upon any

national courts must protect."[11] In other words, the obligation is not unconditional and cannot therefore have direct effect.

However, the Court made it clear that in cases where the latitude is limited in time, the expiration of the time-limit suffices to confer direct effect to Community rules, notwithstanding the absence of implementing provisions whether to be adopted by the institutions or by the national authorities. The Court also found that even in the absence of any express reference to the possible action to be taken by the institutions, the Community provisions cannot be interpreted as reserving to the national legislature exclusive power to implement those rules, since such implementation may be relieved by a combination of Community and national measures.[12]

The fact that the European Treaties have created a new legal order, directly applicable and conferring upon citizens rights which national courts must uphold, was not only ascertained by the Court of Justice, but also recognised by national courts and tribunals. In the first place, the judiciary of all the Member States has implictly recognised this by making extensive use of the possibility offered by Artice 177 to request the Court to give preliminary rulings on questions concerning Community law raised before them,"[13] by doing so they accepted that Community rules apply

act of the Community institutions or of the Member States; that said prohibition therefore is complete and legally perfect so that it can create direct effects in the legal relations between the Member States and their citizens," Case 28/67 *Molkerei-Zentrale* v. *Hauptzollant Paderborn* [1968] E.C.R. 143 at 153. Several years later, in Case 43/75 *Defrenne* v. *Sabena* [1976] E.C.R. at 471 *et seq.*, the Court took a different attitude: "the question of the direct effect of Article 119 must be considered in the light of the nature of the principle of equal pae, the aim of this provision and its place in the scheme of the Treaty."

[11] Case 10/71 [1971] E.C.R. at 730 (14–16).

[12] See, *e.g.* Case 43/75 [1976] E.C.R. at 478, where the Court noted that Art. 119 provides that the application of the principle of equal pay was to be uniformly ensured by the end of the first stage of the transitional period at the latest, *i.e.* December 31, 1961 and thereafter the principle contained in Art. 119 may be relied upon before national Courts and they have a duty to ensure the protection of the rights which this provision vests in individuals.

[13] See, *e.g. Belgium*: Case 83/77 *Naselli* v. *Caisse Auxiliaire d'Assurance Maladie-Invalidité* [1978] E.C.R. 683, requested by the Tribunal de Travail, Brussels; *Denmark*: Case 151/78 *Sukkerfabriken Nykøbing* v. *Ministry of Agriculture* [1979] E.C.R. 1, requested by the Højesteret (Danish Supreme Court); *Germany*: Case 85/78 *Bundesanstalt für landwirtschaftliche Marktordnung* v. *Hirsch* [1978] E.C.R. 2517, requested by the Bundesverwaltungsgericht (Federal Administrative Court); *France*: Case 84/77 *Caisse Primaire d'Assurance Maladie d'Eure-et-Loire* v. *Recq*

within the territory of their jurisdiction and may confer rights which they must uphold, otherwise they would not have suspended the procedure in cases before them in order to obtain the Court's interpretation of provisions of Community law, which they consider necessary to enable them to give judgment. In the second place the fact that Community law constitutes a new legal order has been explicitly recognised by several national courts and tribunals. This was the case, *inter alia*, for the Italian Corte Costituzionale,[14] the German Bundesverfassungsgericht[15] and the

[1978] E.C.R. 7, requested by the French Cour de Cassation; *Ireland*: Case 92/77 *An Bord Bainne* v. *Ministry for Agriculture* [1978] E.C.R. 497, requested by the High Court of Ireland; *Italy*: Case 94/77 *Zerbone* v. *Amministrazione delle Finanze dello Stato* [1978] E.C.R. 99, requested by the Tribunale di Genova; *Luxembourg*: Case 50/75 *Caisse de Pension des Employés Privés* v. *Massonet* [1975] E.C.R. 1473, requested by the Cour Supérieure de Justice; *Netherlands*, Case 15/74 *Centrafarm* v. *Sterling Drug* [1974] E.C.R. 1147 requested by the Hoge Raad of the Netherlands; see also the first request for a preliminary ruling: Case 13/61, *Bosch* v. *Van Rijn* [1962] E.C.R. 45, requested by the Court of Appeal of The Hague; *United Kingdom*: Case 41/74 *Van Duyn* v. *Home Office* [1974] E.C.R. 1337, requested by the Chancery Division of the High Court of Justice.

[14] In a judgment of 1965, the Corte Costituzionale held that "the legal order of the Coal and Steel Community is clearly distinct from the Italian legal order"; a few years later, the same court added that Community law "cannot be considered as international law, nor should it be considered as foreign law or as national law and that the fundamental requirements of equality and legal certainty demand the Community provisions to be directly applicable in all the Member States as acts having force of law without their reception or adaptation by national law being necessary so that they enter into force everywhere and simultaneously and apply equally and uniformly to all the addressees" (December 27, 1973).

[15] Judgment of October 18, 1967: "The regulations of the Council and the Commission are acts of a special 'supranational' public authority created by the Treaty and clearly distinguishable from the state authority of the Member States. The institutions of the EEC exercise sovereign rights of which the Member States have divested themselves in favour of the Community set up by them. The Community itself is neither a state nor a federal state. It is a gradually integrating Community of a special nature, an 'interstate institution' . . . to which the Federal Republic of Germany—like the other Member States—has 'transferred' certain sovereign rights. A new public authority was thus created which is autonomous and independent with regard to the state authority of the separate Member States; consequently its acts have neither to be approved ('ratified') by the Member States nor can they be annulled by them. The E.E.C. Treaty is as it were the constitution of this Community.

The legal provisions issued by the Community institutions within the sphere of competence conferred upon them by the Treaty (the 'secondary Community Law') form a special legal order whose rules are neither international law nor

Belgian Cour de Cassation.[16] All the implications of the autonomy of the Community legal order did not always become immediately clear, it was often a lengthy process of adaptation and learning in which the Court of Justice played an important role. But even as early as 1967 the Commission could refer to the growing penetration of domestic legal systems by Community law and the steadily improving comprehension of the new situation by those working in this field as shown by the pattern of cases dealt with by the national courts.[17]

PRECEDENCE

In retrospect it might seem evident that the autonomy of the Community legal order, the necessity for its uniform interpretation and application in all the Member States automatically implies that the Community provisions have precedence over national legislation in case of conflict. Since the national courts and tribunals are under an obligation, as was just seen, to apply Community rules, besides the provisions of national law, it is not unlikely that conflicts will result from this simultaneous application. The European treaties contain no explicit provisions regarding the solution to be applied in such cases and therefore attempts were made at first to solve such conflicts in accordance with the provisions of national law. Few national legal systems, however, provide for conflict rules of this nature.

In the United Kingdom, for example, the European Communities Act 1972 provides the necessary procedence, by accepting the "legal effect" of Community provisions in the United Kingdom[18] and also the decisions of the European Court regarding the meaning or effect of any of the treaties, or the validity, meaning or effect of any Community instrument.[19] In relation to statute law, this means that the directly applicable Community provisions must prevail over future Acts of Parliament, in so far as they might be inconsistent with those instruments. In practice, this also means

national law of the Member States. Community law and national law of the member States are 'two independent legal orders different from each other'; the law created by the E.E.C. Treaty comes from an 'autonomous legal source'." (Reprinted with permission from 5 C.M.L. Rev. 1967–68, p. 483).

[16] *Minister for Economic Affairs* v. *Fromagerie Franco-Suisse "Le Skier"* [1972] C.N.L.R. 330. This decision will be examined *infra* under precedence of Community law.

[17] First General Report (1976), 463.

[18] 1972 European Communities Act, s. 2 (1).

[19] *Ibid.* s. 3 (1).

that it is implied in the acceptance of the treaties that the United Kingdom must refrain from enacting legislation inconsistent with Community law.[20]

In the Netherlands, the Basic Law (Constitution) not only provides that the provisions of international treaties have precedence over existing national laws and regulations, it also specifies that the same applies to the measures enacted by the institutions set up under these treaties and adds that this precedence applies in case of conflict between an existing Community rule and subsequent national law.[21]

The French Constitution provides in general terms that treaties or agreements, duly ratified or approved, shall, upon their publication, have an authority superior to that of laws, subject, however, for each agreement or treaty, to its application by the other party.[22]

The German Constitution provides that the Federal Republic may, by legislation, transfer sovereign powers to inter-govern-

[20] *Ibid.* s. 2 (4) provides therefore that present and future enactment shall be construed and have effect subject to s. 2. See *Hansard*, February 15, 1972, Vol. 831. This basic principle derives not only from the obligations explicitly accepted by the Member States when they became members of the European Community (see, *e.g.* EEC, Art. 5) but, as was explained, from the very nature of the Community and Community law. The very existence of the Community depends upon simultaneous and uniform application throughout the Community of all the provisions of the treaties and the acts of the institutions. This was clearly stated over and over again by the Court of Justice. See, *e.g.* Case 83/78 *Pigs Marketing Board* v. *Redmond* [1978] E.C.R. at 2371 (56) where the Court held that once the Community has, pursuant to Art. 40 of the Treaty, legislated for the establishment of the common organisation of the market in a given sector, Member States are under an obligation to refrain from taking any measure which might undermine or create exceptions to it and Case 128/78 *Commission* v. *United Kingdom* [1979] E.C.R. 419 at 428 where the Court reiterated that it cannot be accepted "that a Member State should apply in an incomplete or selective manner provisions of a Community regulation so as to render abortive certain aspects of Community legislation which it has opposed or which it considers contrary to its national interests" and the Court concluded that "in deliberately refusing to give effect on its territory to the provisions of Regulation No. 1463/70, the United Kingdom has markedly failed to fulfil the obligation which it has assumed by virtue of its membership of the European Economic Community" (*ibid.* at 429 (13)).

[21] Dutch Constitution, Arts. 66 and 67; these were incorporated in the Constitution in 1953.

[22] French Constitution of 1958, Art. 55. In a judgment of 1962, the French Cour de Cassation held that a contested action had been carried out under an EEC decision and regulation which are "acts regularly published and having acquired force of international treaties" (*Gazette du Palais*, December 9 to 11, 1970, 6–7). See,

mental institutions[23] and refers to the precedence of the general rules of public international law.[24] It is only with difficulty that one can equate Community measures with the latter.

The Italian Constitution is even less precise. It only provides that "Italy's legal system conforms with the general principles recognised by international law."[25]

These German and Italian texts and even the French Constitution form a rather meagre legal basis for the obligation that national courts should give precedence to Community law over national law in case of conflict between the two, to say nothing of those Member States whose constitution contains no provisions in this respect. Furthermore, in certain cases, the above-mentioned constitutional provisions were not accepted by national judges as obliging them to give precedence to Community measures over national rules,[26] even in the case of the Dutch Constitution, which

however, decision of the Conseil d'Etat, *Syndicat Général des Fabricants de Semoules* v. *Direction des Industries agricoles* [1970] C.M.L.R. 395. See also French Cour de Cassation 1975, *Administration de Douanes* v. *Jacques Vabre* [1975] 2 C.M.L.R. 336, where the French Supreme Court clearly stated that the Treaty has an authority greater than that of national acts and is binding on the national courts.

[23] Art. 24 (1).

[24] Art. 25.

[25] Art. 10 (1).

[26] By a ruling of March 1, 1968 (*Recueil Dalloz-Sirey*, 1968, jurisprudence 286) the French Conseil d'Etat dismissed a request for annulment of decisions of the Minister of Agriculture authorising the importation into France of wheatmeal from Algeria and specifying that the imports were not subject to the levies provided for by Reg. 19 since an Order of the President of the Republic of September 19, 1962 had provided for the tariffs in trade between Algeria and France. According to the Conseil d'Etat, the Order prevented the application of the levy provided by Reg. 19. This ruling clearly proceeds from the idea that a French court is bound to ensure the application of the *lex posteriori* whatever the meaning and scope of existing Community law (Second General Report (1968) 453). The Commission considered this ruling incompatible with the legal obligations deriving from the Treaty (J.O. 1968, C 71). *Syndicat Général des Fabricants de Semoules de France, supra*. See, however, Cour de Cassation, October 22, 1970, *Contributions indirectes* v. *Ramel* [1971] C.M.L.R. 315.

In a ruling of July 10, 1968 the German Bundesfinanzhof took the view that in certain cases the German constitutional provisions guaranteeing fundamental rights might be a bar to the application of Community law (Aussenwirtschafts dienst der Betriebsberater, 1968, 354, quoted in Second General Report). This view cannot of course be accepted; if it is thought that there is incompatibility between a Community act and fundamental rights—whether incorporated in a constitution or not—appeal for annulment can be lodged with the Court under Art. 173 for violation of a rule of law relating to the application of the Treaty.

is so explicit about this precedence, if the sole justification for supremacy of Community law over national law were national law itself, this supremacy would be at the mercy of the next constitutional amendment. Other grounds had therefore to be found which would be accepted by all national jurisdictions without reference to their particular national legal orders. This ground was obviously the Community legal order itself, which was accepted by all the Member States which "have adhered to the Treaty on the same conditions, definitively and without any reservations than those set out in the supplementary protocols."[27] The Court had always considered that the provisions of Community law had been integrated into the legal system applicable in the Member States and that the terms and the spirit of the Treaty make it impossible for the Member States, as a corollary, to accord precedence to a unilateral and subsequent measure over a legal system accepted by them on the basis of reciprocity. Such a measure cannot therefore be inconsistent with that legal system. The Court added that "[t]he executive force of Community law cannot vary from one State to another in deference to subsequent domestic laws, without jeopardizing the attainment of the objectives of the Treaty set out in Article 5 (2) and giving rise to the discrimination prohibited by Article 7."[28]

Therefore, "the law stemming from the Treaty, an independent source of law, could not, because of its special and original nature, be overridden by domestic legal provisions, however framed without being deprived of its character as Community law and without the legal basis of the Community itself being called into

[27] Cases 9 and 58/65 *San Michele* v. *High Authority* [1967] E.C.R. 1 at 30.

[28] Case 6/64 *Costa* v. *ENEL* [1964] E.C.R. at 594. The Court also considered that "the obligations undertaken under the Treaty [. . .] would not be unconditional, but merely contingent, if they could be called in question by subsequent legislative acts of the signatories."

This was once again emphasised by the Court in Case 128/78 *Commission* v. *United Kingdom* ("Tachographs") [1979] E.C.R. at 429. "For a state unilaterally to break, according to its own conception of national interest, the equilibrium between the advantages and obligations flowing from its adherence to the Community brings into question the equality of Member States before Community law and creates discrimination at the expense of their nationals. This failure in the duty of solidarity accepted by Member States by the fact of their adherence to the Community strikes at the very root of the Community legal order."

question.[29] To put it simply: either Community law stands by itself, is uniformily applied and has precedence over domestic law or it does not exist. This view now seems to be generally recognised in the Member States, although with varying degrees of conviction and acceptance. Some of the most important rulings of national courts and tribunals should be mentioned here, since they constitute essential steps towards recognition of the Community legal order and its implications. In Belgium reference must be made to a decision of 1971 of the Cour de Cassation in the case *Belgian State* v. *Fromagerie Franco-Suisse* "Le Skier"[30]; in France, the

[29] *Ibid.* See also Case 11/70 *Internationale Handelsgesellschaft* v. *Einfuhr-und Vorratsstelle Getreide* [1970] E.C.R. at 1134 (3).

Mention must be made in this respect of a decision of the German Bundesverfassungsgericht (Federal Constitutional Court) of May 29, 1974 [1974] 2 C.M.L.R. 540, same parties, when the German Court held that it never rules on the validity of a rule of Community law; it added however that it can hold that such a rule cannot be applied by the authorities or courts of the Federal Republic of Germany in so far as it conflicts with a rule of the German Constitution relating to fundamental rights. This view was rejected by the Court of Justice clearly stating that the effect of a Community measure within a Member State cannot be affected by allegations that it runs counter to fundamental rights as formulated by the Constitution of that State (see Case 11/70, *supra*). The Court added that respect for fundamental rights forms an integral part of the general principles of law protected by the Court and that the protection of such rights must be ensured within the framework of the structure and objectives of the Community. In other terms, respect for rights of a fundamental nature must be ensured in the Community legal system and not by the national courts or tribunals when violation of such rights by Community legislation is alleged. See also Case 4/73 *Nold* v. *Commission* [1974] E.C.R. 491, where the Court stated that it cannot uphold measures which are incompatible with the fundamental rights established and guaranteed by the Constitutions of the Member States since the Court is bound to draw inspiration from the constitutional traditions common to the Member States.

[30] See [1972] C.M.L.R. 330 at 373. The Cour de Cassation considered that "[9] In the event of a conflict between a norm of domestic law and a norm of international law which produces direct effects in the internal legal system the rule established by the Treaty shall prevail. The primacy of the Treaty results from the very nature of international treaty law.

[10] This is *a fortiori* the case when a conflict exists, as in the present case between a norm of internal law and a norm of Community law. The reason is that the treaties which have created Community law have instituted a new legal system in whose favour the Member-States have restricted the exercise of their sovereign powers in the areas determined by those treaties.

[11] Article 12 of the Treaty [. . .] is immediately effective and confers on individual persons rights which national courts are bound to uphold.

[12] it follows from all these considerations that it was the duty of the judge to

Cour de Cassation, 1975, *Administration des Douanes* v. *Jacques Vabre et al.*[31] and for Italy mention must be made of a judgment of the Corte di Cassazione of 1972, *Schiavello* v. *Nesci*, although recent developments seem much less promising.[32]

set aside the application of provisions of domestic law that are contrary to this Treaty provision." Reproduced by permission of Common Market Law REPORTS

[31] The French Cour de Cassation considered that the EEC Treaty, which by virtue of Art. 55 of the Constitution has an authority greater than that of statutes, institutes a separate legal order integrated with that of the Member States. Because of that separateness, the legal order, which it has created is directly applicable to the nationals of those States and is binding on their courts. Therefore, the Cour d'Appel was correct and did not exceed its powers in deciding that Art. 95 of the Treaty was to be applied in the instant case, and not section 265 of the Customs Code, even though the latter was later in date. It is interesting to note that the Cour de Cassation also dismissed the plea that the Court d'Appel could not verify whether the reciprocity referred to in Art. 55 of the Constitution did indeed exist; the Cour de Cassation argued that failings by a Member State to comply with an obligation under the Treaty are subject to the procedure laid down by Art. 170 of the Treaty and that therefore the plea of lack of reciprocity cannot be made before a national court. [1975] C.M.L.R. 336.

However, the situation in France is far from satisfactory, since the Conseil d'Etat, although it referred two cases to the Court of Justice for a preliminary ruling (Cases 11/74 *Union des Minoteries de la Champagne* v. *France* [1974] E.C.R. 877 and 48/74 *Charmasson* v. *Minister for Economic Affairs and Finance* [1974] E.C.R. 1383) does not seem ready yet to accept the unconditional precedence of Community law: see judgment of the Conseil d'Etat of December 22, 1978 in the Case *Cohn-Bendit* (1979) C.M.L.R. 701. The French Conseil d'Etat refused to recognise direct applicability and consequently direct effect to a directive on the basis of the theory of the "acte clair," *i.e.* that EEC, Art. 189 was clear in itself and did not need further interpretation: that provision limits direct applicability to regulation.

A similar problem arose with the French Conseil Constitutionnel when it examined the constitutionality of the provisions concerning the direct elections to the European Parliament although it did not raise any objections.

[32] Corte di Cassazione "As the Constitutional Court itself has held, the organs of the internal Italian judicial system—including the Constitutional Court—have no jurisdiction to censure the acts of the organs of the European Communities, which are not subject to the power of the Member-States. . . . the EEC constitutes a legal order of a new type in the international field, in favour of which the Member-States have surrendered, albeit in limited sectors, their sovereign powers and to which are subject not only the Member-States but also their citizens. That has been held by other Member-States; and the Cour de Cassation of Belgium . . . has, most recently, held that norms of Community law, endowed with direct effect in the internal order, must prevail through the very nature of international treaty law over internal legislation, even if subsequent in time." Reproduced by permission of Common Market Law Reports [1975] 2 C.M.L.R. 198 at 202.

The general principle of precedence of Community law over national law having been established, it is necessary to examine some of its more concrete consequences. As far as any national court is concerned, the Court of Justice has described its obligations as follows. Directly applicable rules of Community law are a direct source of rights and duties for all those affected thereby, including any national court whose task it is, as an organ of a Member State, to protect, in a case within its jurisdiction, the rights conferred upon individuals by Community law. In accordance with the principle of precedence of Community law, the relationship, between provisions of the Treaty and the directly applicable measures of the institutions on the one hand and the national laws of the Member States on the other, is such, that, those provisions and measures, by their entry into force, automatically render any conflicting provision of current national law inapplicable. Any recognition that national legislative measures, which are incompatible with provisions of Community law, have any legal effect would amount to a corresponding denial of the effectiveness of obligations undertaken unconditionally and irrevocably by Member States pursuant to the Treaty and would consequently endanger the very foundations of the Community. It follows that every national court, in a case within its jurisdiction must apply Community law in its entirety and protect rights which the latter confers on individuals. Accordingly it must set aside any provision of national law which may conflict with it, whether prior or subsequent to the Community rule. It is not necessary for the Court to request or await the prior setting aside of such provision by legislative or other constitutional means.[33]

See, however, Corte Costitutionale *Frontini* v. *Ministero delle Finanze* (C.M.L.R. 1974, 372) where the Italian Constitutional Court held that protection of the rights of individual citizens against the acts of Community organs is a matter for the European Court of Justice; but added that if ever Article 189 of the EEC Treaty had to be interpreted as giving the Community organs an unacceptable power to violate the fundamental principles of the Italian Constitution on the inalienable rights of man, the Constitutional Court would reserve the right to control the continuing compatibility of the Treaty as a whole with such fundamental principles; see also Court of Justice, Case 106/77 *Amministrazione delle Finanze dello Stato* v. *Simmenthal* [1978] 629, from which it clearly appears that there is a reluctance to accept all the consequences of the precedence of Community law.

[33] Case 106/77 *supra*, at 643–644 (14–18 and 21, 22, 24).

With regard to legislative bodies, the Court indicated that the principle of precedence of provisions of Community law—in so far as it is an integral part of, and takes precedence in the legal order applicable in the territory of each of the Member States—precludes the valid adoption of new national legislative measures to the extent to which they would be incompatible with Community provisions.[34]

As far as other national authorities are concerned, it is clear that the respect of Community law's precedence and the obligations for the Member States under Article 5 not only prevent them from enacting measures, which are incompatible with Community provisions, but also impose upon them the obligation to abolish all existing contrary measures, whatever their nature. Although these measures are inapplicable, their maintenance gives rise to an ambiguous state of affairs by maintaining a state of uncertainty as to the possibilities available to the beneficiaries of the Community rule of relying on the latter.[35] It follows from the above that autonomy of the Community legal order, direct effect and precedence of Community rules over national measures are all aspects of one and the same thing: the particular nature of Community law.

A more recent development in this respect is the Court's reference to the usefulness[36] or effectiveness[37] of Community acts to justify the right of individuals to rely, before their national courts, on the obligations imposed by the act. It concerns cases where Community authorities have imposed on Member States by means of directives, the obligation to pursue a particular course of conduct. These acts are not directly applicable, since the choice is

[34] *Ibid.* (at 17). See also Case 230/78 *Eridania* v. *Minister for Agriculture and Forestry* (not yet published).

[35] Case 167/73 *Commission* v. *France* [1974] E.C.R. 359 at 372 (41); see also Case 159/78 *Commission* v. *Italy* (not yet published). See also Case 61/77 *Commission* v. *Ireland* [1978] E.C.R. at 442, from which it appears that following a Court order (interim measure) the Irish Government simply refrained from enforcing the contested measures since the Court order "has had the force of law in Ireland."

[36] Case 51/76 *Nederlandse Ondernemingen* v. *Inspecteur der Invoerrechten en Accijzen* [1977] E.C.R. 113 at 127: "the useful effect of such an act would be weakened if individuals were prevented from relying on it before their national courts."

[37] Case 38/77 *ENKA* v. *Inspecteur der Invoerrechten en Accijzen* [1977] E.C.R. 2203 at 2211. It should be noted, however, that in the language of this case, Dutch, the expression used is the same as in the case referred to in the previous footnote; literally translated it refers to "useful effect."

left to the national authorities as to the form and method of implementing the directive. The implementation is left, within limits, to their discretion. As has been seen, according to the direct effect theory, the right of individuals to invoke Community acts before their national courts does not exist when the obligation provided for in the act leaves to the addressee a discretionary latitude. The Court now admits the right to rely on such acts in order to have the national court determine whether the competent national authority, in exercising the choice which is left to it, has kept within the limits of its discretion as set out in the directive.[38] In other words, the concept of direct effect as defined stands. Whether or not the national authorities have exercised their discretionary power cannot be subjected to legal review, neither can the material content of the measures, which the national authorities have taken within their margin of discretion. "It is the duty of the national court before which the directive is invoked to determine whether the disputed national measure falls outside the margin of the discretion of the Member State.[39]

SOURCES OF COMMUNITY LAW

As was previously indicated, the Community legal order has its own sources, which consist, not only of the European treaties and the acts of the institutions issued in pursuance of the powers conferred upon them (regulations, directives, decisions and agreements),[40] but also the rules relating to the application of primary and secondary Community law. These rules comprise international law, in so far as applicable[41]; the general principles of

[38] *Ibid.* at 2212 (10).

[39] Case 51/76, *supra* n. 36, at 127 (29).

[40] See *supra*, Chap. 3 IV, 2 (3).

[41] Agreements concluded by the Community with third States or international organisations (EEC, Art. 228) are, of course, governed by the rules of international law. On the other hand, as the Court pointed out: when exercising their rights to lay down Community rules, the institutions are not bound by provisions of international law unless the Community itself has assumed the rights and obligations resulting for the Member States from international agreements to which they are parties, and unless the provisions of those parties have direct effect within the Community. Cases 21–24/72 *International Fruit Company* v. *Produktschap voor Groenten en Fruit* [1972] E.C.R. 1219 at 1227.

See also, Arts. 37 (5) and 234 and Cases 21–24/72 *supra* where the Court found that "in so far as . . . the Community has assumed the powers previously exercised by Member States in the area governed by the General Agreement [on

law[42] including fundamental rights. The latter play an important role as the Court pointed out: "respect for fundamental rights forms an integral part of the general principles of law protected by the Court of Justice," and added that "[t]he protection of such rights, whilst inspired by the constitutional[43] traditions common to Member States, must be ensured within the framework . . . and objectives of the Community."[44] Formulation of fundamental rights is to be found, *inter alia*, in the Convention for the protection of Human Rights and Fundamental Freedoms,[45] ratified by all the Member States, to which the Court has referred in interpreting a Community provision concerning equality of treatment as

Tariffs and Trade], the provisions of that agreement have the effect of binding the Community." (*Ibid.*, 1227 (18)); the Court rejected the direct effect of Art. XI of the GATT and concluded that therefore the validity of Community regulations could not be affected by that article; *id.* Case 9/73 *Schlütter* v. *Hauptzollamt Lörrach* [1973] E.C.R. at 1157 (27).

As for agreements concluded between Member States, the Court declared that the EEC Treaty indeed takes precedence in the matters it regulates, even over conventions concluded between the Member States before its entrance into force (Case 10/61 *Commission* v. *Italy* [1962] E.C.R. at 10). See also EEC, Art. 219.

The precedence of Community law over all other applicable provisions, including international law, is recognised by the European Community Act 1972, ss. 2 (1) and (4).

[42] See *supra*, p. 79.

[43] In this judgment, the Court rejected recourse to either fundamental rights as formulated by the constitution of a Member State or the principles of a national constitutional structure, in order to judge the validity of measures adopted by the institutions of the Community. Indeed the law stemming from the Treaty cannot, because of its very nature, be overridden by rules of national law, however framed (*i.e.* even when provided for in the constitution) without being deprived of its character as Community law and without the legal basis of the Community itself being called in question.

[44] Case 11/70 *Internationale Handelsgesellschaft* v. *Einfuhr- und Vorratsstelle Getreide* [1970], E.C.R. at 1134 (4). See also Case 25/70 *Einfhur- und Vorratsstelle* v. *Köster* [1970] E.C.R. 1161 at 1176 where the Court found that a system of licences for import and export, involving a deposit did not violate any right of a fundamental nature and Case 44/79, *Hauer* v. *Land Rheinland-Pfalz* (not yet published), where the Court examined whether a Community regulation violated the right of property and of the free exercise of a professional activity.

[45] Signed in Rome on November 4, 1950, it entered into force on September 3, 1953. In April 1979, the Commission adopted a memorandum on the accession of the European Communities to the Convention; this accession would bind the Community institutions and would imply recognition of the competence of the European Court of Human Rights (Bull. 4–1979, 16). See Case 4/73 *Nold* v. *Commission* [1974] E.C.R. 491 at 507 (13).

regards membership of trade unions and the exercise of rights attached thereto.[46] Another formulation of fundamental rights is to be found in the Joint Declaration by the European Parliament, the Council and the Commission of April 5, 1977 on fundamental rights.[47]

APPLICATION OF DOMESTIC LAW BY THE EUROPEAN COURT

The question of *applicability of national law* by the Community institutions was raised on several occasions before the Court of Justice,[48] but the Court decided that it lacked the competence to apply the internal law of the Member States and consequently it cannot examine a claim that, by taking a decision, an institution has violated national law, neither can the Court decide on the interpretation of a national provision.[49] Application of national law by the European Court, however, does take place where the Treaty refers explicitly to national concepts.[50] This is the case, for instance, under Article 58 of the Treaty, which refers to companies and firms formed in accordance with the law of a Member State,[51] and under Article 215, which provides that in the case of non-contractual liability the Community shall make good any damage caused by its institutions or servants "in accordance with the general principles common to the laws of the Member States." Similarly, when the Court is called upon to solve a question for which there are no Treaty provisions, it must solve the problem "by reference to the

[46] Case 36/75 *Rutili* v. *Minister for the Interior* [1975] E.C.R. at 1232 (31–32).

[47] O.J. 1977, C 103 and Bull. 3–1977, preliminary chap. See also the European Council Declaration of April 8, 1978 on democracy (Bull. 3–1978, preliminary chap.).

[48] See, *e.g.* Case 1/58 *Stork* v. *High Authority* [1959] E.C.R. 17; Cases 36–40/59 *Geitling* v. *High Authority* [1960] E.C.R. 423. See, however, Cases 17 and 20/61 *Klökner* v. *High Authority* [1962] E.C.R. 325 and more recently Case 159/78 *Commission* v. *Italy* (not yet published).

[49] Case 78/70 *Deutsche Grammophon* v. *Metro* [1971] E.C.R. at 498 (3).

[50] See Case 50/71 *Wünsche* v. *Einfuhr- und Vorratsstelle Getreide* [1972] E.C.R. 53 at 64 (6): "Terms used in Community law must be uniformly interpreted and implemented throughout the Community, except when an express or implied reference is made to national law."

[51] See, *e.g.* Case 18/57 *Nold* v. *High Authority* [1959] E.C.R. 41 at 48, where the Court stated that "under German law a company in liquidation has the capacity to institute proceedings and to indicate its rights for the purposes of its liquidation."

rules acknowledged by the legislation, the learned writing and the case-law of the member countries."[52]

As is shown by the foregoing considerations, the Community legal order grew and developed mainly at the hands of the Community judges. Over the years the Court has played an essential role in consolidating its autonomy *vis-à-vis* municipal and international law, in emphasising its orginality and in imposing its precedence within the national courts and tribunals. It goes without saying this task would have been impossible without the co-operation, understanding and adaptability of the national judge, but the Community Court was and still is the driving force. It should be clear also that the task of this Court is not limited to the applying, developing and interpreting of Community law *stricto sensu*. According to the Treaty,[53] the Court shall ensure that "the law" is observed. Law in this provision and as it is understood by the Court refers to the concept of what is "right", much more so than anything that has been described and analysed in the foregoing pages of this book. Seen in this light, the European Communities appear beyond all the limitations, ambiguities, hesitations and conflicts as a legal, political, social and economic system which, thanks to its balanced institutional structure and inherent potential, constitutes the only possible solution for Europe's problems and the only hope for its development.

[52] Cases 7/56 and 3–7/57 *Algera* v. *Common Assembly* [1957 and 1958] E.C.R. at 55. Another example in the definition of "misuse of power" (EEC, Art. 173) based on a comparative study by the Advocate-General of this concept in the municipal law of the Member States (Case 3/54 *Assider* v. *High Authority* [1954 to 1956] E.C.R. at 74.

[53] EEC, Art. 164.

INDEX